"Last week, an old friend of the family asked me, 'How can I believe that this book isn't just another lie?' I thought about her question for a long time. The answer is that I no longer have anything to hide, and more importantly, I no longer have to hide from myself..."

—Craig Fraser

This poignant first-person account gives us a stunning you-are-there understanding of what it's like to be trapped within the darkest depths of drug addiction . . . and points up the kind of courage and strength it takes to journey back to recovery and "a new start." Fascinating in its candor, Craig Fraser's true-life story offers inspiration and hope to others, and provides invaluable resource "hot-line" listings: where to go, who to call, for help.

"This memoir should be read by parents who never say no to their children."

—Publishers Weekly; BURNT, first edition

Craig Fraser lives in Napa Valley California. He is working with schools creating and implementing drug, alcohol and tobacco programs. He plans on going back to school to get his Masters in social work to continue his work with addicted teens and their families.

Dear Craig,

I am an 8th grade student from a junior high school you spoke to. I've always wondered about drugs—what they're like, what getting high feels like—but most kids here just smoke and drink.

I just finished your book and it turned me around. I now see that drugs aren't as glamorous and fun as people think. Your book inspired me not to try drugs.

I have a friend who also read your book. She was in tears one night and now every time someone talks about drugs, she says she thinks of "HIGH SCHOOL" and says "No" on the spot. Your book helped a lot of kids and some of the teachers too.

There is one last thing I want to tell you. When you came to our school, you cursed. This told us you weren't full of shit. You acted normal, not like a person sent by the state to lecture us. This made the kids listen.

Sincerely, Justin

To, Craig Fraser

Hello, my name is Tom and I'm currently in treatment. I've just finished reading your book and what you wrote amazed me, I've never been able to relate to someone so much and am so happy I was given your book. While I read it I saw myself go through the motions of my own life and see how much I screwed myself up. I can't thank you enough for giving me hope and a will to survive. My thanks go out to you.

Thank you so much,

Tom

Dear Craig,

I wanted to write and tell you that I have never related to any other story as much as yours. I am a recovering addict and alcoholic, but my recovery has just begun. I am in the fellowship of Narcotics Anonymous, but I have only recently been able to admit to my alcoholism. I have six months clean and sober today, and it is the longest period of time I have spent drug-free in years. Before this last time in treatment I thought cocaine was my only problem, but now I know that I cannot afford to stay in denial. I view my recovery as a gift, a second chance at the life I almost ruined. I will be 18 next month, and I will be attending college in Arizona. I never thought my life could be this great.

Your story was a major factor in my initial decision to enter rehab. When you talked about "white outs" and your addictive behavior, I felt as though it was written just for me so I could clearly see my problem.

Thank you so much for sharing your story through your book. I am grateful for its impact on my life.

Sincerely, Steve

Dear Craig;

Hi, I'm very happy to be alive. I am writing you this letter to thank you with all my heart for steering me in the right direction. Your book "High School" was Great!! very vivid and real. I want to tell you and others…that it had a tremendous impact on me. You helped me re-live feelings I thought I had lost and buried so deep in me that they were gone. I am 29 years old and presently serving a 6 year armed robbery due to my drug addiction. Unlike you, I knew I had a drug problem…

It wasn't until after I read your book that I wanted to do something about it. Man I can't thank you enough…your book was like a mirror to me, yeah that's the best way to describe it. I identify with so much in your book and let me tell you when tears came to my eyes in my cell while reading your book I had tears of both grief and joy, joy for the fact that I was able to cry again which has been too long. And grief for feeling for you. Which also makes me happy that I can still feel for others. Thanks man. As of next Tuesday I am going to an N.A. meeting. They have them here in the prison. I could never bring myself to go to one until now. I guess it was shame holding me back from going to them and also facing so many people and let them all know my problem. . . But now after your book I know I can stand up and admit it to a roomful. Again I thank you from the bottom of my Heart.

John

HIGH SCHOOL

A Teenager's Drug Addiction, Treatment and Lasting Recovery

Craig Fraser

Published by AYNI PRESS.
1451 Library Lane
St. Helena, California 94574
(707) 963-1822

First published in 1990 by Signet, an imprint of
New American Library, a division of Penguin Books USA Inc.

Library of Congress Cataloging-in-Publication Data

Fraser, Craig.
   High school : a teenager's drug addiction, treatment and lasting
   recovery / Craig Fraser. —2nd rev. ed.
    p. cm.
   Preassigned LCCN: 97-93835
   ISBN 0-9658466-9-5

   1. Fraser, Craig. 2. Teenagers—Drug use—Biography. 3.
Narcotics addicts—California—Biography. 4. Narcotics addicts—
Rehabilitation—California. I. Title.

HV5805.F73A3 1997   362.29'3'092
                      QBI97-40640

SAN# 299-3597

Text design and production by Teutschel Design Services, Palo Alto, CA
Cover by Tim Gaskin, San Francisco, CA

Printed in the United States of America
10 9 8 7 6 5 4 3 2 1

For a complete catalog of Ayni Press materials,
write AYNI PRESS P.O. Box 335, St. Helena Ca. 94574
E-mail address BuyHSchool@aol.com

Author's note:
This is a true story. To protect the privacy of many of the people with whom I grew
up, I have changed certain details aside from my own. All the names have been
changed except my parents' and new friends once I was sober. Where necessary,
significant characteristics about the different people introduced in this book have
been changed as well. In many cases, the people in this book are composite characters. Similarly, the names and descriptions of certain locations and institutions
have been reworked and, in some cases, fictionalized. None of these changes affect
the essential story.

In memory of Andy Flock, my best friend,
who unlike me, was not given a second chance.

I would like to thank the following people for their continued support: Margaret and Don Newport, Sally Marston, Pat Newport Berra, Otis Marston Jr., Jennifer and Jim Abeles, Jack Fraser, Dianne Fraser, Deidre Sullivan. I would also like to thank, Rev. Richard Mantsi, Patricia Keel, Tom Tompson, Lyndal Walker, Reverends Phillip and Dorthy Pierson, Ric Giardnia, Father John Cruz, Kristine Namkung, Tania Schramal, John Mini, Darlene Dozier, Terry Ogisu, Robert Hsi and Tim Gaskin for their love and guidance. My deepest gratitude goes to the following friends who had faith in me during the times I did not, Lisa Doles, Jefferson Buller, Martin Bucher, Barbra Burnadett, Gloria Clokey, Dan Daugherty, Chris Epting, Trish Flannigan, Laramie Flick, Sally Fletcher, Emil Aruma and Robert Ruddell, Raymond Schnapp, Denen Holler, Mark Haworth, Lanetta Wilsey, Christie Tadiello, Rina Novia, Ava and Derby Wilson, Katie and Hudson Auberlin, Jorge Catalan, Ariane Bigelow, Jennifer Kresge, Tarek Azim, Art Bacon, Cathy Young, Mandy Maddox, Risco Francisco Louis, Kathryn Snavely, James Steel Jr., Louis H. Young Jr. and Paul Young. For all of their sound business advice and guidance, I would like to thank Jerry Ann Jinnett, Anthony Tusller, Gim Meyer, Sarah Teutschel, Lucy Shaw, Mary Shaw, Alex Haslem, Ken Tracey, Bill Dixon, M.D. and Les Addler. Most of all I would like to thank my parents, Donna and Don Fraser.

CONTENTS

Prologue

Eight years have passed since the first edition of this book entitled BURNT was first published. Sometimes I wonder how I was able to write about my addiction back then. I was so new to recovery, I didn't know if I could stay sober as a teenager, or if I wanted to. My time was spent trying to preserve what little sobriety I had. I went to Narcotics Anonymous (N.A.) meetings, talked to my sponsor, and attended personal therapy.

Although I was doing everything I could to have a "text book recovery," I often did not want to keep going. I missed my using friends, drugs, and all the excitement that went with them. Sober, I found myself standing alone in life with no idea where to go. There was no one to lead me, just some Higher Power I was supposed to trust in. People in meetings constantly told me, "Turn it over." I thought to myself, "Turn what over and how?" I had no idea what they meant. I learned with time.

Over the years, my recovery has endured many tests, including long-term negative effects of my drug abuse, challenges in personal relationships, and extreme health issues. The most significant challenge was a short relapse with alcohol I had after several years of sobriety. At the time, my life was great. I thought I was no longer an addict, so I drank. Today, I fully realize the importance of my sobriety. It has returned my life to me and allowed me to follow my dreams and accomplish my goals. Unfortunately, many of my using friends never found out that this was possible.

Out of the sixty people I went through treatment with, only a few were still sober two years later. From the time I left treatment in 1986 to present, seven of my friends have died from drinking or drugging. Each death was preventable— overdoses, AIDS, suicides, drunk driving, the list goes on. Their deaths are a constant reminder to me. My friends continued to use drugs while I was creating a new, sober life. As I worked through the problems my addiction caused, life became increasingly better. Theirs continued to get worse.

The first challenge I faced was creating a life that didn't revolve around drugs or people who used them. The next step was learning to deal with the long-term side effects of my drug use. Paranoia, hallucinations, and depression were just the beginning issues in my recovery. As each new challenge presented itself in my life, I took it one step at a time. Living this way prevented me from becoming overwhelmed by the many challenges I faced.

The years of drug addiction had turned me into a manipulative and paranoid person. Back then, I believed that people always wanted something from me. I did not trust anyone. I lacked the ability to have honest and healthy relationships with people. I had never experienced open and frank discussions, especially about myself. Learning these new skills demanded continual personal introspection, something I had always avoided.

Once sober, I unknowingly switched my addiction from drugs to the people I dated. It took many relationships before I learned how to relax and allow people to be who they were naturally, without wanting to fix or change them.

I came to this realization after contracting a near-fatal illness following a breakup with a girlfriend. After months of medication proved useless, I took my illness and healing into my own hands. With faith, a strong program of recovery, and belief in a Higher Power, I was able to overcome this illness and go on.

Leading a sober life was hard in the beginning. It was much easier to become an addict than it was to work the steps of recovery and take responsibility for my life. I needed to undo many things before I could have my life back. I created more problems by using drugs than I had ever imagined. With time and help from many people, I have worked through them.

My life is now better than I could have ever dreamed. I still attend recovery meetings weekly, and daily spend time sitting quietly thinking about my Higher Power. I have a good relationship with my parents and sister. I am healthy and enjoy the work I do. I wish my friends that died could have known the life I found in sobriety. Drugs felt good, but only for a while. Soon the good feelings and fun times were over, my life was a mess, and there was nobody to clean it up but me. It took hard work and was worth it; I just wish I had known how hard it was going to be to get off drugs before I had ever started taking them.

BURNT was first published two years after I completed treatment. I was going to college full time, studying psychology and Liberal Arts. I maintained an A- average. I was the philanthropy chair for my fraternity, and a member of a psychology honors society. Outside of school, I spent my time going to meetings, running, public speaking, and working for a nonprofit organization.

I have rewritten the last two chapters in this edition to summarize the past five years. I did this to help show the progression of my recovery. Many others I have known in the program have had similar experiences regarding relapse, codependency and illness. A life of recovery is not just about abstinence, it is about becoming whole, taking control of and responsibility for one's life. Drugs and alcohol prevented me from doing this for many years. They no longer do.

From My Parents

When I first read *BURNT*, the original edition of this book, it brought back memories. I was reminded of the frustration my wife, Donna, and I felt, as the mounting evidence led us out of denial and eventually to the conclusion that our "nice" model American family did, in fact, have a drug problem. At first we avoided facing the facts by rationalizing Craig's behavior. Finally the evidence became so overpowering it forced us to seek help.

Our first positive step was taken late one night after Donna and I had gone out to dinner together and talked about all the things we were seeing in Craig as possibly addictive behavior. We called COKENDERS. They suggested we look into treatment programs. We visited a hospital near our home. There, the doctor advised us to intervene in Craig's life. At the same time, Craig's teachers had reason to believe that Craig was heavily involved in drugs. Together we demanded that Craig go through a drug evaluation.

Arranging for Craig's evaluation was the most difficult action I had ever taken in my life. I had to face the fact that our son had been lying to us, that we could not trust him. At the time of our intervention, I was still in denial, hoping and praying that Craig would go in for the drug evaluation and be back in school in a week—with a clean bill of health.

While Craig was in treatment, Donna and I attended a special meetings for parents and other family members of people in treatment. We listened to other families who were struggling to understand how this could have happened. We all asked each other, "What do we do now?"

Driving to the hospital for these sessions was often an emotional roller coaster. I was angry and upset that because of Craig's actions, I had to spend my time listening to and participating in "drug" conversations and education. At the time I was going through an extremely difficult period with my business. And my relationship with my wife was strained for many reasons. Still, I felt the joy that came from having Craig under professional care— with the great hope that these professionals would "cure" him of his addiction. Conflicting feelings of hope, anger, love and even hate, were very difficult for me to handle.

I will never be able to express fully my appreciation to the hospital staff, including the professional counselors, administration and support staff. Craig, like so many kids who enter drug treatment programs, was angry and abusive. How these people can put up with this day after day—and continue to see the good in each of these kids—will always receive my praise and admiration. It takes a special person to dedicate his or her professional life to this kind of service. Because of their loving persistence and their professional ability, they were finally able to convince Craig of the detrimental effects of drugs on him—physically, mentally, and spiritually. Craig was finally starting to listen and learn. Witnessing this change proved to be another emotional experience. I wanted to believe what I was seeing and hearing. At the same time, though, I wondered if Craig was putting on an act in order to get out of the hospital and back to his friends, who were all still using drugs.

The day that Craig "graduated" from the program, I was unable to speak. My tears of joy and happiness were so great that nothing would come out. But this overwhelming joy slowly dissipated into reality. I began to worry about whether or not Craig was strong enough to face his old temptations. Who would be his friends? Where would he find new friends who were sober? Should he return to his old private school or switch back to his local high school? I wanted to do everything to support my child. The question was what to do and how much. Craig needed to live his life and I needed to help—by letting him. At the same time, I had to watch him closely.

The emotional roller coaster ride continued. The question of trust became the most difficult to deal with. I felt guilty for the past and responsible for Craig's addiction. I told myself that I should have looked beyond Craig's words to his actions. Drugs had turned a loving, honest, and thoughtful child into a conniving, lying, thoughtless human being incapable of trusting or being trusted. The questions for me became: At what point do I start trusting again? Do I trust a little or a lot? And, what does that mean? It became a source of great pain. I wanted to help Craig, but I could not—for his good and mine. I found myself watching for any possible sign of a return to his old ways. We worked through this period step-by-step.

Donna and I have always given our children freedom, and encouraged them to make their own decisions. In retrospect, this has been both good and bad. Giving a child freedom can help build independence, but it can also become a way to avoid making tough decisions, like placing limits on actions and activities. Our daughter accepted freedom and did not abuse it. (Ironically, I learned in one of our family therapy sessions that she looked upon the freedom I gave her as evidence of indifference and lack of caring.) But where our daughter functioned well with independence, Craig took his independence and used it to support his addiction.

After treatment, Craig, Donna and I participated in family therapy sessions. One of the first decisions facing us was where Craig should go to school. Craig decided—with our support—that he would return to his private high school. The physical separation left me with mixed feelings. During this period, I was disturbed by the statistics: only 30 percent of the kids who complete a treatment program actually stay sober. That meant there was a 70 percent chance that Craig would go back to drugs.

I wanted Craig to know that my love would always be there for him and that I had forgiven him for his prior actions and was anxious to get on with my life and for him to do the same. Believing that actions speak louder than words, I asked Craig if he would like to join me on a business trip to Milan, Italy. He wanted to go, but at the same time he was saying, "Do you think I'm really worth it—after all I've done?" It made me realize how much guilt Craig was carrying with him, that he had not been able to forgive himself for all of the things that had happened while he was using. Our trip was the beginning of a new and very important relationship between us. We opened up new areas of communication, dealing with our feelings instead of our intellect. Being in a foreign country meant that we were more dependent on each other and were able to share more of our fears as well as our dreams for the future. This trip was the beginning of a rebuilding of "trust" between us.

Soon after this trip, we began talking about Craig writing a book about the experience that had had such an impact on our family. Weeks earlier, Craig had written a term paper for his English class, entitled "Evaluation, My Ass!" After reading this fifteen-page report, I felt that Craig's story would be interesting and helpful to other families who were facing a problem similar to ours. Craig gave the idea a lot of thought, then decided that writing a book was something he really wanted to do.

The writing took a little more than two years. During that time, the emotional ups and downs continued. It was difficult to let go of the past. I continued to watch Craig and at times even doubted him. I also did a lot of praying.

The hardest concept for me to accept during this phase was the fact that we were not going to experience a "cure." There is no magic. True recovery is, in fact, a process that never ends. You hear the terms "day by day" and "one day at a time", and they are true. In recovery programs, people say "First you have to talk the talk and then the question is, can you walk the walk?" This continued to be one of my worries. Craig had learned to "talk the talk", but I was not really sure in my mind and heart that he was "walking the walk."

Time, again, proved to be the great healer.

As the months passed, we found new areas of trust, and success began to build on success. Our conversations and communications as a family continued to be more open and we learned from each other. We also began to accept the fact that our family recovery from addiction would be identical to Craig's—it was going to be a lifetime struggle with no quick cure.

Along with the doubts and fears that kept rearing their ugly heads, we found new joy and excitement as we experienced the wonder of recovery. It brought a new kind of patience and calm that resulted in less tension and a deeper enjoyment of the simple pleasures of life.

Another special joy for me was when Craig said he would like to go to college, that he was ready to give it his best effort. A full draft of *BURNT* had been completed and now he had the time to concentrate on building a sober future. He selected a state university, and within a few months he was rooming in a dorm and living the life of a normal college student.

The reason this was such a joy to me is that when Craig was so dependent on drugs his maturing process was put on hold. Instead of dealing with the real issues of life, he was escaping from them daily. The second semester in college Craig called and asked me what I thought about his pledging a fraternity. I was very excited for him and told him that I, too, had been in a fraternity. In my college days the fraternity had offered me a broad range of activities and friendships that have endured over the years. I wanted a similar experience for my son. Pledging a fraternity indicated to me that he was easing back into a normal growth pattern. I was thrilled.

During this same time, my wife entered an alcohol treatment program. At the time, I was not personally aware of the depth of her problem. The denial I had used so effectively to avoid seeing Craig's problems also helped blind me to Donna's growing problems. During her hospitalization, our whole family participated in family counseling—and the concepts of recovery became all the more real to us.

In my life, I have found a spiritual relationship through the Unity Church, which is helping me deal with my life in a much healthier way. One Unity expression is, "Let Go—Let God." The more I apply this the better it works. My understanding of this simple but profound expression deepens.

It is my hope that this book will help other families avoid the pain of drug addiction. Maybe our experience will give you the courage to face up to the problem and then use the recovery process to build a new life. I've learned that out of the greatest problems can come the greatest opportunities.

—*Don Fraser*

This is a book about a teenage boy's drug addiction. That boy is my son, Craig. As I read Craig's story I was filled with overwhelming sadness for losses and personal relationships that might have been, sadness for a family that had everything going for it but the tools to keep it together, and sadness for lost opportunities for intimacy. As a parent, I wanted the very best for my son, and I wanted to believe the very best about him. This book shows how blind a parent can be to the ones she loves most. For too long, I was unaware of his "other" life and the depth of his involvement in the drug culture.

I was the mother in a "picture-perfect" family living a "picture-perfect" life. I had a lovely home, a successful husband, and two beautiful children who never seemed to misbehave. We took lovely vacations, entertained the "right" people and I tried to believe what others often said—"Donna, you have it all." It was twenty-five years later that I learned that there was so much more.

I took pleasure in being a mother and homemaker. I adored my children and I loved being there for them. I was also class mother, scout leader, and community volunteer. Together, we had many good times. In the winter, when it snowed and the schools closed, the children and I played in the snow and baked cookies. During the spring and summer, the kids and I would often take walks with the dogs down country roads and pick blackberries, go home and make pies and jam.

Birthdays and holidays were especially important in our home. My husband and I put special effort into making Christmas, Easter and Thanksgiving memorable occasions for our children. I enjoyed watching my children grow and mature. They were the essence of my being.

But though there was a lot of love in our household, it wasn't always apparent. Our family relationships were often strained. My husband and I had no major disagreements, but neither did we air our true feelings; it was too difficult to talk about emotional issues. There was little joy. The rule in our family was, "Don't cry out loud. Just keep it inside. Learn how to hide your feelings." We never examined our real selves. I used to think that it was selfish to think of myself. I figured that if I appeared serene, confident, and self-composed then I must be so. I derived my sense of self from making others happy and denied my own feelings. It was in this kind of environment that Craig grew up.

I ached for Craig, although I never understood the depth of his unhappiness. Craig also scared me. I let him strong-arm me verbally because I was afraid of alienating him and losing his love. I reasoned that if I just kept giving and giving, then things would get better. Also, I didn't know how to confront him. I didn't want to risk having him call me a bad mother.

At the same time Craig was active in his addiction, he was unaware that I, too, had another life. I was drinking to survive and was active in the same disease as my son. Hiding my addiction was very hard work. It was important to me that I maintain my facade of a perfect mother and wife. I took great pains to fulfill my obligations, though it became increasingly difficult. I was depressed, confused, filled with shame and guilt; but I was powerless to stop my own destructive behavior.

In the summer of 1988, my daughter initiated an intervention and helped get me placed in a treatment program similar to the one my son went through. I stopped drinking and began my recovery while Craig was completing his work on this book. In the first edition of this book, he talked about my "being in the hospital," I was in a recovery program. At the same time, I was learning that my survival was dependent upon my recovery. I realized that there must be countless other mothers in my spot. Addictions run in families and it is a family disease.

Now I know that if I drink, I will die. Addiction kills women sooner than it does men. Being in recovery means more than just not drinking. It means changing one's behavior and ways of thinking. I now know that it is healthy to feel anger, and I'm learning to communicate my feelings in constructive ways; feelings may hurt but they don't kill. I'm trying to listen objectively to others, particularly my friends and family, and to learn how to discuss uncomfortable feelings. No longer do I keep secrets; in our family, secrets made us sick and kept us sick. Most importantly, I've learned that it is not selfish to think of myself. As I get to know and learn to take care of myself, I can truly "be there" for others.

Like Craig, I have been given the gift of sobriety. In fact, I consider my new life to be a miracle. I no longer hide behind compliance, or numb myself with alcohol. I'm trying to shed my perfectionism. I've also begun to rely more heavily on my spirituality. I know that God's love and healing are flowing through me. Having a sense of spirituality is essential to my recovery.

Before we both got into recovery, being close to Craig was impossible. We each had too many defenses, and thus had a hard time speaking freely with each other. Today Craig and I no longer live in the web of untruth or denials. We are close in a way that I never dreamed possible. We have discovered that we are similar in many ways. He is twenty-eight and I am fifty-eight, yet we are both in recovery, and have been going through the process of self-discovery at the same time. We have nothing to hide from each other. When he does press some of the old "buttons," I can tell him what he is doing and how I am affected. I am learning to set limits with him, and tell him when I feel uncomfortable.

Craig and I have the same zest for life. We participate in each other's lives and give and take suggestions freely. What's more, we are learning from each other. We love to laugh.

As Craig's mother, I am sad when I think that his "carefree" years of youth were spent with little joy or sense of self-worth. I am sad that the only way he could experience those feelings was with drugs. But knowing how his life is today fills me with joy. Of course, I wish I could start over with my children, knowing what I know today. But I cannot regret the past. I can only look back at the pain and learn from it. Happiness and freedom are finally possible for my children and us. In a way, that's what HIGH SCHOOL is all about. I am so proud of my son. I love him more than time can tell.

—*Donna Fraser*

Growing Up

I never thought I had a drug problem. I was on the honor roll at my high school and a member of the student government. I held good summer jobs and played sports. I came across as the kind of teenager that most parents would want to have watch their children or go out with their daughter.

For years I fooled everyone, including myself. As a teenager I felt I could handle drugs like pot, cocaine, and LSD. I thought they added to life, not took away from it. Using drugs seemed like a perfectly natural way to have a good time.

Growing up in a dysfunctional home I did not learn healthy forms of communication or ways in which to build self-esteem. I was taught to be a perfectionist and to stuff my feelings. Until I became sober, I was unaware that there were more than two ways to go through life—ecstatic or depressed. My father was always ecstatic and my mother usually depressed. At the time, I didn't realize this. I thought I had become a drug addict because I was bored and drugs seemed fun and an area in my life where I could be powerful and in control. Now I know I used drugs to find the happiness that my life lacked. I came to depend on them. By the time I was sixteen I did not know how to feel happiness, passion, contentment or self worth unless I was high.

This is the story of what happened to me. This story isn't unusual or out of the ordinary. I could be writing it about any number of my old friends. The only difference between me and most of them is that now I'm a recovering addict and they are either dead, in jail or still getting high.

I'll start at the beginning. My name is Craig Fraser. When I wrote the first edition of this book I was nineteen years old, and I had lived in California all my life. I used to believe that I belonged to the perfect family and that we'd all live "happily ever after," the way I thought other families did. But that's not the way it was.

My mom was a young widow with a baby when she met my dad. Her first husband was a military pilot who was lost at sea during a flight exercise. A few months later, she met my dad while he was finishing business school at the University of California at Berkeley. Like my mom's first husband, my dad had been a fighter pilot in the Marines. About a year later my parents got married and my dad adopted my sister Amy. Five years later, in 1968, I was born.

Up until I was six, my family lived in Palo Alto, a community about fifty miles south of San Francisco. Palo Alto is probably best known as the home of Stanford University and the site of many famous high-tech companies. We lived in a two-story house near the university in an area where there were lots of other families and children. I thought we were a happy family because my parents never argued or raised their voices at each other.

When we lived in Palo Alto, I spent a lot of time with my mom and played with the children of her friends. I helped in the kitchen when she made jams and pickles. I used to love it when she'd read to me from Tom Sawyer or Sixty-Six balloons at bedtime.

I didn't get to see very much of my dad at that time, because he was working long hours as a consultant. I was asleep when he left in the morning and in bed by the time he got home at night. But he always set aside a day for me on the weekends. We went fishing together and spent time outdoors at the state park. Once, he built me a giant tree house in the backyard. Those times I spent with my dad are my happiest memories.

Life with my sister Amy, though, was another story. What I remember most from those early years is our terrible fights. We'd scream and yell, hit and kick each other. Neither of us would ever let up, but Amy always won because she was bigger than I was. This infuriated me; even as a little kid I hated to lose. Amy also liked doing the typical torment-the-younger-brother things. When my parents went out, she would tell me that the "bogeyman" was coming to get me. This scared me, so I'd hide behind a curtain with the dog, falling asleep and staying there until my parents came home.

When I was six, my family moved to a small town in the Napa Valley, about sixty miles outside of San Francisco. The Napa Valley produces some of the finest wines in the world. My parents chose the Napa Valley because they thought it would be a good place to raise their family. This part of California was ideal for my dad because he was in the process of starting a new business and several of his clients were in the area.

Moving to the Napa Valley was a big change for my family, especially for me. Compared to Palo Alto, the Napa Valley is very rural. In Palo Alto, I could run next door or across the street and find lots of kids to play with. But in my new town, the nearest neighbors lived the distance of a football field away and didn't have children. Because we were way out in the country, deer, raccoons, and possums crossed our lawn in the early morning; sometimes, these animals would even wander onto our deck and eat our dog's food. From my point of view, the really good thing about our new house was the fact that it had a pool. Since I love to swim, the pool helped make up for leaving Palo Alto.

I wasn't allowed to join the kindergarten class when we moved to our new home because I had missed the districts birthday cutoff. In Palo Alto, where the rules were different, I'd already been in kindergarten for more than two months. So for almost a whole year, I couldn't go to school. Since I didn't know very many kids in my town, I spent most of my time by myself exploring the creeks and vineyards near by my house, looking for animals. My mom was busy redecorating, and the house was filled with workmen tearing down walls or installing new carpeting. Sometimes the workmen would give me hammer and nails and let me pound on a board. When they used cement, they let me make a print of my hand.

When I got bored with playing outside or hanging around the workmen, I'd watch TV shows like *Gomer Pyle* and *Lost in Space*. My favorite show, though, was *The Beverly Hillbillies*. I liked the idea that the Beverly Hillbillies had endless amounts of money but were still friendly to everyone.

TV was so important to me that I used to get up at 4:30 A.M. on Saturdays and turn the set on to make sure that I didn't miss the first morning cartoons. I'd bring my blanket and my life-size Snoopy doll with me from my bedroom and fall back to sleep in front of the "fuzz" on the TV until the morning shows started. Then I'd glue myself to the set for hours. My dad wanted to teach me how to ride a bike one Saturday, but I had no interest in learning because I didn't want to miss my TV shows. I'd never even hear my mom calling me for dinner until she shook my arm or turned off the TV. In those days, separating me from the TV was practically impossible.

The TV was also a big source of conflict between my sister and me. When she came home from school, Amy and her friends used to kick me out of the family room so that they could watch their shows. This would send me into a screaming rage. When my sister couldn't control me, she'd call her boyfriend; if my parents weren't around, he'd come right over and punch me in the stomach or push me around.

One big problem with living in the country was my allergies. They tortured me every day, all day. After going to a couple of different allergists, I found out that not only was I allergic to all animals with fur and all kinds of grasses, but also to trees, dust, pollen, and molds. I started getting allergy shots twice a week in the first grade. The doctors also prescribed allergy pills, but I had to keep switching medicines because my body quickly built an immunity to each prescription. The pills always made me feel spaced and tired.

In the first years of grammar school, my allergies prevented me from playing soccer and Little League baseball; after about five minutes on the lawn or field, I would start sneezing "like there was no tomorrow." Allergies built a wall between me and the "in" crowd of kids at school, most of whom played sports. It was hard for me to get to know any of the other kids when I had to watch them from a distance. I also felt like I was letting my father down; he'd been a very good baseball player in high school, and I always felt that he wanted me to be a baseball player, too.

Because I couldn't play field sports, I retreated into the world of animals. I got really interested in reptiles because they were the only ones that didn't make me sneeze. I collected snakes, turtles, and lizards. My most exotic pets were a speckled caiman, a small alligator, and a Canadian red-tipped boa constrictor named Noah. At school, I had one friend, Ben, who liked reptiles as much as I did. Sometimes he'd bring snakes that he'd caught to school, and I'd buy them from him with my lunch money. During recess, when the other kids were outside playing, Ben and I would run to the science room to hold the reptiles, or check wildlife filmstrips out of the media center; we watched the same ones over and over again.

I loved dogs even though they made me sneeze, and when I was growing up in the Valley my family always had at least one golden retriever. I used to have conversations with the dogs and tell them what I was thinking. When I was upset, I'd hold the dog and cry. When my uncle died, I sat in the backyard crying into the dog's neck because I realized that I'd never see my uncle again. When my parents made me mad, I used to tell them I was running away. Instead, I'd sit in the doghouse by the garage. There I'd cry and hide with the dog for hours. Doing this made me sneeze like crazy, but I didn't care. I felt the dog was the only friend I could talk to.

In addition to allergies, I also had to deal with dyslexia. In third grade, the teachers noticed that I was having problems with the "fundamentals", and that I was falling behind. Reading, writing, and arithmetic simply weren't coming easily to me. It took me a long time to read sections from books and I constantly mixed up words and numbers if I tried to go at the same speed as the others. Having this problem was very frustrating because I wanted to do everything perfectly. Even though my parents would try to support me by saying, "Just do your best," I had a hard time accepting the fact that I was getting lower grades than everyone around me.

That year, my parents sent me to a tutor three times a week and the school sent me to a "special class" in the morning. I liked my tutor because she helped me do better in school, but I hated being singled out for a special class because it made me feel different from the other kids. What made it worse was that the other people in my special class had really serious disorders. One kid would scratch his tongue until it bled. Another yelled out gibberish and tried to hit the teacher. One girl had so much trouble with pronunciation that she'd spit every time she tried to say a word. Of the whole group, I was the only one who was dyslexic, and I hated the idea that the "normal" kids in my school might see me with my "special class" and make fun of me. And, deep down, I worried that maybe I did have a severe problem and that I wasn't being told the truth.

I compensated for the dyslexia by using my memory to pass my regular classes. I worked much harder than everyone else and still got only "fairs." The other kids in my class would finish their assignments during study hall, while I was still trying to understand how to do the work. I never came close to finishing simple assignments meant to be done in class. Sometimes my smarter friends, the "brains" of the class, helped me finish work so I wouldn't have to stay inside during recess.

Speaking was one of the few ways I felt comfortable expressing myself in school. If a teacher read a story out loud to the class and then asked us a question about what she read, I'd have no problem answering her questions. But if she asked me to read, I'd try to get out of it because I knew I'd make a lot of mistakes. Reading was always embarrassing because after a few minutes, the teacher would say, "Thank you, Craig. That's enough," and pick a "smart" person to continue. I'd feel like an idiot and see the other's faces that confirmed my fear that I was stupid.

At first, when I didn't "get" something, I tried asking questions. But I learned quickly that the teachers didn't like if I kept saying that I didn't understand what was going on. Rather than have them angry at me, I'd pretend I knew what they were talking about by looking at them and nodding okay. Later, I'd ask my "smart" friends what we had to do.

My friends didn't mind helping me out because I was able to help them out, too—with other things. When kids in my class got in trouble at home, they'd call me for advice on what to say to their parents. For some reason, I always knew what parents wanted to hear. I also helped my friends at school. Because I loved an argument, the other kids in my class used to rely on me to get them out of trouble. If a teacher accused one of my friends of getting into a fight on the playground or stealing lunches, I'd speak up for him and try to prove that he didn't do anything wrong. The teachers usually believed me because I was a hard worker and rarely got into trouble in school.

I probably would have been held back in school a couple of times if my parents hadn't been there to help me. At home, night after night, they would sit with me at the dining room table, going over my homework and helping me do my assignments. My mom corrected my spelling and my dad quizzed me on my multiplication tables.

Fifth grade was my toughest year simply because school work got harder. We'd put away the phonics workbooks and started reading real books. Math problems got a lot more complicated, too. Even though I was still going to a tutor, two or three hours of homework a night was typical for me that year.

I was having a rough time socially, too. Getting a girlfriend became important to me because all the people I admired had girlfriends. When I got up the nerve to ask out a girl in my class, she told me straight out and in front of the others that she wouldn't go out with me because I wasn't popular enough. Seeing how hurt

I was, she tried to make me feel better by saying, "Don't worry, Craig. You're an ugly duckling now, but I'm sure you'll grow up to be a swan." This second comment was like a punch in the face. I never forgot what this girl told me, and from then on I worried more than ever that I was ugly and that I wasn't "popular enough."

At home that year, the fighting with my sister got worse. She always said I was fat and stupid; I'd call her an ugly bitch and tell her how gross her acne was. My dad rarely saw us fight, we knew not to even argue around him. He believed that there should be "no fighting and yelling in his house." If my mom happened to witness one of these fights she'd usually take my sister's side because Amy was "older and knows more." I really hated this because I felt like there was no way I could win. Amy always seemed to team up with my mom against me. When I'd argue with Amy, she'd say, "You're just like your father." And my mom used to say the same thing, as if it was a terrible thing to be like my dad—and this confused me. I always felt backed into a corner. I wanted to yell at Amy and say, "He's your father, too," but I never said it to her face because dad had adopted her. I figured that maybe she didn't consider him her dad.

When things got bad with my sister or when I was really in a bad mood about school, I'd take off and ride my minibike. My mom was really frightened by the idea of me on a minibike and didn't want me to have one, but my dad, who piloted airplanes, understood why I loved minibikes so much. And at home my dad always had the last word. I'd ride my minibike on the private roads behind our house. I never went farther than my dad said I could go. Going fast on a minibike was a real high for me. Sometimes I'd wear a walkman under my helmet and listen to tapes while I was riding. As a kid, these were the only times I felt powerful and free.

By the time I was in seventh grade, Amy was out of the house and in college. When my parents' friends asked, "Don't you miss your sister?" I'd think, "No, not at all." Once she was gone, I had the TV to myself. I had my parents to myself. I felt we were a family again. I was glad that she wasn't around to bother me.

School got much better for me that year, too. Instead of one teacher running the class, I had six different teachers for six different subjects. A couple of them really liked me and encouraged me to participate in class; they didn't mind helping me if I had extra questions. I got along best with the women teachers because they seemed to have more compassion. I also knew how to get their sympathy and attention. When I didn't get an answer on a test, I wrote them little notes saying, "This question is tough!" or "Isn't this too hard for a seventh grader?" Later, they'd talk to me about what my problems were with the test. My male teachers weren't as patient with me.

That was the year I learned how to organize myself and take neat notes. This may not sound like much, but it made a big difference for me because I could review the notes at night and make sure I understood what was going on. I got a binder and separated the work for each class into sections. I stopped shoving my homework papers or notes into my books and learned to organize them neatly. At home, my mom helped me; that year she must have typed ten of my papers to compensate for my poor handwriting and constant misspelling. And I knew that if the homework was really hard, I could copy from one of my smart friends. I kept cheat sheets hidden in my desk in case I took too long with a test, since it took me longer to read the directions and questions. That year I finally figured out what it took to get good grades, and for the first time I was getting steady A's and B's.

Unfortunately, even though my grades were improving, my social life was going downhill. In seventh grade, the cool kids in my class, people I'd known since kindergarten, decided to gang up on my best friend, Steve. They'd call him a faggot and shove him around or spit on him to make him angry. This was hard for me to deal with because Steve was my friend—but they were friends too. On top of that, our parents were all friends. Because I decided to stick up for Steve I got picked on too. When my mom suggested that

I invite someone from the cool group over, I couldn't exactly tell her what was going on and that I wasn't getting along with him. If the kids at school heard from their parents that I was complaining to my parents, they'd have picked on me even more.

Nevertheless, my one-time friends soon went from giving me a hard time about Steve to picking on me personally. They made fun of my "bowl" haircut and the fact that my dad manufactured cartoon T-shirts. That year the cool people were into hard core music (a type of punk) and skateboards. But when I went to the record store and bought twenty albums, they ridiculed me for being a "trendy." When I told one of them I wanted to get a skateboard, he told everyone what a "wannabe" I was. I learned quickly that you should either talk about what you know or not say anything at all, that it's better not to pick up a fad than to be late picking it up, and that instead of getting mad, get even.

I hated being picked on. It made me feel like shit. Sometimes, I got so frustrated that I'd browse through the Smith & Wesson firearms catalog and think about buying a gun and rubber riot bullets. My plan was to hide behind a bush and "nail" my "enemies" after school. I never did get that gun but instead got revenge in other ways—by putting a couple of tacks on the seat of one of the people who was giving me a hard time, for example. When that person sat down, he'd scream. The teacher would be furious and the whole class would erupt into laughter. I'd just sit there with the most shocked and innocent look on my face—as if to say, "I can't believe someone would do that." I'd also rip up people's homework and throw away their books. On days that book reports were due, I'd secretly sift through the pile of papers on the teacher's desk and take out the papers belonging to the people that I didn't like. Then the teacher, unable to find the assignments, would either give them an F or make them do the work again.

One of the most effective ways of getting back at people was to switch locks on their lockers. As a result of having to compensate for dyslexia, I'd developed a talent for memorizing things like phone numbers and zip codes. I used to watch kids put things in their lockers and memorize the combinations. During class, I'd go out into the hall and switch locks. This prank infuriated a lot of people because they had to get the locks chopped off their lockers. I was always careful to time my revenge so that it wouldn't be obvious who did it. I was patient. Sometimes, I'd wait a few days or even months to strike at the perfect moment. My personal motto in junior high was, "You burn me once, prepare to get burned forever."

The first drug I ever experimented with was alcohol because it was so easy to get. I was in sixth grade and I wanted to know what it felt like to drink. One year later, I tried pot. That's the way it was with almost everyone I knew. No one did cocaine and then started smoking pot. It was cigarettes, alcohol and pot first. What the doctors say is true—alcohol and cigarettes are definitely the gateway drugs.

Because of the large wine industry, drinking is an accepted, if not required, part of life in the Napa Valley. All my parents' friends collected fine wines—my godfather owns a winery. Whenever I spent the night at one of my friend's homes, my mom and dad would send me with a bottle of wine to give my friend's parents as a way to say "thank you."

When I was growing up, I never thought of my mom and dad as heavy drinkers. They would usually have wine with dinner and when they had guests, my dad would occasionally have a cocktail. My parents always offered me and my sister sips of wine when they took us out to dinner. Each year, after the Christmas holidays, my dad would stop drinking for a month to "clear out his system."

Even though my parents tried to teach me to respect liquor, my attitude about drinking was like my friends: if no one's going to miss liquor or beer, take it and drink it—and when you drink it, get drunk. Every Fourth of July, my family would have a big party. During the day, when no one was looking , I'd take six-packs of beer and hide them in the basement. Other kids I knew would go into their parents' wine cellars and help themselves.

When it was a new thing for me, I'd drink when adults weren't around. At the end of seventh grade, I used to sneak out of my room in the middle of the night on a weekend and meet my friend Ben downtown. We let ourselves into his dad's office, which was in a barn behind the back of his house. There, we'd smoke his dad's cigars and drink hard liquor, usually vodka, straight.

Ben and I weren't the only ones who were curious about alcohol. The same kids who had been mean to me a few months earlier were all interested in partying and experimenting. When it came to drugs and drinking, we were all on equal ground; no one person or group was more experienced than another. Before long, we all started partying together at school. One person would bring his parent's cigarettes or chew to lunch. Someone else would have stolen filterless clove cigarettes from an older brother or sister. I usually brought some beer. We did most of our heavy drinking at night over the weekends when our parents went out to dinner—often all together. A group of people from school would bike to my house and bring a fifth of Jack Daniels with them. We sat around the kitchen table doing shots and took breaks to go outside and smoke clove cigarettes. I liked the numb feeling alcohol gave me. Being drunk made it easier to laugh and tell people that I was glad we were friends.

In seventh and eighth grade, we drank whatever we could get, but I preferred hard liquor because I never really liked the taste of beer or wine. Also, I could get loaded faster on hard liquor. But about a year after I started drinking, I found something I liked a lot more than liquor—pot.

In the Napa Valley, it wasn't hard for a sixth or seventh grader like myself to get drugs, especially pot. Many of the adults in my town smoked pot; some even grew it. Many of my friends had parents who had gone to college in the sixties and kept pot around their homes. The kids whose parents weren't so young usually had older brothers and sisters from whom they could steal pot. A few kids at junior high were selling the pot they got from home.

My family was a little different. My sister Amy wasn't into drugs, although I knew she sometimes drank at parties. Because we didn't get along, I would never think of asking Amy to get me pot from her friends. If I asked her, I knew she could use it against me by telling my parents. My dad is a straight arrow too. I remember him saying that pot was "illegal," end of discussion. My mom, though, was a little more liberal. In seventh grade, I found a plastic bag of green stuff, which I assumed was pot, in the drawer next to her bed. This totally surprised me because I knew that my mom came from a very strict family. My mom couldn't have liked pot very much because every time I went back to her drawer to look at it over the next six months, I seemed to find the same amount in the bag.

Up until that point, I'd thought that pot was for drug addicts. If asked, I would have said using it was "dangerous" and "wrong." In fact, in fifth grade, when someone had been caught selling it at school, I told myself that if that "dealer" had offered me pot, I would have taken it straight to the principal. In junior high, my ideas began to change. I was questioning a lot of things. Pot didn't seem wrong. It seemed "cool." Even thinking about it made me feel older. A couple of people I knew were using it and said it was great. At some point, pot didn't seem all that bad anymore—especially once I knew my mom had some.

The first time I ever smoked pot was on a weekend night when my parents were out to dinner. I was with my friend Ben, and since we didn't know about pipes or rolling papers, we ended up making a joint from a piece of notepad paper. It was pretty awkward, but we lit it up anyway. The pot kept falling out of our homemade joint. When we were finally able to inhale a bit, not much happened. I didn't get "high." I didn't feel "stoned," but this didn't surprise me. A friend at school told me that I shouldn't expect much on the first try, or even the second or third. I decided to try it again a few weeks later. Since my mother didn't seem to be smoking the pot I found in her drawer, I ended up pinching all of it from her, bit by bit, and smoking it with my friends. I replaced what I took with lawn clippings.

My friends at school owed me for sharing all my mom's pot with them. Once that supply was gone, they stole pot from their parents or got it from their brothers or sisters. Ben used to dip into his parents' jars of pot and bring buds—the most potent parts of the marijuana plant—to school. Another friend, Mike, had a dad who stored both pot and "crank" (amphetamine) in their family's refrigerator. (I learned later this keeps crank from melting.) He also grew pot in a closet in their garage. Mike used to bring his dad's buds to school and we would put them in our tuna fish sandwiches.

We soon reached the point where we didn't want to limit ourselves to a few buds here and there, so Ben stole over two pounds of Hawaiian pot from another kid's father. It was the best pot I'd ever seen. The buds were more than eight inches long, and flaked with white crystals. There were no seeds in them, which meant that they were sensimillia and very potent. Even then, I knew that a pound of prime Hawaiian was very valuable, but Ben didn't. When the high school kids found out about Ben's pot, they tried to take advantage of him. Ben wanted friends so he started giving it away or selling it dirt cheap. I wanted those buds myself because it would guarantee me a solid supply, so I went right over to Ben's house with a box of my things I knew he liked and wanted. He was hesitant, but I convinced him to give me a pound and a half of pot for ten hard core tapes, my black engineer boots, and a $100 bill.

I scored this pot the first week of summer and began smoking an eighth of an ounce daily. On top of that, I ended up making about $300 profit just by selling an ounce to older kids who heard from Ben that I now had the buds. This was my first real deal.

People might wonder how a thirteen-year-old got the money to buy pot. I had always saved my money. I was the kind of kid who saved the money his parents gave him for candy when they sent him to the movies. And when I ran errands for my mom, she let me keep the change. Up until eighth grade, I always had an allowance, and I'd save that, too. In first grade it was $2 a week. By fourth grade, I got $3 a week. By eighth grade, it was $10. When I could, I'd collect my allowance from my dad, and later, I'd ask my mom for it, too. I always was careful to save most of my allowance money and I kept it in a special metal box.

I also had jobs. At home, my mother paid me for doing work outdoors. Every time I earned $10 for mowing the lawn or $3 for weeding the tomatoes, I'd put it right into the metal box. In eighth grade I also worked at a student supply store where I got the minimum wage, $3.35 an hour, for selling pencils and chips during mid-morning break and at lunch. Working there was a real honor because only the most trusted students were allowed to run the store. The one problem with this job was that I was not able to work the cash register; I'd get the numbers mixed up because of my dyslexia.

My dad encouraged me to save, too. I'd dump out my metal box every six months. If I had $60 dollars, my dad would match it with $60 of his own and we'd take the money and put it all in my bank account. The money I saved this way would either stay in the bank or I'd use it to buy something "big" like a minibike. For these "big" purchases, I'd tell my dad what I wanted to buy, and if he approved of the idea, he'd contribute half the cost.

The newspapers always say that using drugs is expensive; they run articles about kids stealing from their parents and mugging people on the streets for money. But doing drugs wasn't always expensive for me because I managed to save money on many of my deals. With drugs, as in other businesses, the more you buy, the lower the cost. If I'd wanted to, I could have made a lot of money by selling drugs to my friends. But making money on drug deals was never one of my goals—I preferred the drugs to the extra money.

Why did I start doing drugs? One reason was boredom. The town I grew up in is very small, there were about ten thousand people all together. The high school never had more than four hundred students. Basically, it's not the most exciting place for a teenager. The movie theater, for example, was about two months behind the times. Except for playing video games at the Safeway—which I did for hours after school—there was nothing to do downtown. No boys and girls club, community center or any other place for us to hang out and have fun. Pot changed that. It gave my friends and me something to do—and made boring things like going to the movies seem new and different.

And I liked the way pot made me feel. After just a few hits, time seemed to slow down for three or four hours. Some aspect of reality would always jump out at me. If I were listening to a song, my mind might focus intensely on the music or a particular instrument. Or if I was watching a TV show, I'd usually end up laughing at something that most people wouldn't find funny. On top of that, my worries disappeared when I was high. For instance, when I was in eighth grade, my dad was having some very hard times with his business. Overhearing him talk to my mom about all his problems and about how we might have to sell the house depressed me. I was sure that we were going to have to live in a trailer park, and I thought all the problems were somehow my fault because we never talked about what was going on. This no longer mattered when I was high.

Pot didn't just get me high, though. There were other effects. During my first year of smoking pot, I'd get the "munchies" something fierce and have an intense desire to eat. Since I loved to cook, I really liked getting the munchies. My mother never questioned why my friends and I stayed up all night eating everything in the house and ended up crashed on the couches until the morning. I guess she thought this was normal teenage behavior.

Smoking pot also gave me bloodshot eyes. That's why most pot smokers carry eye drops around with them. My parents never said anything to me about red eyes because of my allergies. Also,

I used to swim a lot and my eyes were red from all the chlorine in the pool—a perfect excuse.

For me, though, the strangest side effect from smoking pot was that it dried up my sinuses. Most of my friends would get "cotton mouth" from smoking pot. But I had not only a dry mouth but also a dry nose. Before I started smoking pot, my nose was always chapped from sneezing and I'd go through a box of tissues on a typical spring day. Once I started smoking pot, my allergies stopped bothering me and I no longer needed my medication that made me feel drowsy.

With pot, I liked that I had access to something that the other kids wanted but few of them had. After getting all that pot from Ben, I was set. Having good buds put me in a powerful position. Because of my dyslexia and allergies, I'd always felt powerless and unimportant. Pot changed that.

Offering pot to my friends was easy. I'd say something like, "Hey, it's a Saturday night. We've go nothing to do. Our parents are out to dinner together. You know how long they stay out. Nothing is on TV. Nothing is happening downtown. I have some pot. Have you ever tried it? Have you ever gotten stoned?" I'd watch to see my friends' reaction to my ideas, then tell them that I'd tried getting high a couple of times and that it had been fun. "You don't get paranoid or freak out. It's like drinking but without the after-effects. And it gives you the munchies."

Had anyone hesitated (although no one ever did), I would have told him that I didn't want to pressure him and that it was okay if he didn't feel like doing it. One of my favorite phrases was, "No peer here," which meant that I wasn't trying to force it on them by peer pressure. Getting people to smoke pot with me didn't take a lot of effort. Most people I knew were eager to try pot. Doing it with someone for their first time creates a special bond, like smoking a first cigarette or taking a first drink with someone. My friends and I could always look back and say, "Do you remember when…?"

After I discovered how much I liked pot, I began experimenting with other drugs. That eighth-grade year, I discovered nitrous oxide. Nitrous oxide is the same gas that dentists give their patients. It's the gas that puts the "whipped" in canned whipped cream. At the Safeway downtown, my friends and I would take the whipped cream cans off the shelves and inhale the nitrous oxide out of them when no one was looking. Then my friends and I would walk back out of the store on a free high. My other trick was to purchase several cans of whipped cream at the gourmet shop where my parents had an account. Then my friends and I would go back to my house and inhale them quickly, one after another. The next day, I'd take the cans back and tell the person at the cash register that the whipped cream cans were defective and had somehow lost their pressure. I'd explain that my sister's birthday had been ruined because we'd had no whipped cream for the ice cream sundaes. The person behind the counter usually ended up apologizing and giving me new cans.

That summer I also started going into my parents' medicine chest, looking for pills with the warning, "Do not mix with alcohol. May cause drowsiness." There were lots of bottles from dentist appointments and torn ligaments (my dad is a runner). I thought that since the pills were prescribed for pain, if I took them when I wasn't in pain then they'd make me feel even better. Rather than swallow the pills, my friends and I chopped them up and snorted them. We'd also do the exact opposite of what the directions said and get drunk while we snorted them. It burned like hell going up, our faces would turn red with pain and our eyes would fill with tears, but we still did it every chance we got. We would pretend that we were snorting cocaine.

In eighth grade, cocaine wasn't readily available to us, but I was really curious about it. I had seen Miami Vice and other TV shows where people were using it. They were always the ones with the nice cars, big homes and beautiful women. Some kids at school called it "rich man's aspirin" or "nose candy." Pretending that we had cocaine was the next best thing to really trying it.

The first thing that surprised me about my pot smoking, drinking, and assorted drug use was my tolerance. I could smoke and drink more than most of my friends. Because I could handle myself when I was "wasted," I got a reputation for being cool among the kids at school. Early on, I learned that the object was to do as much stuff as you could and act as if it didn't affect you. Being able to handle drugs and then even do more was respected. The kids who took drugs and got sick or acted obnoxious were laughed at. They were considered "blow-its." (People who didn't use at all were "uncool.") In eighth grade, I could smoke six bowls of pot and still walk around and be able to talk to adults. I could drink over a pint of whiskey on an empty stomach and not get sick. I could eat an entire pack of stay-awake pills that are sold over the counter in drug stores—and go to sleep. Once, I was camping out in the woods near my house, my friend Ben, who was known for smoking as much pot as people would host, said that he could smoke me under the table. I loved a challenge that I knew I could win, so we ended up passing the pipe back and forth for two hours. I'd take a big hit and slide it over to Ben until he said, "Please, Craig, don't make me smoke no more pot." Another time, when my parents were out and I had a small party, my friend Mike challenged me to a smoke out. We took hit after hit from my special Mexican turquoise pipe until Mike threw up. I kept going and took ten more hits. Mike got hold of himself and tried to take another hit. It looked like he was losing control over his muscles because he threw up again when he tried to exhale. Everyone else thought this was very funny, and I fell down from laughing so hard.

I also drank a lot of alcohol at our family reunion picnics, which took place every year on a ranch in southern California. After my parents went back to their hotel for the night, I'd stay on the ranch and play drinking games like Mexicali and Liar's Dice with my uncles and older cousins. When the beer ran out, we switched to liquor. They were surprised that I was ten years younger and able to keep up with them without ever getting sick.

The only time I ever threw up or passed out during the first couple of years I experimented with drugs was when I visited Amy in Seattle. I was in eighth grade, and hanging out with my sister at college was the most fun I'd ever had with her. We didn't fight at all, and when I was getting baked with her friends, she'd smile and call me the "little stoner." It sure felt better than "little brother."

Even though certain adults in my town used drugs, most people were very concerned about "the drug problem." None of the concerned adults, my parents included, ever seemed to suspect that I was involved in drugs—for a couple of reasons. First, I didn't fit the town's image of a "druggie," a kid who was always getting in trouble with the police and cutting school. If anything, most people imagined I was against drug use because of something that happened in fifth grade. Some friends and I found a large bag of what looked like cocaine. I took it straight to my parents. My dad told me I did the "right thing." A few days later the police said that what we turned in wasn't cocaine but actually a low grade of cut PCP.

Even after I started smoking pot, I had adults fooled. At home, I had a sticker on my door that said, "Are you stoned or just stupid?" I thought it was funny; my dad thought it was an anti-drug statement. Also, after years of feeling stupid, I was finally recognized as a "smart person." I was one of the twenty-three students picked to go on a special week-long trip to learn about biology and wildlife. In addition to doing well in school, I played on the basketball team, and at the beginning of the summer started a business selling exotic birds, called Fraser's Feathers.

Another reason no one suspected that I did drugs was because I knew how to handle myself around adults. My parents, like many parents in the Valley, placed a lot of emphasis on manners. As a little boy, I was taught to shake hands and make direct eye contact with adults. I remembered to use people's names when I spoke with them. I liked being polite, and adults liked it when I was, too. My parents were proud of the way I handled myself; they told me that other adults had complimented me.

My parents always tried to treat me as an adult and to involve me in their lives. My dad would take me out to dinners when his business associates came to town, and when my parents had dinner parties, I always sat at the table with the guests. Starting the bird business put me in the situation of having to talk with many older people. For instance, in order to research the bird market, I had to make phone calls all over the country to find out how much different birds cost and how I could go about buying them. I met with local veterinarians and pet store owners, too. Even though my dad said he was there if I needed him, I liked doing this on my own.

Since talking with adults was second nature to me, I never acted nervous around friends' parents. In fact, I was the kind of young person that my friends' parents would call a "good influence." The mother of one friend, Kyle, kept a close eye on the people Kyle was hanging out with. I was one of a very few of Kyle's friends she allowed in the house. She thought the other kids were a bad influence because she'd seen them downtown at the Safeway smoking cigarettes. Every time I went over to Kyle's house, I spent time talking to his parents. I genuinely liked them. I'd ask his mother questions about her winery, and she talked to me about my bird business. Ironically, only a few of Kyle's other friends were trying pot. I was the one getting Kyle high.

As far as I can remember, I didn't have any confrontations with my parents about pot, liquor, or the pills from their medicine chest. During junior high, the only run-in I had with my parents was about cheating. Three days before eighth-grade graduation, the teacher called me up to her desk and asked me about an answer book, the one that only faculty members are supposed to have because it has all the test and homework answers in it. She said that her answer books were missing and wondered if I knew anything about them. I pretended I didn't know what she was talking about when, actually, one of the books was inside my backpack.

Many of the people in the cool group had copies of this answer book. I'd used the book on earlier tests and sometimes to help me get through my homework, but on that particular day, I'd had a feeling that something bad might happen so I didn't use it. The principal took five of us out of class to "get to the bottom of the situation." We went into his office one by one, and I was the last to meet with him. He told me that my friends had confessed and that I was in serious trouble. He then asked me if I had anything to say. I said that yes, I'd used the answer book on a couple of homework assignments, but no, I hadn't cheated that day and had nothing to say about the others.

None of my other teachers could believe that I had cheated. I had never been accused of anything like that before. I had a reputation as a hard-working, respectable student. A few teachers even came up to me and expressed their support. They said they were sorry and that they were sure it was all a mistake. My parents thought the same thing. I told them how someone protected himself by telling on me and that the only time I ever used the answer book was on a couple of homework assignments, but that I would "never" cheat on a test.

Because of this incident, I was suspended for three days, but was allowed to take the exams I missed in my other classes. During the make-up science exam, the student monitor, who was a friend of mine, gave me all the answers I didn't know. For the math exam, I brought a stolen answer book with me inside a notebook. As for history, I didn't need to cheat because I knew the answers and the teacher didn't mark me down for bad spelling.

Cheating was no big deal. Like going to class and doing homework, it was something most everyone did. I never once felt morally wrong or bad. On the contrary, I really believed it was the right thing for me to do. I worked twice as hard as my friends, I went to tutors after school every day and studied at night to get fair grades, while my friends got mostly perfect grades. I felt that my cheating was justified; I worked real hard so I deserved the best grades.

"High" School

By the time I got to high school, I had a reputation as being cool—that is, as someone who partied. That was because I'd spent the summer before school smoking and occasionally selling KGBs—Killer green buds—to select people in my town—kids one or two years older than me.

At the same time, I had the reputation for being a good student among the teachers. All my new teachers would say, "Oh, you must be Amy Fraser's brother." Because my sister had been a good student, they expected me to be one as well. If my sister had been a dropout, the teachers would have treated me differently.

The public high school in my town had less than four hundred students, many of which came from wealthy families. So my school was high pressure when it came to how you looked, what you wore, drove, and which family you were from. My sister had always said she hated it. I remember her coming home from ninth grade crying and telling my mom that kids at school didn't like her; they didn't accept her even though she'd already been in school with them for three years. Once while Amy was in high school and I was in grade school, she saw me with someone who was overweight. That night, she told me I'd have to be careful about who my friends were because if I had losers for friends everyone would label me as one too, and they would make fun of me. This made me really angry because I liked my friend regardless of his weight. Amy's opinion of the high school prepared me for the worst and, inside, I was worried about being in high school. Being a freshman and in the youngest class was different than being in eighth grade and having the run of the school. Everyone at high school seemed so much older and more mature, like adults. Even before school started, I worried about what the juniors and seniors would think of me.

At my high school, cliques were everything. Usually the only times people from one clique would interact with people from another was when they were playing sports or buying drugs. Drugs were a common denominator, especially pot; everyone smoked pot. Membership in most of the cliques was based on looks and money, and members of different cliques used different drugs. For example, "rockers"—the students, both girls and boys, who had long hair and wore concert T-shirts—tended to be into hallucinogens like 'shrooms (short for mushrooms—psilocybin), LSD, and speed (amphetamine). The "uppers," or the in-crowd, whose parents had money, were usually into beer, pot, and cocaine. Many of the kids in this group belonged to families who owned wineries. The Latinos, whose parents were in California for the grape harvest, always had speed and usually sold it to the rockers. A lot of the Hispanic kids were older than the rest of the students because they didn't go to school regularly. The guys usually dressed in black and wore hair nets. Girls from all the different groups used speed to lose weight. They usually got it from guys in the other cliques who knew the Latinos.

If someone who didn't really know me had to put me in a clique on the first day of school, they'd probably put me into the uppers. After all, my parents were affluent; I dressed well, and my grades were decent. In reality, I was a "sometimes upper" because I preferred having my own group with my own friends. I liked all different kinds of people, but at my high school, if you belonged to one clique, you were supposed to be friends with them and them alone. I was also a "sometime upper" because I could be a leader when I had my own group. If I stuck with the uppers, I didn't have a chance of being in charge—status in that group came from participation in sports, and sports weren't something I did. And, deep down, I worried that the kids might turn into jerks again as they had been in seventh grade. Also, breaking into a clique like the uppers was tough because my "ins" to the clique were gone—two good friends from eighth grade had chosen to go to boarding school instead.

Dealing with the uppers the first week of school was harsh. My best friend, Steve, decided that he couldn't hang around with me because he wanted to join the sports segment of the uppers, a group of freshmen and sophomores from wealthy families who played football and ran track. At first, I couldn't believe that Steve would join up with some of the people who singled him out in seventh grade. I had nothing against the sports uppers; in fact, a couple of them were good friends in junior high. But I hated the idea that Steve felt forced to choose between them and me. I was upset and angry; we had been friends for years and I had always stuck up for him no matter what.

I tried to put this incident out of my mind and focus on making some new friends. Because of my reputation for KGBs, older kids from many different cliques immediately began asking me if I could score for them. This made me feel really important because freshmen were usually considered plebes by the older students. No senior ever threw me in the school pool or dumped me in a trash can as they did to other freshmen. Instead, I got respect from a lot of different people, including some of the senior uppers. They talked to me as an equal because I had something they were always looking for. It also helped that many of them knew me because they knew my sister.

I began to lose contact with my non-using friends. These were the kids who were the smartest in seventh and eighth grade, the ones I worked with in the school supply store and class projects. Sometimes we'd talk in the lunch room, but since most of them didn't party on the weekends, I drifted away from them, until we no longer had anything in common.

My greatest wish at this time was to have a girlfriend. I used to try to figure out what it took to get a girlfriend and how other guys in my class managed it. I'd dwell on this topic for hours, imagining what would happen when I finally had a girlfriend and what we'd do together. In my mind, I practiced being a great boyfriend, someone who was attentive and generous. I'd imagine the many different, deep conversations that my future girlfriend and I would have, and although sex was a big deal to a lot of my friends, it didn't concern me all that much. I just wanted to be close to someone in my life.

Even though I had many friends among the girls and they often wanted to borrow my clothes and hang out, I couldn't believe that I would ever cross the border from friend to boyfriend. All the girls I grew up with knew that I had gone to a special class in elementary school. They knew me when I wore cartoon T-shirts and had a bowl hair cut. I thought that they would never change their image of me from those years. And the girls that I was attracted to would only go out with the older uppers. Plus I still saw myself as the fat and ugly child Amy had always told me I was, even though it wasn't true any more.

In October, I convinced a new girl in my class to go out with me. Our relationship consisted of holding hands and talking on the phone. After two weeks, she told me that she couldn't see me any more, and that "it was over." I wanted to die. After school, I went to the drug store and bought a bottle of over-the-counter sleeping pills. I went home, told my mom I was feeling sick and was going to sleep until the next day. I locked myself in my room, took a handful of pills and went to sleep. When I woke up the next day and felt like crap, I stayed home wondering why I hadn't died. It had always worked for the people on the soap operas and in the movies.

Back then when life sucked I would always think, "Just end it." I was sure I was going to die from nuclear war anyway. My life pretty much sucked during that time. I hated school and most of the people in it. I felt intimidated by them, not because they were mean to me, I was just insecure. So I tried to always look confident, which people interpreted as being a snob. I didn't know how to express the feelings of anger, confusion and loneliness I was going through unless I was fucked up on drugs.

My mother would often try and talk to me when she picked me up from school. She would ask, "Did you have a good day?" I'd end up yelling at her because I never had a "good" day; I had horrible days. I rarely understood what the teachers were saying in class, so I felt stupid. The "uppers" I was supposed to be friends with would start shit with me for no reason or spread rumors about me that were never true. So I'd take it all out on my mom, the one person who was trying to help me but didn't know how. I'd bitch her out for bothering me and when she started to cry, I'd ignore her until we got home, then I'd just watch television or ride my minibike.

Yelling at my mom was something I did without thinking. I'd just see red and start to yell, and I was never told not to, so I continued to do it. My mom never fought back. She just took it quietly. Sometimes, she told my father about our fights, but since he traveled a lot and usually wasn't there to witness what was going on, he'd just tell me not to yell at my mother.

I couldn't and I wouldn't talk to my parents about my girlfriend problems or how I hated school. I didn't think that there was anything that they could do to improve my situation, and we weren't the kind of family that talked openly about our personal problems.

Once, though, I shared some of my concerns and feelings with a seer. My tutor, an older woman who lived in my town and the only person who I trusted, took me to Berkeley to hear a seer speak. I was blown away by what I heard and saw. The seer, a woman in her early fifties, radiated what I can only describe as loving and comforting energy. She talked about a shift in our global consciousness that was currently taking place and said that the day would soon come when people would be able to commu-nicate without words and would no longer be able to tell lies. When the seer asked if anyone in the audience would like to say anything, I was the first person to stand up and speak into the microphone. I said that I felt a lot of life's problems could be solved if people were more open with each other and stopped try-ing to keep everything locked up inside. She nodded her head encouragingly and said, "You are right, that is the first step we must all take." A week later, the seer contacted my tutor to tell her that her young friend (me) was more than "highly intuitive" and that she wanted to help foster the growth of this "gift" with some tapes of her lessons. I received them a few weeks later. I was so moved that someone had really seen who I was and uncondition-ally accepted me for it. I had known for a long time that I had special intuitive abilities and her letter confirmed it. I listened to her tapes over and over.

Academically, high school started out okay. Although I was smoking a lot of pot on the weekends, I made sure that I never got stoned on Sunday so that I would be able to deal with class on Monday. My grades that first semester were mostly B's. I applied what I had learned the year before—half of getting good grades came from being organized and having a good attitude.

I made a point of asking questions and contributing to discus-sions in class. Now that I was in high school, I didn't have to ask for "extra" attention. I simply saw teachers during their office hours. This sometimes made the difference between a C+ and a B. As I had in junior high, I kept my class work organized in a binder and kept a special note pad on which to write down my homework assignments, so nothing got lost or mixed up. I still had a tutor and went for help three to four times a week after school.

Cheating, of course, was still my back-up for getting good grades. In high school, as in eighth grade, cheating was no big deal. Most everyone did it. For example, the medium-smart people—and most of the uppers were in that category. They had a sort of give-and-take system going. Sometimes I'd copy from them; sometimes they'd copy from me. But, on occasion, I'd also share my work with a couple of Latino friends. One thing that really helped me cheat during freshman year was my new asymmetrical haircut. My bangs were cut right across my eyes, down the side of my cheek, and teachers couldn't see where I was looking.

English was my best class. Even though I had a hard time spelling, I loved to write and put a lot of effort into class discussions. Because of my dyslexia, the school put me in the low-level English course with the Latinos, rockers, and the people who didn't care. Usually, I was the only one contributing to discussions because I was the only one who bothered to read the material. It wasn't hard to stand out in that particular class. The teacher used to make comments like, "It is a pleasure to have Craig in class," on my report card.

Although English was easy, my favorite class was health—because we spent part of the year studying drugs. The teacher, Ms. O'Donnell, knew a lot about the properties and effects of all different kinds of substances. Ms. O'Donnell had gone to college in the sixties and she knew what was up. She used to say, "I'm not here to make moral judgments. I just want you to know what you might be getting into should someone offer you drugs at a party."

Since this class interested me so much, I put extra effort into it. My goal was to learn as much as possible about what I was using. I listened carefully and retained most of what Ms. O'Donnell said. Sometimes I went to the library with a friend to look up more information about the drugs we discussed in class. I also bought

High Times, a magazine for drug connoisseurs, to get more specific information on the active ingredients and chemical composition of these drugs. All this knowledge helped me a lot when it came to negotiating deals with kids who were older than I. This way, I knew what to look for in terms of quality.

Ms. O'Donnell taught two sections of health to the ninth grade, and one day, both classes were held together in the school library because Ms. O'Donnell had invited a "narc"—a county narcotics officer—to give us a talk. This was something she did each year. Word got out on campus that a narc was coming to school, so the library was jammed with people from all the grades. Everyone wanted to check him out.

The narc was about thirty-six years old and reminded me of a hippie from the sixties. He brought a large box filled with recently confiscated drugs and paraphernalia. While holding up different items for us to see, he talked about the laws governing drug trafficking and use. My friend Mike let out a yelp during the talk because the narc held up a pipe and a bag of weed that Mike had recently lost. The narc explained that a large part of his job consisted of going undercover to catch suspected drug dealers. To be accepted by these people, he said he had to do drugs with them. He said the government even gave him his own supply of high-quality drugs. I wondered if he really cared about catching dealers or if being a narc was just a way for him to do great drugs and beat the system legally.

During the presentation, people raised their hands and asked innocently, "Officer, what is that?" Their questions were bullshit; everyone was familiar with the different items he was showing us. The narc then passed around a few pipes and a processing kit for cocaine. I saw a senior, one of the older uppers, examining a "sno seal" bindle that was being passed around. These are slick sheets of 3 x 5" white paper with pictures of little light blue seals on them; they are used to package coke or crystal meth and are available at any head shop. There is a special way to fold the paper to "seal" in the "sno"—the cocaine or speed. Since this senior clearly knew how to do the fold, I knew that he did coke.

After the discussion, a bunch of us went up to the narc and asked him questions about his work. Because so many people were crowding around him, he was distracted and students were able to help themselves to his supply of drugs and paraphernalia. One friend got a small ball of hash and a quarter gram of cocaine packaged up in one of those sno-seal bindles. I took a little hash pipe and Mike's bag of weed as a present for him. I didn't steal any drugs for myself because I always liked knowing where drugs I did came from and I felt there was a good chance that the drugs in the narc's box were cut or laced with cheap or toxic substances, such as strychnine, PCP or paraquat.

One of the best things about health class was that the teacher could answer just about any question I had about drugs. So when I decided to start growing pot, I asked her the basic questions like how fast the plants grew and how often they needed to be watered. Ms. O'Donnell never suspected what I was up to because I told her that I was working on a paper for English about C.A.M.P., California Against Marijuana Production, a special task force that flies through the northern counties trying to catch pot farmers and spraying fields with paraquat, a cancer-inducing substance. I got serious about the project and ordered books through High Times to learn the specifics about male versus female plants, how to cultivate the plant to create a potent bud, and how to identify a good seed.

Growing pot is very common in my town because pot thrives in the northern California climate. To start my small crop, a friend gave me some Afghani seeds from his father's last harvest. Then, I went to the hardware store and charged a high-powered sodium light to my parents' account and rigged it up in my bedroom closet. Within a month and a half, the plant had grown a foot tall and my whole room smelled like a skunk. One Saturday morning my dad opened the closet and barked out in a harsh tone, "Craig, what is this?" I was quick to answer in a calm voice so that he wouldn't be suspicious. I told him that it was a plant for a science experiment. He said that he had a hard time believing that this was a school assignment and that the whole thing looked pretty suspicious. I told him that the plant was a species of hybrid tomato and showed him my textbook. But my dad was still skeptical, so I pretended to be really indignant and said, "Let's call the teacher. She'll explain." My sister happened to be home on vacation and I involved her into the discussion knowing full well that she might turn against me. I told my dad that Amy had to do the identical experiment when she was in school. Amy gave me a really dirty look and then verified my story. I was relieved and then started to talk to my dad about cross-pollination, grafting, and temperatures—stuff that would confuse him and throw him off the track. I remembered him trying to explain new math to me when I was little and knew that he hated talking about something he didn't understand. I kept talking and totally frazzled him. He left the room and told me to complete the experiment immediately. Later that day, I took the plant out into the woods and tied it onto the branches of an oak tree. This is something local growers did to escape attention of C.A.M.P. Once the plant was out of the house, my dad never mentioned it again.

In the middle of the first semester, I made friends with Ryan, a junior in my Spanish class. Ryan was different from my other friends. He was Latino, although he spoke and dressed like someone whose father owned a winery. Ryan also seemed a lot older than most of the people at school—maybe because he was the only seventeen-year-old I knew who was living and sleeping with a 32-year old woman.

Ryan taught me a lot of useful things, like how to deal better with girls and how to dance. I used to be petrified of going to dances, I didn't want to look stupid or give people another reason to mock me. Ryan showed me how to listen for and find the rhythm in songs. He had learned it from his girlfriend who taught aerobics. He made me listen to music and snap my fingers over and over again until I caught the beat. This helped to give me confidence and soon I no longer feared dances, but looked forward to them. Ryan would tell me it didn't matter what others thought and that it was up to me to have a good time.

Ryan also helped me pick out clothes. Ryan had lived on his own in San Francisco the year before and knew all the trends long before they came to the Valley. A couple of times, Ryan and I cut classes to go to San Francisco where we'd explore the Asian and Italian districts, which had cool stores. There we found great deals on baggy pants, beat-up bomber jackets, things that weren't sold in stores at home. Then we'd usually go have a couple of daiquiris at a bar that didn't check IDs. Back at school people would ask, "Where did you get your clothes, they're really cool?" At times my clothes felt as if they were more important than I was. I felt proud to have cool clothes—in style. Somehow it protected me from the negative attitudes the uppers often had towards me, because I had something they couldn't find. Ryan felt the same but would often have to steal the things I would buy.

Ryan seemed to know everything and had done more than I would ever do. One day I asked him if he could score me some cocaine. He said that he would keep his eyes out for some. A month later, on a Monday, Ryan came up to me in the lockers during lunch while I was putting away my books. "Come with me, I've got something to show you," he said. We walked out to the baseball field and into the dugout. There he opened up a bindle like the narc had in his box. Ryan scooped a line onto a razor blade and had me snort it into my nose with the bottom half of a pen. Even though this was my first time, I did twice as much as he did. I didn't feel much, except a little numbness in my nose and mouth. My next class was typing and I spent the whole time talking. I didn't care that the teacher had told me, "Get to work."

Two weeks later, Ryan bought a half-gram of coke and came over to my house to watch some movies that I'd picked up from the video store. Before the movie, Ryan and I went upstairs into the bathroom and emptied out some coke onto a mirror. I watched him very carefully as he cut up the coke. Then each of us did a line. This time the coke really hit me. My heart opened up and the only thing I wanted to do was talk and share my thoughts and feelings, two things I rarely did. I had no inhibitions whatsoever and felt great. We talked freely all night about girls and what I was looking for in my ideal girlfriend—a subject that greatly preoccupied me. Ryan, who was very experienced with women, gave me a lot of advice and built up my confidence. I felt that he really understood me. When we finished the coke, I was sad because I wanted to keep talking and doing more. Since I couldn't sleep, we went outside and smoked a few bowls—pipe loads of pot—to help us come down. I felt that cocaine had given me what I had been missing in life—the courage to express my true self.

Ryan was able to get more coke cheap from his connection in San Francisco. He suggested that we start selling it to select students and adults we knew in the Valley. We paid $200 for an eightball (three and a half grams) and then sold it for $60 per half gram. Even without cutting the coke the way most dealers did, we made a profit of $160 that paid for our share. Although our business never took off because the dealer in San Francisco got busted, we did sell coke to some juniors and seniors. Dealing such good blow gave me further credibility with the older kids. I looked up to these people and wanted them to accept me. Even though many of them had good connections, knowing they liked "my" coke made me feel important.

After Ryan's source got busted, my main connection for cocaine was the older brother of one of the kids in my class. Even though this guy was in his twenties and made it a rule not to deal to ninth graders, he didn't mind selling coke to me because I didn't act immature. I always bought at least a gram and sometimes more. My friend's brother was a pretty reliable source, but I did get burned. I gave him $500 for two eightballs, but didn't get my coke because his connection stole both the money and his car. I never got a cent back. The car was found stripped in Los Angeles.

This event taught me a good lesson—never to "front" money to someone in a third party deal unless I knew and trusted him.

When I couldn't get coke, I'd settle for "crystal meth" or crank. Both crystal meth and crank are types of speed, or amphetamines, and in my town, they are usually snorted. However, I knew one freshman that would slam (inject) it. People at school used to call these drugs "poor man's coke." A quarter-gram of crystal meth cost $20, a quarter-gram of crank $15. Meth is more potent, and a good quad, or quarter-gram, could keep two people wired for over two days. The same amount of crank would only last about a day. Other types of speed I liked were "cross-tops" and "black beauties." These came in pill form, and the Mexicans sold them for thirty cents apiece at school. That year, I got a better connection and bought cross-tops at twenty cents a piece from a security guard at my parents' country club.

Speed was my energy drug, and one of my favorite things to do was snort crystal meth and work out. Since there was no health club in my town, I'd get my friend Dave, who worked at the local hospital, to sneak me into the hospital's physical therapy unit, where there was a heated pool and a weight room. I usually went at night when the hospital was quiet and brought another friend, Dirk, with me. In the physical therapy unit, we'd snort lines of crystal and lift. On speed, I could bench press more than 200 pounds. As it turned out, I made a great cocaine connection because the hospital ran a very well-known treatment program for drug addiction and there were a lot of "recovering addicts" working out in the gym. I became friendly with one of the addicts, Tony, who was both going through the program and having his nose reconstructed. While he was still in treatment, Tony hooked us up with his connection in a nearby town to score some "blow."

Dirk and I continued to go to the gym even after Dave got fired from his job at the hospital for stealing medical supplies. We found a couple of good connections for pot and sometimes got the security guards high. Rarely did anyone in authority question us. If someone did, I'd put on a very disturbed expression and explain that I was Doctor so-and-so's son. I knew one of the doctor's sons from school and we had similar features. So this story always worked. In fact, anyone who questioned me usually ended up apologizing.

During my freshman year, I also began experimenting with hallucinogenic drugs. The easiest to get were 'shrooms because they grew wild in the nearby states of Oregon and Washington. And anyone could grow their own. Special psilocybin kits, costing less than $100, were advertised in *High Times*. Typically 'shrooms are sold by the gram. If they are potent, an eighth, which usually sold for $15, was enough to get three people "tweaked."

LSD was a different story. This was a drug that people at school talked about all the time. They said it was "wild" and "exciting," but it was rarely available. Ryan, the friend who first lined me up— gave me coke—had done LSD and said it was fun. To me, trying LSD was like taking a step into the great unknown. I was curious, but I was also scared because of all the stories going around about kids on LSD jumping out of windows or going insane.

Most people in my school took mushrooms before they tried LSD because 'shrooms were much milder and "natural." I did it the other way around. The first time I actually fried (did LSD) was on a Friday after a football game. Earlier in the week, Greg and I had both scored a few hits of Fry-LSD, at $3 a dose from a friend who scored it in Berkeley. Greg had done his during school with another friend when he first got it, but I saved mine for the weekend. Greg went to the game with me on Friday night and we'd both drunk a fifth of vodka and smoked a few bowls of weed before I drove us to the game. That night, I asked Greg if he felt like frying—I didn't want to do it alone. When he said he didn't, I told him that I had dosed his slice of pizza. After about five minutes, he began waving his hands back and forth in front of his face and said, "Yeah, I feel it. I'm seeing tracers." I told him that I was only kidding. Telling him that he was already on it was my way of psyching him into wanting to do it. The plan worked and he decided to fry with me. Greg dropped one hit. I dropped two. An unforeseen problem was that we took the acid so late that we tripped all night.

After about two hours, the drug kicked in. Greg and I tried to explain what we were experiencing to each other. It seemed I could relate in almost a seer way to what Greg was feeling and our conversations consisted only of fragments of words. Greg would smile and I'd get his thought right away. I knew exactly what he was trying to communicate and vice versa.

Since Greg had already tripped, he showed me a few neat mind games he had learned. For example, he told me to pull my hair slowly. When I did this, the hair felt as if it was growing because of the sensation created by me pulling it. And when I stared at my hands, my fingers seemed to grow, too. As the night went on, more strange things began to happen. For example, the sounds of elephants and dogs seemed to be coming from my father's study. When we tried to play a video game, the characters seemed almost alive. But the trippiest thing was when I looked over at Greg and he appeared to have turned into a three-dimensional grid and was levitating.

These hallucinations were hysterically funny to us. We were laughing so hard that we had to put our faces into the pillows on the couch. This went on for two hours until it dawned on us that maybe we were making too much noise. My parents and my grandparents, who happened to be visiting that weekend, were asleep upstairs and the last thing I wanted to do was wake them up. Going outside for a walk, away from any adults, was one idea we had. But on that night the outdoors seemed really foreign— like it was a place I'd never been before. I thought if we went outside, we would get lost or caught by my parents. Instead, we decided to go up to my room. The two minutes it took to climb the stairs seemed to turn into two hours. We took each step of the stairway very carefully. Every little creak sounded like a crash.

Vines seemed to hang from the ceiling and eyes seemed to peek out from every corner. Getting to my room was like walking through a scary jungle. For awhile, I thought we were lost and would never find our way up stairs and to my room.

By the time we got upstairs, I was exhausted. Sleep was impossible though because the acid had been dried with speed. I was certain of this because our hearts were racing. Also, I didn't know that the trip was still in its early stages. I thought tripping on LSD would last only a few hours. I was wrong.

I tried closing my eyes but every time I did I saw hundreds of little multicolored cartoon alligator heads going back and forth making "waka-waka" noises like the old video game Pack-man. The trip was getting too intense and I was getting frightened. I kept silently telling myself, *It's all right. You are in your room at home. Everything is going to be okay.* Repeatedly, I asked Greg to make sure that I didn't fall asleep. I was certain that if I fell asleep I would stop breathing and die. Greg was having a bad trip, too. He thought that nothing was his in life, that nothing belonged to him. So he made a girl that we both knew, Sarah, his reality and concentrated on her. When Greg began to see the little alligators going waka-waka, though, we both were afraid that we were going to loose it—trip out forever.

When I woke up after only two hours of sleep, all my joints ached. Greg went home and I went to the hospital gym to work out and take a sauna to sweat the poison out of me. I couldn't concentrate; no matter how hard I tried focusing, my mind would wander from thought to thought. I continued to hallucinate mildly. In the sauna, patterns emerged from the wall tiles and then sort of jumped out at me. All day, I kept seeing tracers. When someone moved an arm quickly, I'd see twenty-five arms following the real arm. The tracers didn't stop after one day—I had flashbacks for weeks, especially at night. If a car drove by, the tail light would stream behind it as if I were looking at a photograph taken on a slow-exposure time delay. I also had a recurring hallucination. In biology class, everytime I saw the teacher, I saw a three-dimensional black rectangle levitating over her head. This hallucination lasted for many weeks. Sometimes I saw lights where there weren't any. I remember looking at the blackboard in Spanish class trying to read what the teacher had written. The only thing I could see was bright white light. When I tried to read, a similar light would jump off the pages of books. This made reading doubly difficult.

My ability to concentrate was shot. I'd look at teachers as if I was paying attention, but my mind was always someplace else. I had to ask them to repeat questions. Reading an entire chapter was tough as well. I kept losing my place; my mind wandered as I tried to eye and mouth the words. Nothing would sink in. Spacing out like this forced me to make copies of other peoples' notes; in my hardest courses, I relied on cheating a lot to get by.

When I first realized what was going on, I stopped doing any drugs for a week. When I tried smoking pot again, nothing happened. I'd smoke bowl after bowl of pot and not feel a thing. I did 'shrooms and they didn't affect me. Then one day a couple of weeks later, I smoked some pot and all of a sudden I felt like I was tripping on LSD again.

Because of that one trip, my grade-point average ended up dropping that quarter from a B+ to a B-. My grades were very important to me, and I didn't like the idea that they had dropped. And I hated not being able to concentrate in class. LSD had been as wild as I expected, but it wasn't worth losing good grades over. I decided not to do this drug for a long, long time.

Except where drugs were involved, my life that year wasn't very thrilling. I'd go to school, come home, ride my motorcycle, and do my homework while watching TV. Sometimes I went out with my friends.

During second semester, I probably smoked an eighth of pot a week. I did speed a couple of times a month. Occasionally, I took 'shrooms, which would usually make me laugh and hallucinate mildly. I didn't drink much because I preferred drugs. My favorite drug was coke and this I'd do only occasionally—maybe once a month because even though I loved it, coke caused me some problems. After binges of more than a couple of grams, I'd vow that I'd never do coke again because my heart would ache so hard in my chest that I felt like I was being stabbed. Usually I'd do it until I couldn't walk or barely breathe. Sometimes I'd get a bloody nose. The worst thing about coke, though, was how I'd crash when it was all gone. I felt like yelling with frustration because I needed to do more. I'd feel emotionally drained and completely dead inside. It was so awful that I had to smoke massive amounts of pot so I could be numb. To help me come down I would listen to one of the tapes that the seer from Berkeley had given me. And I would use visualization to help me relax and ease out of the crash.

Although I preferred hanging out in groups, at the end of second semester I began to do drugs by myself. Usually, it was pot or speed. Going off on my dirt bike and smoking a joint was my way of relaxing. It helped take my mind off things like finding a girlfriend and being accepted at school. I kept thinking that everyone had me labeled for who I used to be, not who I was. I really worried that no one liked me and that they were saying bad things behind my back or laughing at me. When I got high, I'd forget my problems. It was an escape, even though I didn't realize it at the time. I thought using drugs was perfectly natural and okay.

My parents had no idea how much partying I was doing. We never talked about drugs. They assumed that drugs were something that I'd never be involved in, and neither of them asked me, or checked into what I was doing. They always trusted me to tell them the truth. They thought I was very responsible because I used to do things like call home when I was going to be out late. I don't ever remember having any in-depth conversation or family meetings while growing up. If my dad asked how school was going, I'd say fine and mention a bit about a book from English class or some good test score I had in history. Only good news was acceptable in my home.

While I was in ninth grade, my dad was traveling a lot, mostly to Japan, and we didn't do much together except to play tennis on Sundays. Even though I was usually recovering from a night of heavy partying, I always managed to drag myself onto the court and play a decent game. Usually we played doubles with some friends of his from the Valley. They'd always comment on what a handsome young man I was becoming and ask me what I was doing. In between sets, when we'd sit down and have iced tea, I'd talk to my father's friends and try to learn about their businesses. Sometimes, I'd ask their advice about college and law school. My dad liked bringing me to these tennis matches, and I think he was very proud of the way I acted. Although I genuinely enjoyed talking to his friends, I knew what my dad expected from me and I knew how to give him exactly what he was looking for.

I got along pretty well with my mom during that second semester because by then she knew that I needed time alone in front of the TV after school in order to unwind. Sometimes she'd take me shopping to buy clothes—something we enjoyed doing together. When my dad was traveling, we'd often eat dinner in front of the TV together. This was a treat for us both because when my dad was home we would all have to sit at the table. Sometimes after dinner, I'd leave the room to get high and then return to try to make my mom laugh by imitating people from TV or school.

I really don't think my mom could tell when I was high or on something. One time when my mom was helping me with algebra, I excused myself to go to the bathroom where I did a couple lines of coke. Then we worked together at the dining room table for the next hour. I'm sure she had no idea why I wanted to talk instead of do my homework. Late one night, while my dad was asleep, my mom and I shared a clove cigarette in the living room—

the one place my father let her smoke. It was as if we were sharing a secret. Because of this I felt closer to her, more like we were equals and that I could trust her. I then told her that I had tried pot in order to see what her reaction would be and gauge how much I could actually discuss with her. She did not look shocked until I told her that the first pot I smoked had been hers. She told me that she didn't like pot and had forgotten about the present—the bag of pot in her room, from her friend. We talked about the fact that some of my friends' parents got stoned. Before I went up to bed, my mom said I should "use my best judgment," because I was running with a "fast crowd."

My "best judgment" was to do what made me feel good. When I needed to use one of their cars, it was usually to go score drugs. I wasn't old enough to drive by myself, so I told them that the law in California said that a fifteen-year old with a learner's permit could drive with friends who were over twenty-one. They believed me because I'd just taken drivers ed. When I wanted to miss a test, I'd tell my mom that I had a headache and felt like throwing up. Then I'd call my friends that night and find out what the questions were. If I needed money for drugs, I'd ask my mom for money to go to the movies and then ask my dad as well. Usually I got whatever I wanted from my parents because they always believed me and they rarely said no.

Summer Time

The summer before tenth grade was an in-between time for me. I didn't want to go to camp, and my parents didn't pressure me to get a job because I'd had such a hard time in school the year before. Plus none of the uppers worked in the summers, they partied. In July, they let me go to Phoenix, Arizona to visit my old friend Colin, who I hadn't seen since he had moved in third grade. In Phoenix, Colin introduced me to his friends. They'd all say, "You're from California? Do you smoke weed?" With pride I told them yes, everyone does. They just laughed and said, "I knew it!"

Colin was the first person from outside the Napa Valley I corrupted. In fact, before I got there, alcohol and chewing tobacco were the only "substances" he used. But that first week in Phoenix, I introduced him to whipped cream cans. The second week, we took his sister's bong (pipe), and I scraped the bowl with a penknife for any excess resin. This is something desperate pot smokers are known to do when they run out. I hadn't brought any pot with me because I was afraid that if Colin were really straight, he might freak out. So we smoked the resin and both got headaches.

While I was in Phoenix, Colin's family threw a going away party for Colin's older sister who was leaving home to travel around the world for a year. There were a lot of college kids at this party, and I convinced Colin's sister to let Colin and me get high with them behind the pool house. Even though I was seven or eight years younger than most of the college students at the party, I could take longer and bigger bong hits than any of them. When I got back home, I sent Colin a big green bud inside a thank-you note.

I spent the rest of the summer doing chores outdoors for my parents. I enrolled in a course for lifeguard certification, which met five times a week. Since I was a good swimmer and swam laps in my family's pool almost every day, it didn't take too much effort for me to do well in the course. Life guarding further secured my alibi for red eyes. When the course was over, I missed the final exam and never became officially certified.

I also bought a new Honda 250XL, an on/off road motorcycle, that summer. To afford this, I traded in my old dirt bike, and my dad supplied half of the rest of the money. Because my town is so rural, he gave me permission to ride this bike in the vineyards and on the back roads, even though I didn't have a license. As long as I wore a helmet, the local cops never questioned me.

Besides riding my motorcycle and doing chores for my parents, my standard summer activity was sitting outside by the pool, getting tan and smoking pot with my friends Dirk, Greg, and Ben. Even though we were all good friends, I was definitely the leader, and they looked to me for ideas on what to do or where to get drugs. I also spent a lot of time with Dave, the friend who had worked at the hospital. Since Dave was twenty-one and could drive legally, we'd do things like go to the movies in a nearby town, or go to the pizza parlor to play video games. Most of the time, though, we'd just cruise around downtown getting high and doing speed.

TV and videos were a big thing for my friends and me that summer. Some of our favorite videos were Cheech and Chong movies like *Up In Smoke, Still Smoking,* and *Nice Dreams.* Whenever Cheech and Chong lit up a joint, so would we. We sort of acted out the movie. My favorite film of that summer was *The Big Chill.*

More than anything, I wished that I had a group of close friends like that; people who would get together for the weekend, hang out, and reminisce. I also admired the William Hurt character— the guy that drove the old Porsche and dealt drugs. As with the Chech and Chong movies, when the actors got stoned or did cocaine, I did it along with them, as if I were one of them.

By this time smoking pot was as natural as breathing. I'd get high in the morning and I'd get high in the afternoon. The more I smoked, the more enlightened I thought I was becoming. It wasn't a conscious thing; I wouldn't think "Oh, in January I knew this and by June, I felt that..." I just thought pot was helping me become more aware and intuitive.

My big preoccupation was analyzing all my thoughts to a "t." I thought about conversations I had and how I could have made them better. I would think about what people said and what they really meant. One of my favorite subjects to dwell upon was creation and how human beings began. For awhile, being constantly high seemed to make me a seer because when I was stoned, it seemed like I could always guess the exact time or price of something. And often, it seemed that I knew what people were going to say right before they said it.

I'd also become a real pot connoisseur. Just by taking one hit, I could tell exactly what kind of pot I was smoking. Good Green, which was around a lot, grows in northern California and Hawaii and smells sweet or skunky, sort of like a Christmas tree. Mexican or South American pot, on the other hand, smells like hay. Then there were "Thai sticks"—"chocolate Thai" and other strains of pot from Southeast Asia—and "purple kush," which comes from the Himalayas. Also popular in my town, was opium laced pot. The only kind of pot I avoided was paraquat sprayed pot because I had seen some rockers cough up black and bloody chunks after smoking it a few times. They would still smoke it though, because it was "good green" and cheap. It was cheap because it had been sprayed by C.A.M.P. helicopters so people wouldn't use it, but kids still did. We were told it would give us lung cancer by Ms. O'Donnell, but no one cared.

That summer, though, the drug I really wanted more of was cocaine. My most reliable connection at this point was through my old friend Ryan, who'd decided to drop out of school and move back to San Francisco to live with his 32-year old girlfriend. He got a job waiting tables at a seafood restaurant down at the wharves. Even though we hadn't been in contact for several weeks, I called Ryan to see if he could score some coke. When Ryan said he'd try, I took the bus down to San Francisco to spend a few days with him. In addition to my regular spending money, I brought six $100 bills with me to pay for the coke.

The day after I got to San Francisco, Ryan took me to a run-down auto body shop to meet a guy named Carlos, who was going to sell me three eighth-balls at $200 apiece, a bargain by Napa Valley standards. Being able to get so much really excited me, it was like buying the feeling of being in love. Since school had ended, I had been obsessed with the idea of scoring a quarter ounce or more of coke.

Ryan and I got to the auto body shop around noon; Carlos was waiting for the coke to arrive. He was about six feet tall and looked to be in his late twenties and was "ripped,"—strong from lifting weights. He told us that his family, who lived in Ecuador, sent him cocaine to cover his living expenses. He wore a beeper on his belt. Having to wait was something I sort of expected; with drug deals, waiting was always part of the game. Carlos began hosting lines from his personal stash. Though the lines he gave us were tiny compared to those he did himself, the quality made up for it. Carlos also took out some pot and we smoked a joint.

At 4 P.M., Ryan had to leave to work at the restaurant. I decided to wait with Carlos for the coke. Carlos went to the liquor store and bought a pint of 151-proof rum. He drank it down in three gulps. I didn't want any because I hadn't eaten anything. Coke had cut off my appetite. While we waited at the auto body shop,

Carlos and I kept doing lines. We talked about the going prices for large amounts of cocaine and he offered to get me a kilo for $10,000. My mind raced to figure out how I could raise the money. I calculated how many birds I'd have to sell, what I could get for my motorcycle, or how many people I'd have to get to invest in this deal. While we talked, I worked out the profit margin in my head. A kilo, 2.2 pounds, was around 10,000 grams. My net profit would exceed $100,000. The more lines I snorted, the better the idea sounded. I began to make mental lists of friends I'd call and how I'd put the whole thing together. By 9 P.M., we were both very "amped" (coked up). Carlos started saying things like, "You know, man, I don't trust that Ryan, man," and "I think Ryan is a fucking narc, man." I thought to myself, *Oh shit, he's getting paranoid.* I tried to calm him down by asking him questions about cars from his uncle's auto body shop. Did he ever get any good deals on hot cars—stolen vehicles? I also asked him about his homeland and what it was like. Carlos began to relax a little and he took out some photographs of Ecuador to show me.

The score still had not gone down by 1:30 that morning, Ryan had not come back, and Carlos was acting strange. He was totally fucked up, he had drunk a few more pints of 151 and had not eaten a thing. I started to get a bad feeling that the deal was never intended to go through. He started talking paranoid again about Ryan and then about me. I didn't know what to do, so once again I started talking to him about his home. Then something happened I was not ready for at all. He jumped on me, pulling me off the couch, he forced me to the floor. I was so wasted from all the drugs that I didn't realize what was happening. He was trying to rape me.

Now I was terrified and angry. I had a surge of energy and pushed him off of me. He grabbed me again and threw me onto the couch. He was much stronger than I was. I still had my butterfly knife in my pocket and I was debating whether or not to use it. I was afraid if I did, and missed, he would kill me. He tried to force off my pants as I was pinned to the couch. My face was shoved into the cushions and it was hard to breath, I began to panic. I kicked with all my might and hit him. He let go just long enough for me to get to my feet and tell him to *"Get the fuck away from me!"* His eyes went wild and he lunged at me again, but now I was no longer feeling groggy, I was terrified. I dodged him several times. He told me that I was not going to get out and that I just better give in. I knew he had some guns in the house and if I didn't get out quick he was going to make good on his promise.

I relaxed and looked him in the eyes. I said, "You're right," he smiled and also relaxed. In a blink of an eye I rushed past him and out the front door and into the night and back streets of San Francisco. I was running at a full speed, I was running for my life. By the time I hit the main street by his house I heard his door slam. In an instant he was right behind me. I broke into an all out sprint, scared to death I was going to be raped and then killed. I ran for several blocks, past the liquor store and the auto body shop. He was still on my heals. A couple times I felt him grab at my shoulder. He was yelling at me to *"Stop !"* I just kept running.

It was pitch dark aside from the occasional street lamp. All the stores were closed and I was alone. There was no one around. My feet hurt from hitting the pavement so hard as I ran, I could taste blood in my mouth as my heart pounded in my chest as I gasped for air. He would not stop and I knew I couldn't run much further.

I turned onto a street that was downhill and found another burst of energy. I saw a car coming, ran directly toward its lights and yelled out to Carlos, "I'm not stopping until I hit this car or you stop." I swerved away from the car at the last moment and kept going. I could no longer hear him behind me, but I didn't stop. I kept running for several minutes, through more deserted streets. Eventually I got into an area where there were cars and I jumped into a cab and handed the driver a $100 bill and told him to get me out of there.

That night I was in shock! I could barely talk, but when I finally did I yelled at Ryan for leaving me with such a sick fuck as Carlos. Ryan didn't seem to care and told me that it was not his fault, and the only important thing was that I got away. "It just comes with the territory Craig," he said casually.

I made Ryan call Carlos the next day and try to make the score himself. Carlos was now sure Ryan was a narc and threatened both of us. It was so important that I get the coke that I was able to forget about what happened and tried to convince Ryan to call again. I didn't want to be a failure in the eyes of my friends who were waiting on the blow. Plus I wanted that high more than anything else. I was willing to do almost anything for it, but was not going to be some guy's coke slut—person who trades sex for drugs. I really wanted to kill Carlos for what he had tried to do to me.

Later that week, at home, I was really scared that Carlos was going to come after me. I'd heard that South American coke dealers did terrible things to people and their families. He called my house once and I picked up the phone. I hung up as soon as I heard his voice. Then I called my friend and asked him if I could borrow one of his dad's nine millimeter pistols and a full clip. I wanted to blow Carlos away if he came anywhere near me. We went up to Ben's grandparents house where his dad kept the guns, but couldn't get one. I had to settle for my butterfly knife that never left my side for the rest of that year.

Over the summer, my parents and I got along well—basically because I didn't see them very much. We did, however, have one major run-in regarding drugs at the end of the summer. My parents rented a house at Dylan Beach, along the northern California coast, for a week, and said that I could invite a friend to come along. I brought Dirk.

One afternoon, Dirk and I were down in the garage doing lines. My dad heard us and tried to get into the garage, but the door was locked. When he knocked, we didn't answer but instead, did the lines quickly and went down to the beach for awhile so that we could enjoy our high. After our walk, we came back into the house and I saw my box of drug paraphernalia lying on the kitchen table. My first thought was, *Oh shit. Did I leave that there?* Then I realized that my dad must have found it. Dirk and I were more concerned about getting high to help us come off the coke than with dealing with my parents, so we went back down to the ocean and smoked a couple of joints that I had taken out of the box. On the way back to the house, I made sure that we had a story down pat. We planned to say that we found the box at the beach and were curious about it.

My father was upset and confused. He couldn't understand why I would be using drugs. I told him about finding the box by the sand dunes. But when he said, "Don't lie to me, Craig," I admitted that the box was mine.

My dad started asking us a lot of questions. I told him what I knew about marijuana: its long-term and short-term effects, how much it costs, the laws in California and so on. He asked me if I was involved in dealing and I told him that I wasn't. I explained that I didn't drink—which was true; I preferred drugs. I said I didn't smoke tobacco. But I did admit to using pot every now and then. I had half a pound of buds in my closet at home.

Then my mom started to cross-examine me, too. To stifle her questions and because I was getting angry I said, "The first pot I smoked belonged to you." My mother looked as though she had been slapped. My father clearly didn't know about the pot that had been in my mother's drawer. I succeeded in transferring his attention away from me for a few minutes so I could collect my thoughts. My mother looked scared because my dad wanted an explanation from her. She said that she'd gotten the pot from a friend and that she'd only smoked it once. My dad was at a loss for words, so he redirected the conversation back to Dirk and me. When my dad asked Dirk how he would feel if his father knew he were smoking marijuana, Dirk told him that his father smoked pot, too.

Again, my dad was stunned. I offered more examples of prominent adults in the community—from local officials, to law enforcement and many business owners—that I knew for certain smoked pot and did other drugs. My dad said, "You aren't doing heroin or cocaine, are you?" With no facial expression whatsoever, I looked him directly in the eye (something I was very good at doing), and said, "That stuff is a waste of money and highly addictive. I wouldn't touch it." My dad said he was relieved.

The final result of all this was that the confrontation turned into a discussion that I was able to lead. In a way, my parents knew nothing and I knew everything. I didn't give away any information that might incriminate me. I only told them what I had to. After all was said and done, my parents left the box out on the table and I took it back. The joints and a quarter ounce of buds were still in it. I knew then that I had won a clear victory. I was lucky and feeling very relieved that my dad hadn't found the cocaine. That would have been very difficult to explain.

Tenth grade got off to a bad start simply because I didn't really want to go back to school and have to deal with all the people. I loved the summer and being in my own world, where no one bothered me and I could do what I wanted and see whom I wanted to see, and I could party whenever I felt like it. Needless to say, being back in class took some getting used to. I felt really burned out from smoking so much pot over the summer and I'd forgotten nearly everything I learned from the year before. Grades, as always, were important to me, though, so I tried to pay attention as best I could.

My favorite class that semester was biology because the teacher spent a lot of time talking about animals—a subject I knew a lot about. In fact, as a kid, books about animals were the only ones I'd ever read. All this early learning paid off because in biology class, I'd mention something I'd read as a kid and no one except the teacher would know what I was talking about. I brought my boa constrictor and birds to class for a presentations on the anatomy of animals. We also studied the human body in biology. Raw eggs, I learned, can rebuild the stomach lining. From then on, whenever I did speed, I'd always eat a couple of raw eggs the morning after. Before, using speed had trashed my stomach and left me unable to eat anything for a few days afterwards without feeling sick.

I signed up for three classes of choir—concert choir, pre-jazz, and combined choir. These classes met at 7:15 in the morning, an hour before the regular school day started. I didn't mind getting up early to go to them because I enjoyed singing. I had been doing it since fourth grade, plus the teacher was really fun, and we were able to laugh a lot in his class. Every couple of years all the choirs would come together and record an album to sell in the valley.

Although I no longer took health, I still had Ms. O'Donnell for the non-jock phys. ed. class. Since the jocks weren't there to compete with, I got to be captain and pick the teams whenever we played volleyball. I made a point of choosing people from all the different cliques to be on my side. For an hour, no one was mean to anyone else; we all worked together. My team got to be so good that Ms. O'Donnell suggested that we challenge the jock class to a match. We did, and we beat them. This made us all feel great. I only wished that my school had a boys' volleyball team because I knew that I was good at it. I had fun playing and the sport didn't bother my allergies.

My other classes weren't as interesting as biology or as much fun as phys. ed. I was sick and tired of being in remedial English. I hadn't minded the class the year before, because I did a lot of talking and got an easy A. But in tenth grade it was a pain; the people who were in the class—mostly rockers and Latinos—were disruptive and rude. The teacher spent half her time yelling at people and often handed out extra homework because she was mad.

Geometry was very difficult for me and I had to get a tutor. I spent most of my time trying to catch up, and when I couldn't catch up I cheated. Typing class was especially frustrating because I had to keep checking to make sure I was spelling the words right during the timed tests. I ended up dropping independent Spanish because I had too much homework in my other classes.

Even though my grades averaged out to a B, I felt very frustrated and almost out of control. I'd be ahead in one class, behind in another. In one class, I'd need a tutor; in another class, I wouldn't even have to show up. I was good at volleyball, but there was no team. I didn't seem to fit in at all. I knew that I wasn't living up to my potential and it bothered me.

Things weren't much better socially. I wanted to have a girlfriend, but I still wasn't confident about what it took to get one. Ryan wasn't around anymore to answer my questions or tell me what I was doing wrong. There was no one I could really talk to about girls unless I was on cocaine.

To make matters worse, one of my other friends, Greg, told me that he wasn't allowed to associate with me anymore. Greg's father, the owner of a local winery, had heard a rumor that I was using cocaine and didn't want Greg to be corrupted by me. Little did Greg's father know that his son had not only tried coke, but was selling speed. In fact, Greg was the person I took my first LSD trip with. Greg's father was very much opposed to people taking drugs and every time I saw him downtown, he would look right through me, as if I weren't there. This bothered me a lot because I really liked Greg and his family. Even though Greg and I continued to sneak out and do things behind his father's back, it wasn't the same anymore.

The person I spent the most time with was Dirk. Until we became friends, Dirk had been a very unobtrusive and quiet guy; I brought out the rowdy side in him. It was easy to make him laugh. It was like having a little brother who looked up to me. Dirk wasn't part of any clique, unless being friends with me constituted being in a clique. In a way, I was to Dirk what Ryan was to me. In the way that Ryan introduced me to a lot of new things in ninth grade, including cocaine, I taught Dirk about them the next summer.

A lot of people, particularly the uppers, gave me a hard time about being friends with Dirk. They'd say he was a "loser" and ask me how I could hang out with him. I hated it when they said things like that; it made me feel like I was a loser and that I had to choose between my friends. On one hand, I wanted the uppers to accept me. On the other hand, I liked Dirk. He was dependable and didn't act stuck up like most of the uppers. I felt comfortable around him. Even my parents questioned my friendship with Dirk. He was so shy that he rarely said anything to them. I had to tell him to at least say hello, good-bye, and thank you. Even though they never talked about it, I knew my parents associated Dirk with pot because of the incident at the beach over the summer. I could tell they preferred that I hang around the uppers.

Ever since I can remember, I've always gravitated to people like Dirk—people who seemed to be victims. For example, that semester I became very good friends with Jenny, a really smart new girl in my geometry class. Jenny got straight A's and I admired her for this. Since she was new, she kept to herself a lot. None of the cliques really even noticed her—probably because she didn't dress well or drive a BMW. She was a loner.

During free periods, Jenny and I used to hang out and talk about her problems—most of which centered around her parents, who had just gotten divorced. Jeannie's dad, a doctor, lived in the midwest. Jennie's mom drank and took ludes and was usually out of it. Even though her mom had a housekeeper, Jenny was the one who ended up watching her little brother. Things got so bad that she used to sign her mother's name to checks in order to pay the bills. All this depressed her and she cried on my shoulder about her life.

I would help Jenny sort out her options and try to show her that her life wasn't worthless. We used to talk for hours about how she should handle her mom's irresponsibility. Once she said that she wanted me to be her boyfriend. Jenny wasn't my type, but it made me feel good to know that someone actually wanted to go out with me.

During the first part of tenth grade, if someone had asked me, "What do you like most about your life?" I'd have said, "Drugs." After all, academics at school didn't thrill me. My love life was nonexistent. But where drugs were involved, I felt I was in control and having fun.

When the kids at school were scrounging around for drugs and scraping their pipes for resin, they'd come to me because I never ran dry. In fact, people at school wondered how I always seemed to have a supply. For me, it was easy. In fact, half the fun of doing drugs was finding and then scoring them. Sometimes at night, I'd drive with some friends into a large town nearby and check out who was hanging around the square. Rockers were often a good bet for speed and LSD, so if I were going to look for these particular drugs, I'd "dress down" and probably wear a concert T-shirt and ripped jeans to look more like them. Then I'd take out my hackey sack (a leather ball-shaped bag of beans), and look for people to "sack it up" with—kick it around. Then I'd start a conversation.

In addition to knowing how to dress, I prided myself on being able to act in different ways toward different kinds of people. With rockers, I always spoke in a monotone, never used big words, and mainly spoke in slang. By changing my act, I was quickly considered cool and more likely to score. With my steadier connections I applied the same "no threat" philosophy, and it worked every time. I met a young couple named Sam and Mary who dealt coke out of the back of a gift shop they owned. Sam and Mary were usually very jittery, so I made a conscious effort to act completely relaxed in front of them. Since they were very generous and always cut me heavy grams, I'd visit them even when I didn't want to buy drugs. Once I even helped them move to a new house.

One of Jennie's mother's crazy friends turned out to be a great connection. His name was Jerry, and he was a three-hundred pound former pro-football player who lived in a big house in the hills with several dogs. Jerry, who reminded me of Grizzly Adams, dealt pot, hash, and pills. His ironclad rule was to never sell drugs to kids—high school students, but Jenny convinced him to change that rule for me. So I made sure that whenever I bought drugs from him, I used large bills. I showed up on time and I didn't talk more than was necessary.

Sometimes I'd also buy and trade drugs with Jennie's mom. I remember being at Jennie's house studying in their huge sunken living room; Jennie's mom would walk in, usually in her bathrobe, and say, "Craig, honey, can you find me something to smoke?" I would usually give her a joint or small bud and she'd give me a great deal on cross-tops. In my mind, I separated buying drugs from Jennie's mom, from Jennie's mom's drug use. They didn't seem related and Jenny never said anything. I figured, if Jennie's mom had drugs to sell, I should buy them because if I didn't, somebody else would. All my steady connections counted on me to keep my mouth shut and I did. The last thing they needed was a bunch of high school students knocking at their door. Talking about your dealer is the fastest way to lose one, and possibly your life too.

People in my school also sold drugs to each other. Buying and selling drugs was one way I could associate with different people from different cliques. If I scored an eighth of pot on a Tuesday night from an upper, he'd expect me to get him high that Wednesday in school. Or if I bought some speed from one of the Latinos, I might offer to "line him up." No one really ever saved their drugs for later. Once we scored them, we did them.

Even though I was careful never to get high on days when I had a big test or presentation, doing drugs in school was part of the game. On days when I didn't have first-period choir practice, I'd drive my motorcycle to school, meet one of my friends in front of the entranceway and then drive down to the football field to smoke a bowl before homeroom. Sometimes we'd just leave during a lunch break and walk up into the vineyards. Occasionally we'd get high in the school hallways by putting our heads inside our lockers and lighting up a small pipe called a "sneak a toque." This pipe didn't let any smoke escape aside from where you inhaled. Even though the pipe was smokeless, the challenge for us was to make sure that no smoke would escape from our lungs as we walked out of the locker bay to the doors leading outside.

At school, we didn't limit ourselves to pot. We also did cocaine in the bathrooms. One of my friends would stand guard at the door while I would "line up" on my little mirror. Then we'd take turns guarding the door and snorting lines. We'd line up crank in the glove compartment of my mom's car before gym and leave it there. Then during our two-mile run, we'd make a pit-stop and do up the lines.

Whenever we did drugs in school, my friends and I had to be on the lookout not only for teachers, but for the "Kiddie Cops"—students who were part of a police auxiliary program. Kiddie Cops were out to bust other students who were involved in anything illegal. Once a week after school they'd attend lectures at the police station and then ride around in the squad cars. They were anti everything, and the principal would praise them for turning troublemakers in. In fact, the Kiddie Cops once tipped off the police about some pot plants that my friend Mike was growing in his basement. One Saturday morning, the police showed up at his house and took away thirty plants. Needless to say, the Kiddie Cops weren't very popular with their fellow students.

One of these Kiddie Cops actually became a police officer. His brother, Tim, was a connection for good buds and always high, but now that his brother was a cop we had to be extra careful. One day when we were taking bong hits in Tim's room, his brother kicked open the door wearing his full uniform. He looked at both of us in disgust, then took out his gun and forced it into his brother's mouth and said, "There is no difference between what I could do with this gun and what you are doing right now. I should end your miserable little life." He cocked his gun, and Tim began to cry. Panicked, I ran out of the room. Tim called me later and said, "You better stay clear of my brother." I agreed, but it didn't prevent us from getting high at school the next day.

In December, my friend Ryan, who was still living in San Francisco, told me that he had enrolled in a self-discovery program called Est. I'd never seen Ryan so excited about anything before. He said that Est taught him how to "be committed and follow through." He said that it was "transforming" his life and giving him a more "total view" of humanity and his role in it. I still idolized Ryan. He was still the big brother I had always wanted. I thought to myself, *If Ryan thinks Est is so great then I should check it out too.*

During the first weekend in December, he brought me to an Est introductory meeting in San Francisco. After one morning of Est, I was sold and immediately signed up for the formal training. I felt that Est could help me understand the reasons my life was so empty and why I always felt frustrated. I hoped that Est would help me live up to my full potential and learn to express myself more openly. When I told my parents about my interest in Est, they discussed it between themselves and told me that I would have to pay the whole $500 fee myself. I lied about my age on the application because you had to be eighteen or older to register for the training. That month I turned sixteen.

The training was held every weekend for four weekends in December. One of the rules was that the participants were, under no circumstances, to take any drugs or drink during that entire month. I never broke this rule. In fact, during that month, not doing drugs was easy for me. In a way, Est offered me something better than drugs. It gave me a natural high and people to share it with.

The training helped me a lot. Before Est, I never considered my problems as obstacles that could be removed; I always thought they would be there forever. I soon learned that dyslexia is what I made it and that it doesn't have to be an obstacle if I don't want it to be. I began to examine my role in both creating and resolving my problems. I learned that every breakdown creates the possibility for a greater breakthrough. I also learned how to recognize different ways of communicating. We talked about roles people play and the masks they wear. The training leaders said that everyone has an act because they are afraid of being hurt. This made complete sense to me—and seemed to apply to all the people I knew at school. This knowledge made the uppers seem a lot less scary. It was the first time I had ever thought that other people were as self-conscious as I was, and that no one was perfect.

By the second weekend, I realized my "act" was always having to be right. As part of the training, I had to figure out what I gained from my act and what it cost me. I got up in front of four hundred participants and said that not being smart made me feel like I was always wrong and stupid.

About three weeks after the training began, I made a commitment to talk to my family. I called my sister Amy and told her I was sorry for being such a mean little brat to her. I also decided to talk to my parents about what was bothering me at school. I told them that I felt inferior and that I thought I let them down (especially my father) because I didn't play sports, do well in school, or have many extracurricular activities. These were things that I'd never even mentioned before. Talking like this made me break down and cry, something I also never did or saw my family do. The subject of drugs never came up because this was one area of my life that I felt good about.

My parents were stunned that I was telling them so much because we never talked about upsetting things, especially ones that were personal. During this conversation, they both kept saying, "We love you for who you are." That night was the beginning of many frank conversations between us. My mother suggested that I might be happier at a different school. She mentioned a neighbor who'd gone away to boarding school and loved it. Although we'd talked about boarding school once before, I'd never really seriously thought about it. I had never thought I was smart enough to go to a private school. My mom said she thought it might be a good idea for me and for the first time I was willing to admit that she might be right.

Changing Schools

knew that getting into a good boarding school was going to be tough, but I knew that I wanted to go and that somehow I would get in. My grades were solid mid-B range. My record of extracurricular activities was fair, especially chorus and my bird business, Fraser's Feathers. I was counting on my personal interviews to help a lot. Making a good impression was one of my best skills.

My mom helped me send away for applications and apply to three schools—Webb in Los Angeles, Hawaii Prep in Honolulu, and Monticello in Mendocino County. I especially liked the idea of Monticello. It wasn't too far from home; it was supposed to be very liberal; and my sister told me that there were a lot of drugs at Monticello.

It wasn't too long after sending out the applications that I received the generic, "We-are-sorry-but-our-school-is-full-at-the-moment-please-stay-in-touch" responses from Webb and Hawaii Prep. I kept my fingers crossed for Monticello. I was really excited when they sent me a letter inviting me up to the school for an interview and a tour.

My parents and I went to visit Monticello in January, and once I'd been there, I knew it was where I wanted to go to school. Monticello didn't look anything like a public school, and I liked that. The girl who acted as our guide told me and my parents that before Monticello was a school, it had been a working ranch. Remsen Hall, the school's main building, had been the owner's home. As we walked around I noticed the big windmill next to Remsen Hall; our tour guide showed us a teepee that had been built by the Native American studies class.

My mother was impressed that Monticello had such a big vegetable garden—and our tour guide told us that students at Monticello took care of the garden themselves as a community service project. Then she took us to look at the animals. I was stoked to find out that Monticello had cows, chickens, and even horses—even though I knew that the animals would probably make me sneeze a lot. Our tour guide mentioned that many students brought their own horses with them to the campus and that each spring the riding club sponsored week-long horseback camping trips into the hills. She said camping and cookouts were very popular at Monticello and that completing a three-week backpacking trip was a graduation requirement. My dad and I both liked the emphasis on outdoor activities.

The dorms looked like ski cabins but I didn't care. Inside, the rooms were all paneled with dark knotty pine and had high ceilings with cross beams. The room we saw had both a Jimi Hendrix and a trippy Pink Floyd poster on the wall. I checked out one of the dorm bulletin boards and saw announcements for a Greenpeace meeting and a sign-up sheet to audition for the Arthur Miller play, *The Crucible*. After visiting a classroom and checking out the computer center, we wound up our tour by taking a look at the pool. I told our guide that I'd just finished my lifeguard training; I didn't tell her that I had not taken the written exam. She said that was good because Monticello needed more lifeguards.

That afternoon, I had an interview with the dean of students. He told me to call him by his first name, then asked me questions like, "What are your favorite subjects?" and "What are your best qualities?" We talked for about twenty minutes and throughout the conversation, I made sure to look him in the eye and speak clearly. When the interview was over, I shook his hand and thanked him.

All day, wherever I went, I tried to figure out what the clique situation was like, without being too obvious. I noticed a group of guys playing hackey sack, and several people wearing tie-dyed shirts. I wondered if tie-dye at Monticello meant the same thing it did in my town: "I do LSD." That day, as we walked around and passed students lying out on the green or working in the stables, many gave me the casual head jerk, a quick upward movement of the head that meant "Hey, what's up?" I returned the gesture tentatively; at public school, it took a couple of years before most people would even acknowledge a new person. I wasn't sure if the friendliness I was witnessing was sincere.

In February, I received a letter saying I'd been accepted at Monticello. Even though I was really happy to be going, I told all my friends at public high school that my parents were forcing me to go. I was embarrassed to be leaving, and didn't want to hurt anyone's feelings. I also didn't want the other kids to ridicule me as they had Karen, a girl who went to an East Coast boarding school after junior high. Once she left, the cliques spread mean rumors about her. People said that she was a stuck-up bitch and a loser. When she came back for summer vacation, no one would talk to her.

Around the same time I was accepted by Monticello, my popularity and social standing at school changed radically because I started going out with one of the most beautiful girls in my class. Her name was Katherine and she was a exchange student from Denmark. Katherine had piercing green eyes, a beautiful smile and was always laughing. She also had a great body. Her incredible good looks and foreign accent made her popular at school right away—she was the first exception to the "strangers should remain strangers" motto at school. That Katherine was obviously very wealthy, and that her grandmother was rumored to be a countess also helped. Katherine was like no one I had ever met before.

The Est training I'd had gave me the self-confidence to approach Katherine. I knew that if I never took risks, my life would never change. I told myself that there was no reason why we shouldn't go out together. At first, though, Katherine didn't pay much attention to me. A few months before, I'd have given up on her and become depressed. My attitude had changed, however, and I didn't give up on her or us. I called her every night to ask about homework—really I was just trying to show her that I was different from the others and that she should go out with me.

It didn't take long before the feeling was obviously mutual. She would sit behind me in all the classes we had together and pass me notes or play with the back of my neck. She drove me absolutely crazy. I was in love, really in love. Katherine was the fist person I ever felt loved me for just who I was. I had no control over my love for her. I sent her a dozen roses the first week we were going out, wrote her countless poems, and drew her pictures. At night we would whisper into the phone for hours until the sun came up. Then, when we saw each other at school we would laugh hysterically about how tired we were. I had finally found someone I could love who also loved me.

One reason that I focused my energy on Katherine was that she was an exchange student and new to school, which meant she had not known me my whole life, like all the others in school. Also, the fact that she was a foreigner really appealed to me, too. From spending so much time with my dad's foreign business associates, I always got the impression that foreigners generally had a deeper sense of friendship. I believed this to be true of Katherine.

After that first week of being completely infatuated with each other, I learned that her best friend, Maura, whose family she was living with, had told Katherine not to go out with me because I was stuck-up. Maura couldn't stand Dirk, either, and said he was a loser. I expected to hear something like this; it proved I was right about the other girls and their ideas about me. After Maura spent some time with me, she realized that I wasn't stuck-up at all; she even told Katherine that she was lucky to be going out with me.

Katherine was the first girl I had slept with. Before her, I hadn't even really kissed anyone. Having sex had been her idea. She came over one night when my parents were out to dinner, we got stoned, and went skinny dipping. Afterwards we drank a bottle of champagne she brought and had sex. I didn't know much about sex, let alone have a condom. She assured me that it was okay, and not to worry. In that moment, stoned, and buzzed from the champagne, I didn't think about her getting pregnant or giving me a disease.

Since we were going out, it was generally assumed that we were sleeping together; even if we hadn't been, everyone would have thought we were and said that we were. She thought that I wanted sex because that's what all the uppers required from girlfriends, but I would have been content just holding and kissing her. I wanted someone to share my feelings with more than I wanted to have sex. She was surprised at this and loved me all the more for it. Some of my guy friends were jealous of me; I enjoyed knowing that they wanted Katherine, but that I was the only one who could have her. And, I felt even better when Katherine told a couple of her friends that I was great in bed.

Katherine smoked French cigarettes and hung out in the smoking section, an outdoor porch area behind the cafeteria. Even though kids from all the cliques—the rockers, the Mexican's, the stoners—hung out there, the uppers always took the best seats. Among the uppers, the smoking area was the place to be. I felt intimidated by the people who hung out in the smoking section, and since I never smoked cigarettes, I had no reason to go there. But now, because Katherine was my girlfriend, I went to the smoking section to be with her. I automatically became better friends with Katherine's friends, most of whom were the uppers.

Katherine was also friends with many junior and seniors, like Maura. I too ended up hanging out with the older students—people I'd admired since freshman year.

At first I couldn't believe that these people accepted me so readily. I was shocked when Katherine said things like, "You should do stuff with Matt. He thinks you're cool." Matt was the leader of the athletic uppers in my grade and our parents were good friends. Everyone at school admired his natural talent with all sports; and all the girls wanted him, and most had him—had sex with him. I didn't know how to react to the idea that Matt might want to be my friend; I'd always thought that the people I didn't know well had a bad impression of me.

Regardless of how friendly they were to me personally, the uppers still gave me a hard time about Dirk, whom I considered my best friend. I didn't want to deal with this because I liked having Dirk for a friend. The previous year, I wouldn't have known how to respond. But Est gave me the confidence to say, "He's a great person. You just don't know him," and let it go at that.

Besides, even though we were spending less time together because I had a girlfriend, Dirk sold hash for me that semester. The hash came from Jerry, the ex-pro football player who lived in the woods. I had bought a small brick of it for myself but there was just too much, and I didn't care for the high. So I gave what I didn't intend to use to Dirk to sell. Dirk was stoked to sell drugs for me because he didn't have to front any money and got to keep several grams of hash for himself as commission. And selling drugs gave him power to choose who could buy and who couldn't. Those who had been mean to him at school and needed a high couldn't get it.

Mike was another friend I made that semester. He was the one person in my class that I thought did too many drugs. Mike's parents had died in a plane crash when he was ten, and he lived with his uncle, who was only thirty-one. Mike's uncle had made a fortune with a high-tech company and owned one of the more up-and-coming wineries. He gave Mike a lot of freedom. Although Mike could have been an upper, he spent most of his time with burned-out rockers and Latinos. We were alike in that respect: both of us had friends from lower middle-class families—people like Dirk, who weren't anything like the uppers.

Mike was different from me in one major way—he didn't care about school at all. That's what I mean when I say he did too many drugs. He had the typical "I-don't-give-a-shit" attitude that Ms. O'Donnell said was the sign of someone who smoked too much pot. Occasionally, I would torment teachers too, by making funny comments from the back of the class—where I always sat. My statements were always a bit disrespectful, but usually more funny than anything and even the teacher would end up laughing. I was often the class clown. Mike would be blatantly rude, defiant, and get kicked out of class; then everyone would laugh, but not with him, at him.

It wasn't just the teachers who didn't like Mike. He also pissed off people when it came to cheating. Most of us would cheat to raise a C to a B, or a B to an A. But Mike cheated simply to pass. Also, Mike was a "taker" and never had homework to share. People got really tired of giving their answers to him with no return of the favor. But it was with drugs that Mike showed himself to be a true pain in the ass. In fact, he gave the word cheap *new* meaning. To people who weren't his close friends, he'd sell a third of a gram of coke for the price of a half a gram. If anyone complained, he'd tell him that the quality of the coke more than made up for the small amount. People usually shut up because Mike came across like he knew what he was talking about. He also was one of the few people at school with solid cocaine connections. Because his uncle was a big partyer, Mike knew older professional dealers. He would never reveal these connections. People at school who wanted coke were forced to deal with him.

Because of drugs, I hung around with Mike. That he was able to get good drugs, especially coke, made the rest of his bullshit tolerable. Mike also knew more about drugs than I did. I had something to learn from him, and that year, I used him as a teacher.

The fact that we both had money to spend on cocaine was a key part of our friendship, and we'd often go in on deals together. In the past, when I'd do cocaine with someone like Dirk, I always paid for it. I never minded paying for coke alone. But since Mike and I both had money, our friendship was more mutual. The fact that he usually tried to take more than his share when we went in together on deals didn't really bother me because I wasn't paying for all of it.

That semester, I went from buying a gram or a sixteenth to buying eightballs for myself. I began to build up a heavy tolerance for cocaine. Mike and I liked to put out big lines—over two feet long—on a full length mirror, then try to snort it all up in one breath. One night, Mike and I did several of these two-foot lines. Mike threw up as I did one more line. Another time, I did coke with Greg, the friend who wasn't supposed to associate with me, and had a strange experience. Greg and I had done about a gram of coke really quickly and went outside for a walk. I snorted and felt a big coke drip flow down and numb the back of my throat. As I felt the coke hit my empty stomach, I became light headed, and it was hard to breath. I was scared. Then my vision went blank and all I could see was white fuzz—like on a blank TV screen. For about four or five minutes I was in a state of total bliss. But then my heart slammed against my chest and I was having a serious problem breathing—my throat seemed to be numbed shut. The same thing happened to Greg; he said he couldn't see anything either and that he was really scared. I focused on helping Greg instead of my own problem. I told him to focus on breathing in deeply and slowly. Then holding his breath and releasing it slowly. Soon he felt better.

I was less scared because I felt that no matter what I did, no harm would come to me. I truly believed this. I was convinced that I had some sort of karmic protection that prevented me from dying. Believing that nothing bad would ever happen made me feel it was perfectly fine to take outrageous risks, like the time I drove Matt and a group of uppers to a bridge that spans a reservoir near my house. After I'd had several beers and a few bowls of pot I climbed the scaffolding under the bridge. We all knew that jumping off the bridge in June was dangerous because the water level was very low and the rocks were exposed at the bottom. At least two or three people die every year as a result of jumping.

Matt and I had watched some of the others jump earlier in the day and said that we would jump once our buzz was in effect. We sat on the scaffolding for fifteen minutes looking down at the water, then at each other. The water was more than 70 feet below us. I thought, *Oh, shit. Am I really going to do this?* Then Matt said, "Fuck it," and jumped, screaming all the way. After he hit the water and his head popped back up, I jumped, swinging my arms six times before I hit. Falling so fast through the air was a real rush. Matt and I went back up on the bridge and jumped several more times throughout the day.

Like most of my friends, I drove like a maniac. I told myself that I'd never get a ticket and relied on my sixth sense to avoid being snagged by the cops. When I drove a car under the influence of drugs I thought that I could not hurt myself or anybody else. I truly believed that having an accident was not my destiny.

One Friday night, Dave, Dirk, and I smoked an eighth, and I drove us all to Napa in my mother's Fiat with the top down and Iron Maiden blasting on the car stereo. On a windy road near my house, I downshifted and accelerated to 80 miles per hour in order to pass the car in front of us. I went on to pass the next car at 100 miles per hour, the car after that at 110, and gassed it to over 120 around a totally blind turn in order to pass the fifth car. My friends were yelling, "Oh, fuck!" all the way. Suddenly, a truck hauling grapes came at us from the other direction, just missing our Fiat by a hair's breadth. Coming that close to death didn't bother me a bit and I looked for it everywhere I went.

Another time, Matt and I split a quarter ounce of 'shrooms and went driving in my mother's Fiat on a road that zig-zagged through the vineyards and hills between Sonoma and Napa counties. It was dusk, and since we had taken mushrooms, all the colors seemed especially bright. We were going about 80 when I suddenly hit the breaks and cut the wheel, making the car do a 360-degree turn. Both the car and I were completely out of control. The car came smoking, screeching and snapping to a halt. Matt turned totally white, I looked over at him, grinned, and pealed out to continue down the hill.

Like driving recklessly, shoplifting gave me a natural high. Since I didn't really need anything, I'd steal for the challenge, then give what I'd stolen to my friends. I rationalized my stealing by thinking that if the store owners weren't good enough to catch me, they weren't good enough to keep their merchandise. I also thought that if certain things were overpriced, I had the right to take them. If I bought a shirt at normal price, which I thought was too high, I would also take one or two more. Once I took a handful of silver bracelets while a person was wringing me up. Later I'd give the bracelets or shirts to Katherine. Other times, I'd go to the record store with my friends, buy a couple of tapes and then browse around for some more. While I was browsing, I'd pocket six or seven more tapes. My friends would do the same, in fact they taught me to steal. At first I had been scared to do it, but soon realized that it was easy and a fun challenge—like Robin Hood, stealing from the rich and giving to the poor.

Stealing tapes was a meager challenge, though, because all I had to do was rip the electronic beeper device from each package when no one was looking. Since I didn't have a stereo at this point and since I wasn't into music as much as the other kids in my school, I'd usually end up giving the tapes I'd stolen to my friends, or trading them for a butt or a line. But I never stole from local stores because I knew all the owners, and I never stole from people I knew. I just did it for the challenge. Stealing was easy for me.

No one ever caught me shoplifting and I never got arrested while I was driving. That semester, the only time the police ever questioned me was when I had already pulled over to the side of a mountain road with Katherine. I was rolling a joint on the driver's manual. I did what I always did when confronted by an adult—I reacted quickly and talked my way out of it. On that particular evening, I funneled the pot into the bag, and shoved it down my pants. When the police officer came to my window, I looked him in the eyes, and asked him if there was anything wrong. Not expecting this, he paused for a moment to gather his thoughts and then asked me if there was anything wrong. I told him that I was just enjoying the view with my girlfriend and that I didn't think it was a crime in this state. He laughed and told us to have a good evening.

Lying was becoming second nature to me. It was as if I were simply switching gears and going into a different mode. I'd speak smoothly and clearly. I made myself believe what I was saying. Since Est taught me how to manipulate conversations to get what I wanted, I knew that my lies were good. In fact, my lies sounded more believable than what most people called the truth, at least to me they did.

At the end of the school year, the idea of leaving for boarding school really began to depress me. I finally had a girlfriend. I knew that once I left, our relationship would be over. Also school was going better than ever. My grades were great, all A's and B's. I didn't even need a tutor anymore because Est had taught me how to apply myself and follow through on my work. I made the most of the skills I had and it paid off. I had made a lot of friends in all the different groups. It seemed a shame to leave just when things were going well. But, the plans for boarding school were already set—I had promised, no matter what, if I was accepted, I would go. The gains I'd made in communicating with my mom and dad no longer seemed real, and I didn't tell them how ambivalent I now felt about boarding school. Over the summer I only saw my parents in passing, and when they asked how everything was going, I'd tell them some little detail and leave it at that. Sometimes, they'd take Katherine and me out to dinner, but we never had much serious personal conversation. Now and then I'd play tennis with my dad and occasionally I'd play dominoes with my mom, but that was the extent of our contact. Instead, I plunged into two summer jobs and a very busy social life.

My typical weekday would begin at 5:35 a.m. I'd get up and be at work in the watercress fields by six. There I'd meet five other guys my age—two rockers from my ninth-grade English class; two Latinos who worked there year round; and Greg, whose father didn't know we worked together. Our job consisted of building hydroponic trays for growing watercress. We also dug irrigation lines and drainage ditches.

Smoking pot made the work go easier. At around 9 a.m., before the doughnut break, I'd get stoned with Greg out behind the barn. We'd work until 1 p.m., then call it a day. After having lunch and smoking a few bowls at Maura's house, where Katherine was living, I'd call Dirk and we'd score an eighth of pot and smoke part of it together. At 2:30, I'd drive my motorcycle to my landscaping job, which consisted of weeding, mowing, and cutting down branches at an old woman's estate. Since she wasn't ever at home and there was no one there to tell me what to do, I always took a few hits while I was watering and cleaning up the lawn. At six o'clock, or whenever I finished, I'd go back to Maura's, take a shower and eat dinner with Maura and Katherine. Most nights we'd sit at her house and watch videos until I fell asleep on the couch. I would often drive home at two in the morning.

On weekend nights, Katherine and I would go out with the uppers. Occasionally, I'd go motorcycle riding with my non-upper friends. Sometimes, I'd party with the rockers who worked with me at the watercress fields. I loved having so many friends. But with so many different friends from different groups, I felt like I was being pulled in too many directions—that I had too little time to devote to each of them. I didn't want to be forgotten or ridiculed when I left for boarding school so I did my best to please everybody. I didn't want to lose what I'd gained second semester.

During the first part of my summer, Katherine was everything to me. I never thought that I could love someone so much and I poured myself completely into our relationship. Even though I knew that it would be over once I went away to school, I thought of her constantly. I wouldn't let myself dwell on the end of the summer.

Katherine wasn't as involved with drugs as I was, but she always did them with me, especially coke. Katherine loved cocaine. One night after we'd done a couple of lines, Katherine said that she thought she was addicted to coke because she loved doing it so much. This blew me away because whenever we bought coke I'd always do twice as much as she did. All that summer, we'd stay up late at night snorting cocaine and talking about how we felt about each other. Sober, I felt I could tell Katherine anything, but after a couple of lines of cocaine, I wanted to bare my soul. When I was with Katherine, I never crashed. But if I ran out of coke and she wasn't there, I'd feel totally depressed, as if there were an eighty-pound emotional weight on my chest. I guess that being with her and feeling loved took the crash away. For all the talking we did, though, one topic we never got into was my boarding school and her leaving for Denmark. I think it was easier for both of us to ignore the fact that our relationship was going to end.

In July, I took two weeks off from work and went to New York with Katherine to see her father, who had business in the United States. For this trip from San Francisco, I packed an ounce of KGBs in my bags. I also had a sixteenth of crank hidden in the seam of my shirt so that I could easily get to it. Once the plane took off, Katherine and I started doing lines of crank on our seat trays. In New York, I smoked the ounce of buds in twelve days—with help from Katherine and her brother, who was also visiting from Europe.

I went home to California alone. Katherine had decided to stay with her father for another two weeks because they so rarely got to spend time together. Alone, and on my own, I tripped on LSD again. One Friday afternoon, when I got off work early from the watercress fields and didn't have to work on the old woman's property that day, I drove to Santa Rosa and picked up my friend, Ben. That night we went to the Santa Rosa Fair, a carnival with rides and animals.

I only had a little pot with me and wanted to get some more, so Ben and I drove to the "Alley," a space between two buildings. Outside the Alley, I recognized a punker I'd seen there before, and asked him if he knew where we could get any buds. The guy's pupils were dilated. When he tried to sell us a bud for $13, I offered him $10.

"For fifteen," he said, "I'll give you the bud and three hits of acid." Ben immediately said, "Lets do it."

Tripping on LSD wasn't something I'd planned on. I wasn't hot on the idea because of what happened the first time I tried it. We stepped away from the guy with the drugs for a moment to talk about frying. Ben kept begging and nagging me to "do it." While he was jabbering a number of reasons to fry—*take LSD,* ran through my mind: It was summer; my parents were twenty miles away; I didn't have grades or classes to worry about; the pressures that bothered me before didn't exist anymore; LSD could be fun. In the back of my mind though, I was worried and thought about merely pretending to take the hit, or only taking half of it. Then I decided to give in and said, "Okay, let's trip."

We took one hit each that evening and drove around Santa Rosa in my pick-up truck, tweaked out of our gourds. When we started to come down at 4 a.m., we each took another half-hit so that we could fry a little longer. We didn't go to sleep until eight in the morning. This trip changed my mind about LSD. Ben and I joked and laughed all night. Hallucinating was fun, not scary. Having no responsibility took all the pressure off my mind.

LSD was that summers "in" drug, but in my town, it was practically impossible to score. Never one to give up a good connection, I kept in touch with the guy from the Alley in Santa

Rosa and began selling LSD to my friends. Wendy, a girl from my town who had lots of friends at Monticello, once bought a couple of hits from me. She told me that girls at Monticello like to "blaze" (to trip). This astounded me because in my home town tripping on LSD was considered a strictly male thing to do; I only knew one girl at school who did it, but she had lived in Berkeley where a lot of acid is made. The girls in my school would do 'shrooms every now and then, but never acid. I thought, if girls at Monticello fried, then there *must* be a lot of drugs up there. I felt confident about my knowledge of cocaine, speed, and pot. Since I was rapidly learning more about LSD, I figured that I'd be able to hold my own where partying was concerned at Monticello.

Selling LSD was very profitable. I could buy a sheet, (100 hits for $100), then sell each hit for up to $5 and potentially make 400 percent profit. And LSD was very easy to move. Mike, for instance, would buy twenty-five hits in advance and then sell them to his friends for a higher price. I needed Mike for coke. But with LSD, the tables turned.

Katherine came back from New York in the beginning of August, and I felt very uneasy when I was with her. I hated the idea of leaving her, and despite our closeness, I didn't want to discuss our impending break-up. So I began to spend more and more time doing LSD and other drugs with my male friends. I didn't return her phone calls or make much of an effort to see her. "Nothing counts when we're on this," my friends always said, referring to LSD. What I was doing to Katherine, then, "didn't count."

As with the other drugs I took, I never did a little LSD. I always did a lot. I'd take five hits, sometimes eight. One time, when my parents were away for the weekend, I took fifteen hits in one day. This happened by mistake and I was flying high for three days. I had scored some acid and Dirk and I both took a couple hits and started smoking pot to help the effects along. Well, we didn't feel anything for a long time. So we took more and still no effects. Assuming the acid was bunk (ineffective), we took what was left.

He took ten and I took fifteen. Suddenly it hit us with full force. We spent the days driving in the back hills, parking and hiking through the woods, laughing. Somehow we managed to find our way back to the car and back home each day.

Dealing with my parents while I was frying on LSD became second nature, too. The first time I tripped, I had been certain that if my parents had seen me they would've known instantly that I was on drugs. This early worry rarely crossed my mind anymore. Once after frying in the hills all day, I walked into a small dinner party at my parents' house. Because I'd done so much acid, I'd trained myself to snap out of tripping when necessary. That night, I talked to my parents' friends for a half hour telling them about my summer jobs and plans for boarding school. When my friends came to pick me up, I ran out into the driveway and burst out laughing.

Sometimes, I had weird experiences on LSD—like the time I kept hearing devil voices on a Rush record. Another time I drove my scooter while tripping and thought that the bushes growing along the roadside were trying to reach out and grab me. Experiences like these were a little unnerving, but I put them out of my mind.

By the end of August, I was totally avoiding Katherine. She wrote me a couple of long letters asking me what was wrong and saying that she was worried about me. I looked at these letters for a long time and then threw them out. I didn't know how to deal with the feelings I was having, so I just did more drugs and tried to erase the memory of loving her in the first place. One day I saw Katherine and I told her that our relationship had to end. I said that I needed to make a new start and that I felt repressed by the public school cliques, even though I had been accepted by them at this point. I didn't tell her half the things I was feeling, like how sad and worried I felt about going away. During this time, I was constantly frying, getting stoned, and doing coke or speed. I felt like I was in another world. I was losing control and was not sure if I really wanted to get it back.

After the breakup, I tried to focus on the future and began to wonder about what my new school was going to be like. Even though I was nervous about making new friends, I was also getting really excited. Monticello represented a fresh start for me. No one knew me there. No one had any preconceived notions of who Craig Fraser was or who Craig Fraser should be. As I'd learned at Est, I could make myself into anything or anybody I wanted to.

I soon learned that all the rumors I heard about drugs at Monticello were true. One afternoon I saw Wendy, the girl who knew a lot of people from Monticello, at the country club both our families belonged to. I was with Mike; she was with a bunch of people I'd never seen before. Wendy called Mike and me over and introduced us to her friends. There were two guys and one girl. The girl, Katie, said Hi. Dexter, a tall black guy, gave us the head jerk. Zack, who had a full ponytail and wore a crystal around his neck, smiled. Wendy told them that I was going to be at Monticello in the fall. They all said things like, "Great," and, "That's cool, you'll like it." I had the impression they meant it.

Strewn all over the ground next to Wendy's table were whippit (nitrous oxide) cylinders. Zack was holding a device used for inhaling whippits. Mike and I sat down and began doing cylinders with them. This had the same effect as inhaling from whipped cream cans, but it lasted longer and no cream spilled out. When the waitress came over to take our lunch order, she looked at the cylinders and said that she was going to report us to the manager. I gave her a dirty look and asked what her name was. She said, "Kathy, why?" Everyone at the table was listening carefully, so I told her that what we were doing was entirely legal and that I would hate to see her get in trouble for bothering the children of club members. When she said that she was going to tell anyway, I told her that one of the owners was a family friend and that I would have to mention this unfortunate encounter with "Kathy" to him. She gave me a worried smile, took our orders and asked if we needed anything else. I said "No, but thank you, Kathy."

As we left the table and walked toward the parking lot we agreed to "match" pot, which meant the group from Monticello would roll joints and that Mike and I would "match" them joint for joint. I went back to the glove compartment of my car to get some, and Mike, cheap as usual, ran after me to tell me to roll a "Pinner," a thin joint. This wasn't my plan at all. I wasn't about to let him short these people.

We hung out in the country club parking lot, playing Bob Marley tapes on Zack's car stereo and getting high. Katie mentioned that she was going over to Gary's house in the afternoon. When Mike heard this, his eyebrows jumped right up. We both knew that at school Gary was the middleman for speed between the Latinos and the rockers. As we all got talking, Zack asked me if I could score an eighth of pot that we'd just smoked. I said I could, so he and his friends pooled their money and gave me $24. Wendy said that her parents were in Hawaii, so we all agreed to meet at her house in an hour.

After picking up three eighths, Mike and I drove to Wendy's. On the way there, Mike checked out the bags and tried to make sure that he got the heaviest eighth. He even tried to pinch some from the other bags. I wouldn't let him rip these people off and told him to stop being so cheap. After all, I didn't want to have a reputation as a snake even before I got to Monticello. When we arrived at Wendy's house, the two guys from Monticello were sitting out by the pool drinking beer and talking. Dexter asked if we wanted to match pot again. Mike declined, but I took out my pot, and rolled a big fat joint. Once I lit it up, of course, Mike was the first to want some.

After about an hour, I told everyone that I had something to do. The something I had to do was pick up a half a sheet of acid at the Alley in Santa Rosa. My connection was going to be waiting there with some "blotter"—LSD "hot off the press," meaning that it was just made. No one asked where I was going, but each of them said, "Come back when you're done."

After I picked up the acid, I went home and took a shower. There was a note from my parents saying that they were out at a party. As usual, under the note was $20 for me to buy a pizza for dinner. I went back to Wendy's and brought the acid with me. When I walked into her house, I saw that she and Katie were snorting lines of speed and doing shots of Jack Daniel's at the kitchen table. They were talking very fast and constantly changing the subject. Mike was in the kitchen getting a beer. When they offered to turn us on to some speed, we both declined. Behind their backs, Mike gave me a disgusted look because we usually did coke. To Mike, snorting speed was low budget.

Out by the pool, Mike gave me a raised eyebrow look and said, "Let's see it." I unwrapped the LSD to show everyone. On the serrated paper, the hits were marked off by little pink elephants. Dexter laughed and asked if it was "clean," meaning, was the LSD dried with speed or strychnine? Not only was it clean, I told him, but it was fresh off the press. Dexter looked impressed, because acid loses its potency as it ages. Both he and Mike wanted to buy some from me. I told them that I could probably "let a few hits go." My regular price, I said, was $5 a hit. But, I offered to give them ten hits for $35. I told them if they didn't have great trips, I'd refund their money. Zack and Dexter negotiated between themselves about who was going to pay for what. Dexter explained that the others had bought quaaludes from him earlier in the morning.

Mike bought eight hits from me, under the condition he and I would trip together that night. Then we all went into the kitchen. By this time, Katie and Wendy were playing a drinking game with dice. Dexter suggested that they fry with us. I put four hits on my tongue, grinned and said "See ya'll later." Mike took three hits. The people from Monticello each took two apiece. Our trip lasted until six the next morning.

Two weeks later, I began packing for boarding school. I had spent the entire night with Dirk doing the half gram of speed he had bought for me as a going away present. We had talked until early morning about all the fun we had that summer and all the fun we would have next summer. I was sad about leaving and scared to go to a new school. I couldn't stop wondering, "What would the other kids be like?" and "Would they like me?" That morning I pretended to be asleep in my bed even though I had not slept one minute the entire night. At 5 a.m. I was feeling pretty sick. My entire body shook uncontrollably: I had cold sweats; my jaws were aching from grinding my teeth—a common result of doing speed; my stomach felt as if I had just swallowed a cup of liquid bleach; my nose was raw; and my mouth tasted like blood from my torn nasal passages. A night of speed or coke always ended this way and I swore to never to do it again, but I would, usually that same week.

I lay there in bed, my heart pounding so loud the pressure hurt my ears. My mind was going a mile a minute—I couldn't stay on one thought. I kept going back to Katherine and how much I wished she were with me. Then I'd think about leaving for school and then about how bad I felt. I lay there in bed until 7 o'clock and then went to my parent's bathroom to take a shower. Before getting in, I took out a hand held mirror and laid it down on the sink. I then scraped the remaining residue from the bindle of speed Dirk had given me. It wasn't much, but I needed whatever there was. I scraped it off and on to the mirror with a razor blade from my dad's shaving kit. My stomach wrenched and I ran to the toilet and threw up white foam. I was glad that I had thrown up before I did the last of my speed. I wiped my mouth off and snorted up the line, then licked the bindle and flushed it down the toilet with my vomit. I was ready for the new day, new school, everything suddenly felt like it was going to be great. I showered and packed.

A New Start

On my first day at Monticello, I was surprised at how nice everybody was to me. John Schmidt, the dorm head, introduced himself to me and my parents and told us to call him by his first name. Then he helped us unload my heavy stuff into my room. While I was unpacking, students who lived in the dorm stopped by the room and introduced themselves to me and my parents. One student loaned me a hammer. Another showed me where to park my Honda scooter, which I'd bought after trading in my motorcycle during the summer. That would never have happened at my public school, where new people were usually ignored.

My room, a single, was a good size and had tall ceilings and dark walls. That first morning, I set up my stereo—I'd bought one with part of my summer earnings—and put my Mad Max movie posters on the wall. While I was organizing my clothes, my mom kept saying that she was going to miss me. Even though I was excited and still a bit nervous about being at a new school, my main thoughts focused on how sick I felt. My teeth felt loose from grinding, my jaws ached too, for the same reason. It was now two o'clock and I was crashing hard from the night before. My stomach fortunately was empty, otherwise I would have thrown up. I needed to get high; pot would help me come down. But I hadn't brought any pot with me that day; I thought there would be a lot of adults around. Friends of mine at other private schools had been expelled for drug use based on hearsay. I wanted to make sure that Monticello wasn't that kind of place before I brought in any drugs.

After my parents left, I went down the hall to visit Zack. Once again, Zack confirmed what he had told me before: getting high at Monticello was no big deal. He asked me if I'd help him hang some stuff up on his wall, adding, "Then we'll smoke a bowl." I helped Zack with all his things. I was impressed with the way he was setting up his room. He'd brought a small refrigerator and a large beanbag chair from home. He had a futon instead of a bed. He strung up colored lights and Indian tapestries on the walls and ceiling. He put his electric keyboard on top of his desk. Later, I learned that this was typical; most students put a lot of effort into making their rooms really cool.

After we nailed up the last tapestry, Zack dug deep into a large trunk filled with clothes. He pulled up a wool rag sock and from that, another sock. After the third sock, he pulled out a plastic bag of buds. When he opened the bag, a heavy skunk smell filled the room. I knew immediately that the pot was from Hawaii. Zack handed the bag to me. Inside were several large bright green buds with red hairs intertwined in the leaves. Each bud was about five inches long and three inches wide. I felt a mild wave of excitement. After all, I had been at Monticello for fewer than three hours and already I found some KGBs. All that I had seen in Napa Valley for the past couple weeks was Mexican pot or chocolate Thai— lower grades of marijuana.

I was very conscious of the situation. When drugs were being shown, it was uncool to act impressed. To show any excitement would imply that I wasn't used to smoking quality pot. So I calmly told Zack that I thought it "looked good," when inside I was wondering where in the hell he'd gotten it.

Though I was on my guard and still in my Napa Valley frame of mind, it was clear that Zack was in a different mode. When I looked at the buds, he didn't watch me to see if I would pinch any out; at home, people never took their eyes off each other when someone was showing drugs to someone else. Zack, though, just kept unpacking and talking. Then he said, "Help yourself anytime during school if you want to get high. My door is usually unlocked." I was blown away by his show of trust.

While we were talking, there was a strange rap on the door. I was startled because the buds were out in plain view. Zack's expression was calm as he motioned for me to put the buds into a nearby shoe box. (Later I learned that the rap was a special signal, the way that students indicated that they weren't a bust.) Zack opened the door and in walked a guy wearing a leather biker's jacket and ripped jeans. His head was shaved above his ears, leaving small spiked points on the top of his scalp. With him was a girl who looked like his opposite. She had long straight brown hair and wore jeans, a designer sweatshirt, and riding boots. I figured she must be one of the people who kept a horse at school. The guy with the spikes inhaled deeply, clearly enjoying the skunk aroma as much as I did. Then he smiled slyly at Zack.

Zack hugged them both and introduced them to me. The guy was Brett. His girlfriend was Faith. Zack said they were going out. It amazed me that two such different looking people would be friends, let alone be dating each other. I wanted to relate to Brett, so I told him about a story I'd heard about someone in England who'd gotten fired from his job for having spiked hair with Super Glue in it. His employer considered the spikes an occupational hazard. Both Brett and Faith listened and then discussed the case with me; they had both read about it. Then Brett took out a pipe and waved it in front of the rest of us. "Let's spark a bowl," he said.

We went outside and began walking up the steep hill behind the dorm. The sun had been down for at least an hour and the stars lit the sky. Behind us were the ranch buildings of the school. All around us were giant oak trees that reminded me of mythical creatures. We walked up beyond the stables and into the hills for about fifteen minutes. By this time, I was physically exhausted and running on adrenaline, still suffering the effects of a night of speed. Before I could get too caught up in being tired, though, we arrived at our destination—a large flat area with a backstop to one side.

The wind was blowing off the hills, so we went over to the backstop in order to shield ourselves. Brett and Zack tried without luck to spark a bowl. After about half a pack of matches were gone, I asked if I could see the pipe. It was a strange device. I'd never seen one like it before although I'd been making pipes since eighth grade. It looked as though it had been made from parts from a hardware store. Brett looked at me doubtfully as I fiddled with his pipe and put it back together in a new way, switching a few pieces around to shield the pot from the wind. After two matches, I was able to light a bowl. I was relieved and happy to be getting a good hit. By cupping my hand, I shielded the bowl from the wind so that the others could do the same.

Zack then twisted something in his hand and I heard a short hiss. He handed me a whippit dispenser, just like the ones we'd used a couple weeks earlier at the country club. He said to take a blast and run around the bases—"Monticello Baseball," he called it. We chased the pot with a big hit of nitrous the way some people chase a shot of liquor with beer. Without exhaling either the pot or the nitrous, I began sprinting. As my foot slapped first base, my head started feeling really light and numb. As I rounded second, my whole body was vibrating and tingling, I felt light as a feather. I heard distant shouting from the others rooting me on. I hit third, still managing to hold my breath. I felt as though I was in a silent movie and that every step I took was a different frame. The bases turned into a blur and my head throbbed as I hit home. I knew that I was on the verge of passing out.

While I tried to regain my breath, I heard the others laughing and noticed that Zack was clumsily running around first and then second, wearing those heavy L.L. Bean boots. On third, he exhaled. I walked over to the backstop and prepared a whippit for Brett. Faith did hers while Brett was rounding second. We each did a round of whippits again and then smoked a final bowl of pot.

I no longer felt tense or in pain from the speed I had done the night before; the pot and the whippits blocked out those sensations. I could finally think about food without feeling sick. In fact, I would have liked to smoke more pot—but I wasn't the host and Zack had decided that he'd had enough.

That first night at Monticello, I felt content. I was really happy to have been admitted to a school where the people seemed so nice—if the four of us had been in pubic school together, instead of Monticello, we would have been in different cliques and never would have spoken to each other.

It didn't take me long to get into the swing of things at Monticello. Because of my Est training, I knew that I could be whatever I wanted to be; that I could recreate myself. I had always been insecure about what others thought of me, and how I fit into different groups. At public school it was easy to say, "Oh, that person is a jock," or "That person has a lot of problems." In a small town, reputations followed people from year to year. But at Monticello no one had known me when I was in third grade and had to go to special classes. No one knew that I had terrible allergies and always had to carry around paper towels for my nose.

In addition to coming to Monticello with a clean slate, I had the advantage of having partied with Zack and Dexter over the summer. The fact that they liked me smoothed my way socially. They endorsed me as being cool—a partyer. At the same time, I wanted my new friends to know that I had high academic standards, so I told them that I got mostly A's during my last semester in public school. From Est, I really believed that "stating it" was the first step toward "being it" and no one questioned who I was. Growing up alone, after Amy had gone away to college, had left me wanting other brothers and sisters. It wasn't long before it was as though I had more than a hundred siblings. It was like being part of one big family and I loved it. There were never those uncomfortable feelings that I had back home with my family. Finally there was no daily tension, just fun.

My day-to-day schedule was pretty standard. Monticello's academic year was organized on a trimester plan. I was required to take four courses each trimester; twelve courses each year. That first trimester, I had two periods in the morning and one in the afternoon. From the first day, my favorite class was Spanish. I spoke it pretty well from having spent the summer in the watercress fields, where two of the employees were from Mexico. I had been the interpreter for the boss. Because we were friends, Carlos and Enrique would buy beer for me sometimes or I'd get them stoned.

The classes at Monticello were small—my biggest class had ten people in it—and I loved that. Because the classes were small, I talked and contributed more than ever. Not only did I ask the questions I thought the teachers wanted to hear, I'd also ask what I wanted to know, and for a change the teachers at Monticello took the time to fully explain my questions. This changed my whole attitude towards learning. My goal shifted from getting good grades to learning and getting good grades. I knew my parents were paying a lot of money for this private education and I wanted to get the most out of it.

I had always had trouble relating to my teachers before. Most of them were about to retire and they had little in common with their students. At Monticello, many of the teachers were under thirty, and most of them lived on campus, either as dorm heads or in faculty housing. If I was having trouble understanding an assignment, I could go to them for help. In fact, at least six faculty members, one for each subject, were on "academic duty" for just that purpose each night. Schoolwork aside, the teachers at Monticello were friendly and a lot of fun—I liked being on a first-name basis with the teachers and students alike. Monticello didn't believe in artificial "barriers."

Sometimes, as a surprise, my Spanish teacher would cancel class and take us downtown for doughnuts and coffee. My English teacher, who lived on campus with his wife and baby, invited students over to watch movies on his big screen TV. The dean of students, who happened to be my academic adviser, would occasionally take all his advisees out for a Chinese dinner.

Because I had so much respect for my teachers at Monticello, I made a decision not to cheat in their classes and pretty much stuck by it. This may sound unbelievable since I cheated so much in public school, but it was true. Monticello was different, the teachers made me want to learn and to enjoy learning. If I needed help, they were there to give it, always. In a way, the teachers were friends, and I'd always tried to be honest with friends. Other students at Monticello had the same attitude. There was little cheating except in emergencies.

I especially liked my dorm head, John Schmidt. John was a mellow man. He usually wore a baseball cap and cutoffs. Before coming to Monticello, he had been in Africa with the Peace Corps. He kept a collection of unusual hand-crafted musical instruments and masks in his apartment. John's policy was to let us govern ourselves. During the first week of school, he gave a talk to the entire dorm. He told us that he wanted the dorm to run as an autonomous unit and that he didn't want to be chasing after us. He said that he expected us to do our dorm chores, keep our rooms reasonably neat, and observe the "quiet rule" during study hours. He also told us that he would buy us condoms if we were too embarrassed to buy them ourselves. Then he went back into his room. I only saw him in the dorm five other times that year during scheduled "room checks."

The dorm in which I lived, Boys Dorm C, was known as being the school's big party spot. Its location, away from the other dorms, against a large hill, made it easy for people to get high. There weren't any adults around on that part of the campus, other than John our dorm head, who it was rumored smoked pot himself. So we would hang out behind the dorm in the designated "smoking section" and smoke pot, hash, coke and occasionally opium-laced buds.

Counting myself, sixteen guys lived in Boys' Dorm C. Since we all lived together, many of us quickly became good friends. At night, we'd stay up late getting high, listening to music, eating Domino's pizza and studying. Since most people had stereos, music was always playing. During the first month of school, the delivery man at Domino's told us that Boys' Dorm C was his number one customer.

Boys' Dorm C didn't isolate itself from the other six dorms. If we didn't have people from the other dorms over, we'd go cruising and visit friends in the other dorms. That was what I loved most about Monticello—the freedom to socialize with anyone and everyone.

Back then, if I'd had to describe the Monticello student body to a visitor, I'd say it was mellow and laid back. In fact, the nicest thing about Monticello was that cliques weren't important. Day students got along with boarding students, seniors were nice to freshmen. That's not to say that there weren't certain easy-to-identify groups; there were. It was just that the people who were part of a particular group didn't limit themselves to a few friends in that group. What's more, at Monticello, it wasn't cool to be mean or stuck-up.

A lot of people in my class at Monticello were "Dead Heads"; they listened to Grateful Dead music religiously and went to the Dead's concerts. Some would even follow the band from show to show during their vacations. Dead Heads usually go barefoot, dress like hippies and wear things like tie-dye or paisley shirts and pants. All the Dead Heads I ever knew did drugs. A lot of Grateful Dead's music is geared toward tripping on LSD, and it's easy to score great acid and 'shrooms at their concerts. In fact, if you hold Grateful Dead concert tickets under a light and tilt them in a certain way, you can sometimes see the word "TRIP" embossed right on the tickets. In general, the Dead Heads at Monticello were mellow and friendly—never critical. Many of them worked in the school's vegetable garden for community service and took classes like woodworking and pottery. At Monticello, Dead Heads were less a clique than a way of life.

Another big group at Monticello were the students—mostly girls—who brought horses to school. Some rode English style and practiced jumps in the riding ring by the stables, but most rode Western and rode on the trails behind the school.

Besides a small punk contingent in the freshman class, the most visible group at Monticello was the "pit crew," or the losers group. Pit crew people were rumored to never shower. They kept to themselves and most of them were wizards with computers and liked to work on their restored cars. The difference at Monticello was that no one was ever publicly cruel to them or even rude as they would have been back home. Most people just accepted them.

One of the things that made Monticello so unusual was that one quarter of the student body came from foreign countries—including Hong Kong, Japan, and Saudi Arabia. In fact, more than half of the guys in Boys' Dorm C weren't American citizens. All of the foreigners had a lot of money, and when you walked through the campus you could hear their high-powered stereos blasting. One kid from Taiwan came to school after his parents gave him $40,000 and sent him to the United States to learn English. He enrolled at Monticello, bought a Turbo Saab, and lived with his aunt in a nearby town on the weekends. Most of the foreigners stayed away from drugs. One of the Thai students told me that in his country drugs were only for the lower classes, and one of the Arab students said that drugs were an "assault on his religion," and if you were caught with them you would be killed. But because they had so much money, the foreigners who did get involved with drugs usually got into a lot of trouble.

I soon had friends from every group, from the foreigners to the Dead Heads. Socially, I was having the time of my life. I never thought school could be such a blast. After the first two weeks at Monticello, I decided to run for student government representative. It was a very competitive race because most members of the student government had been elected the year before and only one seat was left open for new students. To my astonishment, I won the election. I remember the dean of students congratulating me by asking, "Are you sure you're a new student? You got a lot of votes."

Winning the election made me feel great; I had lost whenever I ran for student government in public school. At Monticello, as at most schools, only the most popular students were elected to the student government. The first activity that student government organized was a campus-wide blackout that shut all electricity off for twenty-four hours. The goal was to make the student body more aware of how much energy could be saved if we did things like turning off stereos and lights when we weren't in our rooms. We also put together a "closed" weekend, when all the day students were required to sleep in the dorms for Friday and Saturday nights in order to build school solidarity. The whole school ate meals together and played games like "Capture the Flag." We also began organizing a school camping trip for later in the semester.

I also signed up for Peer Counseling, a program in which specific students advise and help other students. Being a peer counselor really appealed to me because I loved helping people with their problems. Students came to Peer Counseling sessions and confided things like, "I'm really depressed about my boyfriend," or "School's too hard. I want to leave," or "I think I'm pregnant." Then they'd ask my advice.

During the first few weeks of school, I was on top of the world. I was being accepted as the "new Craig"; the person I really wanted to be. The only reminder of my past was Katherine. She kept calling me on the dorm pay phone, crying and saying how much she missed me and loved me. I didn't want to deal with her.

Thinking about the way I'd dealt with her only depressed me; no matter how much I tried to ignore her or get high to put her out of my mind, I still felt really bad for the way I treated her over the summer. I didn't want to think about the fact that once she left to go back to Denmark, I'd probably never see her again. Even though it was very difficult, I just wanted to leave her in the past and start my life over again at Monticello. After awhile, I had my friends say that I wasn't around whenever she called.

There was no specific drug culture at Monticello; there was no "drug" crowd. Instead, drugs were the norm and an accepted part of life at school. In fact, most people at Monticello were very much like me—good students who partied a lot. For the first time in my life, I felt I was in a place where I truly belonged.

The priorities of my day were to go to class, do my homework after school, get high, and then go swimming or hang out playing hackey sack. A lot of my friends followed the same schedule; doing well in school was important to us. In fact, I adopted this homework-first-drugs-second routine from Zack, who was quickly becoming my best friend at school.

Getting high in the dorm was a given. Zack's room was considered a cool place for getting high because it was so comfortable. He had several toys—executive playthings—to fool around with, and a great stereo, so everyone hung out there at night. The teachers didn't walk around on patrol. In fact, they pretty much left the students alone. Trust was a big concept at Monticello. It was the kind of place where you checked books out of the library yourself and were expected to bring them back on time.

Casual as Monticello was about drugs, none of us were careless. It wasn't as though we sat around in Zack's room doing giant bong hits with the door open. Monticello wasn't *that* liberal. Since pot has a very distinctive odor, we'd blow the smoke into designated "hit" pillows. Because my lungs were so strong from swimming all summer, I didn't have to use a hit pillow. Most people sprayed air freshener or hair spray around the room after smoking pot. That's why our dorm used to smell like the beauty products aisle in a department store.

Another fairly safe and popular place to get high was outside in the smoking sections—areas behind the dorms designated for cigarette smoking. We used pipes in order to keep the smoke down to a minimum and then blew our hits into the air while other students smoked cigarettes to mask the odor. The safest place of all to go and get high was Bob's Bunker, a fort built into the hill behind the stables by a group of seniors who graduated five years earlier. Ten people could fit comfortably down inside and someone had figured out how to rig up a light inside with a generator. The outside of the Bunker was camouflaged with branches and leaves. Since it was dug into the ground, the Bunker was practically impossible to find unless you knew exactly where it was.

Like doing drugs, scoring drugs at Monticello was no big deal. Going to boarding school didn't limit anyone's access to drugs. In fact, four dealers lived in my dorm alone. Pot was always easy to get since it was grown locally. I used to buy most of mine at school from Cam, a junior who was on student government with me. He had a great connection for bud in a town nearby. Now and then, Cam would also get blow. What most people like Cam did was to buy a lot of whatever drug they wanted to get at a lower price and sell some in order to pay for their share.

For alcohol, we depended on Blake, who was very tall and had to shave every day. He never got carded at liquor stores and bars. He used to take orders from all of us for gin, whiskey, or whatever else we wanted and then get a ride downtown to the liquor store. Sarah, a sophomore, was the campus hash connection. She had a sister living in Amsterdam who sent it to her hidden in "care packages." A day student named Mike was a good source for Ecstasy, MDMA, and his roommate, Tom, who was hyperactive, used to sell his prescription for Ritalin to other students. Like my other school, Monticello was a supermarket for drugs open twenty-four hours a day.

The scarcest but most talked about drug at Monticello, was LSD. It seemed to me that everyone liked to trip. After my summer of continual frying—I had taken over fifty hits in the past three months—I felt I knew a lot about LSD. Since I'd already tripped once before with Zack and Dexter and had a great time, I thought tripping at Monticello would be fun. After about a week and a half of school, Zack and a couple other people, including a girl named Kumi, a foreign student who happened to like drugs, asked me to blaze with them. I was grateful, because I believed that sharing a trip with people was the best way of becoming better friends, real friends—ones that would last.

When we dropped the hits, a couple of negative thoughts crossed my mind. First, I thought that the LSD might be "bunk"—bad—because Zack had said that he wasn't sure how good it was. Then later as we watched the sunset, Zack started to hang on everybody in a "buddy-buddy" way, and I started to get paranoid that people at Monticello were all gay and this freaked me out inside because of what happened with Carlos in San Francisco. Although I felt pretty certain that it wasn't true, deep down the gay question concerned me. I had been thinking about this since I'd tripped with Zack and Dexter over the summer; when we were all in the hot tub, Zack had accidentally touched my friend Mike's leg. After Zack left the hot tub to go swimming in the pool, Mike kept saying, "That guy's a fag." I tried to tell Mike that I didn't think Zack was gay and that he just had a lot of energy. Mike, though, wouldn't let up and he kept calling Monticello that "fag school up north".

Even though I was sure that Zack wasn't gay, the idea that he might be threw me a bit. I was also worried about what was expected of me with the two girls we were frying with. I had heard a rumor that there were orgies at Monticello during the sixties, and that even now when guys and girls tripped together, they usually went off in couples and had sex. But, I wasn't attracted to either Kumi or Amy, the other girl who was with us. The thought that they might expect me to have sex with them bothered me. I was still in love with Katherine.

The acid kicked in while all five of us were walking on the horse trails behind school. I felt a huge wall inside me crumble and a wave of worries flood into my conscious mind. All my insecurities started erupting. I wondered, Do I really have friends? Does anyone really like me for me? How could I have been elected to student government? Does Kumi expect me to have sex with her? I was confused and upset. And to make it worse, we ran into a group of senior guys who said, "Hey, Norton. Fuck me up the ass," to Zack. Because I was tripping, this comment totally tripped me out; it took me several minutes to realize that they were imitating an Eddie Murphy comedy routine.

I ended up going back to my room and listening to a Peter Gabriel tape by myself. I really needed someone to talk to, but I felt I had nowhere to turn. I really didn't want anyone at my new school to see me in such a flipped-out condition. Then, Kelly, a girl I liked, stopped by my room, and for some reason I felt that I could trust her. I tried to ask her subtly about the scene at Monticello. I couldn't blurt out, "Is Zack gay?" or "Do people here have orgies when they trip?" So instead, I tried to dance around the topic and asked her questions like, "Did Zack have a girlfriend last year?" I think Kelly could see that I was upset, so we talked about Monticello for a long time. She calmed me down and said that Monticello was a lot less wild than people thought. After our conversation, I felt relaxed enough to go back to Zack's room, where everyone I'd been tripping with was hanging out. We listened to some trippy CD he had ordered from some spiritual magazine. I ended up having such a good time that I figured my worries were just inside my head, that it was just me. And it was.

Drugs Drugs Drugs

Since I was one of the few boarding students with access to transportation—my Honda scooter—I often volunteered to drive other students here and there. Thus I was nearly indispensable. If our destination was a place to get drugs, which was often the case, my new friends would repay me by giving me a bud or a line or a portion of whatever was being purchased. More often, I was in on deals and got a bulk discount.

Whatever our destination, I knew that my karma would protect me and that I wouldn't get caught or hurt no matter what I did. The strange thing was that I never thought the things I was doing, such as stealing, using drugs or dealing them, was wrong. It was all surreal to me, as if I were in a dream or watching someone else do the things I did. All my activities seemed perfectly normal to me since most of the people I knew did the same things and I had never seen any of them get hurt or into trouble. I had no fear, sense of guilt, or shame when it came to lying, stealing or breaking laws if somehow it helped me or my friends.

For instance, I used to walk into the local Safeway and steal cartons of cigarettes by stuffing them in the back of my jacket. Then, back at the dorm, I'd either sell the cigarettes or open the carton and start throwing packs around the smoking section. I did this several times a week. My favorite Safeway trick was to inhale the gas from the whipped cream cans in the store and put the cans back on the shelves, then go bouncing down the aisle in a cloud of numbness, as if I had just done the most natural thing in the world.

My best sources for drugs were back in the Napa Valley, where I could get pretty much anything—coke, acid, buds, crank, whatever. Every other weekend, I'd go home and buy enough drugs so I had some left over to take back to school. This arrangement worked out well. I was able to keep up my old ties and party with old friends, which was important to me; I didn't want to be forgotten. I also managed to create a drug pipeline so that when Monticello was dry, I still had plenty of pot and other drugs to share with select friends.

It wasn't that I suddenly became a dealer. I wasn't into selling drugs to make money. People would ask me if I knew where to get any drugs and since I did, I'd help them score. It was a very casual arrangement. There are plenty of people who deal drugs but don't use them; these kind of dealers made a lot of money. That wasn't my goal. I sold drugs or bartered for them so that I could do more myself. Any potential profit literally went up my nose or into my lungs every time.

One of my favorite things about selling drugs was putting the deal together. I liked to think that I had developed a pretty good business sense. I always made sure my product was excellent; otherwise I wouldn't buy or sell it. I enjoyed haggling with bigger dealers at home, who were usually much older than I was. Because I knew so much about drugs, I felt confident about bargaining and making sure that I got my money's worth. Ripping me off was a tough job. I had learned my lesson the hard way in the past—with three deals that went bad, I lost over $1,000. Since I usually managed to drive a hard bargain and more often than not would get a nice bulk discount, I was able to pass the savings on to my friends at school. I regularly brought back pot from my rocker friends and fry from my connection in Santa Rosa. Although I wasn't ready to fry again, I loved it when other students would tell me that they'd taken one hell of a ride on my LSD. Occasionally, I'd bring back cocaine. But I'd usually do it all instead of selling any. My philosophy was, "Do a little, feel a little. Do a lot, feel it all!" I never opted to feel just a little. In fact I would pass up using it if I couldn't get enough to really get high on it.

How did I fund all this? I was very resourceful when it came to money. I'd made a lot of money at my various summer jobs and managed to save almost $2000. My parents put money into an account at a nearby bank for me every month. They didn't check my withdrawals; they trusted me, and since it was my money, I didn't feel guilty using it for what I wanted—drugs. Also, I lied to them from time to time about how much money I needed. I'd tell my dad that I needed money for new shoes or that my biology class was going on a whale-watching trip and that I needed $200. I made up excuses spontaneously and I pretended to be completely sincere, to the point, where at times, I couldn't remember whether or not something really happened or if it was just a story of mine. I felt that getting that gram of coke was even more important than having new shoes.

I tried not to lie to my parents about money as best I could, because I knew my school was expensive. My rationale was that I deserved whatever drugs I took as a reward for doing well in school. My attitude was, "I'm getting great grades and doing really well—what more could my parents want?" Besides, I didn't see my parents all that often so they weren't on my mind an awful lot.

I'll never forget one particular incident. The school psychologist, Mary Kay, came to a Peer Counseling meeting and told us that she wanted to do a presentation about alcohol to the ninth grade. She asked us if we would be willing to organize a research committee to collect information on this topic. I immediately volunteered and suggested that we also include a discussion on marijuana. I was confident that I could give a perfect lecture on the effects of pot and other drugs. I thought that giving a speech was a good idea because I knew so much about drugs. I thought I knew exactly what I was doing when it came to drugs. I had read everything I could find at both the school library and public library. Not to mention, I got an A in Ms. O'Donnell's health class. Since there was no health course at Monticello, I thought the freshmen—particularly the partyers—would benefit from my knowledge.

A week later, we gave the presentation to the freshmen. I talked about some of the myths surrounding marijuana. Then we had a question-and-answer period; the freshmen wrote their questions on slips of paper and passed them up to the people giving the talk. Most of their questions were about heroin, LSD, and X—MDMA, and I ended up answering the majority of them. I talked about the same kind of things I learned in public school about drugs—that is, these are the drug's effects; these are its negative consequences; this is what it looks like. I truly felt that it was important that the younger kids know about what they might be getting into. I thought I was doing them a favor, the way a big brother might. During my speech I could see some of the freshmen giggling. Knowing that I was a partyer, a couple of them asked serious questions. Giving them a stern look, I answered their questions in an even tone of voice. Mary Kay was surprised at the questions. She thought that the freshmen would ask questions about "gateway" drugs like alcohol and marijuana, but she never expected they'd want to know about hard drugs. She didn't seem to realize that most of them had already experimented with pot and alcohol, and that a few of them were small-time dealers.

Later, Mary Kay told me that I had done a great job and that she was impressed with the amount of effort I'd put into the presentation. I was glad that I could help, and I honestly liked being involved in school activities. At the same time, I was certain that my anti-drug speech put me one step ahead of the game. It gave me insurance in case anything happened at school that would potentially connect me with using drugs.

During the first semester, I also helped organize a campus-wide Holistic Health Day, and worked with the other Peer Counselors to set up a seminar program. We wrote letters and made phone calls to doctors, nurses, and other health experts. Ten people ended up coming to school for the day. They gave speeches on topics like acupuncture, herbs, stress management, birth control, and meditation. Holistic health was big at Monticello and the seminars went over really well.

By mid-quarter, I had racked up more community service hours than most people in my class—I had a total of fifty hours and was only required to have twenty. One week, I helped organize a clean-up campaign for the smoking areas. This involved not only picking up trash, but also raising the money to buy new garbage cans and benches. As a final touch, one of the Dead Head students in advanced art painted a trippy mural on the brick wall overlooking the community smoking area. Life guarding also counted for community service and since the head of Physical Education had accepted my word that I was a certified lifeguard, other students were allowed to swim in the school pool as long as I was with them. I was usually stoned. No one ever checked to see if I was really certified. They trusted me to tell the truth and in my mind I had. I knew all the techniques for CPR and water rescue, I just had not taken the official written test. Life guarding was my favorite type of community service. After all, getting a tan by the pool was much more fun than picking up garbage or weeding the school's vegetable garden.

I also made a good impression academically. By mid-October, it was clear to both teachers and students that I was good at more than just contributing to class. On my first test papers, I pulled in all A's and one B+. It felt great! Grades were one of my ways of proving to myself and everyone else that I was responsible and in control.

I rarely cheated, but I didn't hesitate to manipulate teachers when I thought it would help boost my grades. For instance, when a wimpy English teacher gave me a B+, I pretended that I was devastated and told him that if I didn't get all A's, my parents wouldn't let me come back next year. I even used my dyslexia to gain additional sympathy—something I rarely did—and stressed to him how hard it is for someone with a learning disability to get good grades in English, which I believed was true. I worked hard every day and night on English and felt that I deserved an A. I convinced him to give me an A- if I redid an old assignment.

In mid-October, I had a near miss with the faculty. About two weeks after I first tripped at Monticello, Kelly walked into my room looking very grave. She said, "I have to talk to you." We went up to the smoking area behind the dorm. She lit a cigarette and stared at me. I asked her what was up.

"Carol came up to me today," Kelly said. Carol was the assistant headmistress and sports coach. "She asked me if I knew anything about you using a lot of LSD." Kelly went on to explain that Carol had attended a volleyball conference and had run into one of my former teachers from public school, who apparently said a few things about me. "Carol wants to speak with you. She's going to leave you a note," Kelly said, "and, I'm not the only one she's been talking to, either."

Trying to remain calm, I pressed Kelly for exact details but she didn't seem to know much more. I was scared because I'd done over ten hits with my old friends while I was at home the weekend before and brought a half sheet back to school to sell. After she left I pieced everything together in my mind. The teacher Kelly referred to had to be Ms. O'Donnell. A lot of students, including me, liked her. Many students talked to her about their problems. Before I'd left for boarding school, Katherine told me that she was worried about me partying too much. I knew that in the beginning of the year, she had told Ms. O'Donnell that a good friend was using LSD and that she was worried about the long-term effects. When Ms. O'Donnell pressed her for details, Katherine admitted that it was me.

As soon as the note from Carol appeared, I went straight to the gym to nip the problem in the bud. I mustered up my best attitude because I knew that I had to put on a strong performance; as second-in-command at Monticello, Carol had a lot of power. Since Carol liked me and I'd been to her campus apartment for a cookout earlier that week, I felt comfortable enough to approach her while she was coaching a volleyball scrimmage.

Carol immediately mentioned meeting one of my old teachers. I felt a weight fall from my shoulders; I knew exactly where the conversation was going to go and knew that I could control it. My main concern had not been about selling drugs. Using them was a far less serious offense at Monticello. When Carol mentioned LSD, I did my best to look shocked and then concerned, not worried. As she spoke, I tried to look hurt, as if to say, "How can you think this about me?" and then acted as if I were really angry. I told her I'd left public school to get away from the gossip and the cliques, and now it was following me to a new school. I said that it was unfair for me to be labeled as an LSD user just because certain students at my old school were. When she asked me about my old girlfriend, I said that she was mad at me and had spread a rumor and talked to Ms. O'Donnell just to get me in trouble. I remember Carol looking at me with sympathy and telling me that she had been worried because she felt the whole thing was "out of character" for me. I thanked her for her concern, and she thanked me for my honesty. When I said good-bye, Carol gave me a little hug and said, "I knew it wasn't true."

I left the gym with a serious face, but once I got outside, I smiled a smile so wide that the corners of my cheeks hurt. A perfect ten for a perfect snowjob, I thought. Then, I went back to my room and smoked a hash cigarette.

The thing I wanted most in life was to have good friends, and I thought I had found them at Monticello. Hanging out in people's rooms, going to meals together, swimming at the pool, studying at night together, getting high every day—all this was really fun for me. It felt like being part of a big family and, unlike home, I was never lonely.

Because I had so many friends, having a girlfriend wasn't as important to me as it had been before. Plus I was still in love with Katherine and sad about breaking up with her. Even so, a lot of girls at Monticello wanted to go out with me. This blew my mind because I'd always had to make an effort to get girls to like me. Even though I didn't really need a girlfriend, I ended up going out with Allie, a day student and one of the most beautiful girls in the senior class.

Being around Allie made me feel really young. She was a model and would often take time off from school to go on "shoots." She was also two inches taller than I was, and this bothered me. And, I didn't like the fact that she had a car at school while I had only a scooter. I felt like less than a man in our relationship. I grew up believing that the man should drive the car, as my father had always done. I felt sort of out of control not having a car.

When I first started going out with Allie, I was smoking pot all the time. Allie rarely did drugs. I avoided her when I was stoned—which was most of my free time—because I wasn't sure how to act. This confused and upset her. Allie also wanted to sleep with me immediately—something I didn't want to do so soon because I was nervous. It had been several weeks since I'd had sex with Katherine and I wasn't sure if I'd be up to par with a new person. I didn't want to be less than perfect in bed. Allie might go around school comparing me unfavorably to her previous boyfriends and ruin my image. I also felt guilty about Katherine, and I wanted to take my time getting to know someone new. But instead of talking about my feelings, I concentrated on telling Allie how beautiful she was. Our relationship never got past kissing and holding hands.

Even though I had trouble feeling comfortable with Allie, a group of her friends sort of adopted me. They were some of the most beautiful girls in the school and I really liked them. I was usually very comfortable with them; it was very easy for me to relax. We all liked to talk. I sincerely enjoyed hearing about their problems and trying to help them come up with solutions. The only time I was ever uncomfortable with them was when they'd try to find out how everything was going with Allie. Answering personal questions like this made me uneasy so I'd put on a poker face and say very little. In fact, I prided myself on being able to control my emotions or keeping a poker face—especially around adults or my guy friends.

One of the only guys with whom I could lower my guard was Zack. I never felt that I had an image or a standard to uphold with him; he was never judgmental towards anyone. I was proud to consider Zack my best friend at school. He was cool and relaxed; he played baseball and the keyboard in a band, but was not caught up in any of it. He had a girlfriend, too, by this point.

Not all my friends were as popular as Zack. Brad, the freshman assigned to me as a "little brother," initially struck me as a total loser and maybe even a bust—narc. But, as it turned out, Brad became one of my closest friends.

Brad had grown up in a small town in Nevada and was really into computers. He could write his own programs and do all sorts of wild stuff on his PC. In fact, Brad was one of the smartest people I'd ever met. But he was also one of the unhappiest. Brad claimed that his parents were forcing him to go to Monticello. It was hard for me, though, to understand how anyone would not want to go to Monticello, which I thought was the greatest place in the world. During the first few weeks of school, Brad alienated a lot of people by being obnoxious,. He'd hide out in his room or in the computer science hall. I told him straight out that he didn't have to be such an asshole to everyone and that Monticello wasn't an awful place. But what really brought us closer together was the fact that Brad was curious about drugs.

His pre-Monticello experience was limited to smoking a few stems and seeds from his friend's father's stash, but he had never really gotten high. After I figured that he wasn't a bust and could be trusted, I made it very clear that I knew a few things about drugs. He used to ask me a lot of questions like, "What happens when you take LSD?" and "Is opium dangerous?" Sometimes at night we'd stay up for hours just talking about all this stuff. His questions flattered me, and anyway, I loved to talk about drugs—especially with someone who had so little knowledge.

I loved talking about drugs, period. I loved having them in my possession. Most of all, I loved doing them. That first quarter, my all-time favorite drug was cocaine and I used it to cement my new friendships.

Most people acted differently toward someone who had coke. They'd be nicer to him or laugh harder at his jokes. I liked being the person with the coke to offer because people naturally paid more attention to me. More importantly, I needed to do coke in order to be able to fully express what I was feeling. Keeping a poker face wasn't necessary when I did coke; everyone else let down their defenses and talked freely. I felt comfortable and in control.

My coke use at Monticello followed a pattern. I'd do some, want to do more, keep going till I ran out, and then go out looking to score. One Sunday night, after I had spent the weekend at home doing LSD with my Napa Valley friends, my dad offered to drive me back to school because it was raining. Throughout the entire ride, I couldn't get my mind off the gram of cocaine I had with me in my duffel bag. I had already done over two grams that afternoon and managed to save a gram only because I ran out of time—my dad wanted to get going early. I couldn't wait to get back to my room at Monticello and line it up. I really wanted to do some. I was obsessed with my body's need to get high because I was crashing fast.

That night at the smoking section, I met up with Sandy, a girl who lived in the dorm down from mine. I suggested we go back to my room. We took out a mirror from my desk and I dumped all the coke on it. I chopped up the rocks with a little gold razor. I really enjoyed the ritual of chopping and lining up the coke. My pulse rate would go up and my hands would sweat and shake slightly from excitement. For me, anticipation was half the high. I arranged five large lines for us to snort and a few other little lines for us to put in cigarettes and do as coke smokes, or "mokes."

I quickly snorted two lines with my gold straw and didn't leave a trace of coke behind. My heart began to beat fast as I watched Sandy do her line. When Sandy was done, she commented on the coke's excellent quality; I snorted a beefy third line. I leaned my head back against my bed and pinched my nose lightly. Then I breathed in deeply through my nose and I felt the coke flow back into my throat and where, before, my sinuses had been clogged and hurting, now I only felt numbness. Finally, my head, throat and body was good and numb. My body's craving for the high was satisfied for the moment.

Sandy tore the filter off a cigarette, and rolled the paper between her fingers so that some of the tobacco would fall out. She handed it to me and I sucked one of the smaller lines of coke into the cigarette. Then, Sandy and I did "numbies" by rubbing cocaine all over our gums so our mouths would be completely numb before we smoked.

By now I had stopped shaking, but my body was seriously sweating and I couldn't stop grinding my teeth. Soon, a wave of desperation swept over me; all the coke was gone and I was coming down really fast. We went outside to the smoking section. My jaws felt like they were swinging from side to side. I couldn't feel any sensation in my mouth, but I felt it opening and closing involuntarily. The whole upper half of my body was numb and felt as if it were asleep—the same sensation when your foot falls asleep and then tingles when you move it. Big coke drips were running down my throat from my nose, the taste was metallic and bitter, it made me grin with pleasure. Then, because I hadn't eaten all day, my stomach turned over, and I had to keep swallowing and contracting my throat muscles so that I wouldn't throw up all the coke I had just swallowed. To feel better, I lit up a coke smoke by slowly waving the flame in front of the cigarette so that the coke wouldn't burn, but instead turn to a sweet and synthetic-tasting gas. The coke smoke delivered a punch to my foggy head. I half sat and half collapsed onto a bench, my head falling back to lean against the building. I stared up to the stars, I felt as if I might die, my body was gone, I was comfortably numb.

Sandy was talking a mile a minute about what she had done over the weekend and how her roommate owed her money for drugs. I was listening to my own thoughts and waiting for the moment when I could talk about what I was thinking. I took another drag and thought I was going to pass out completely; the stars became blurry, and I felt like I was going to puke for sure. As I tried to regain my bearings, we lit another moke. After we talked for a few more minutes, Sandy went back to her room for dorm check and I went back to mine. There, I took out the mirror we used to snort the coke and examined it closely. I licked the mirror hoping to pick up any stray traces of coke. I did the same with the bindle the cocaine came in, then spit into my gold straw and sucked out the coke caught inside. It wasn't enough, I was *needing more.* I snorted hard to produce another sinus drip, but nothing happened. Next I went to the bathroom and put my hands under the faucet to catch some water. I tipped my head back and let the water from my fingers drip into my nose. When I snorted, it hurt. I did this a few times until I got a few meager drips of diluted coke. I also could taste a strong metallic flavor now. I snorted from my nose to look at my spit in the mirror before swallowing it, it was lined with strands of thick blood. I wasn't surprised or upset. I just wanted more. I needed more.

I went back to my room and listened to Pink Floyd. My body was aching. I felt like throwing up from all the nicotine in the cigarettes. My hands were like ice and my nose felt like it had been scraped raw. My heart was pounding in my chest as if I had just finished sprinting a mile; I could see it pushing up and down in my rib cage like a prisoner trying to get past the bars of his cell. My testicles were severely contracted, like they had just been kicked. Every now and then, a sharp pain would jet up from my testicles into my chest, I kept wishing that I had another line to make myself feel better. I desperately wanted more coke, but stayed huddled in bed shaking and thinking about all the other things I could have done with the three hundred dollars I'd just spent. Then I prayed to God to make my heart stop pounding so loudly. I promised God that I would never do coke again if he would just let me go to sleep.

I shook and sweated until 3 A.M., when I finally fell asleep. The next morning, I had solid discs of mucus in my nose. I had to breath through my mouth. In the bathroom, I blew my nose and out came a bloody mass of nasal tissue—I wasn't shocked or surprised, it was the price I paid every time I did blow.

Losing Control

Toward the end of the first semester, before Christmas, I had a couple of close calls with some teachers and even with my parents. But I never once thought anything was wrong, and I continued to feel that no matter what I did, I'd always come out fine.

The first close call happened at home. After a full day of getting stoned, snorting coke and hiking in the local hills, I dropped five hits of LSD with a group of my old friends from public school. That night when the acid was just kicking in, we ended up at a party for the girls' volleyball team. When we got to the party, I thought that everyone was pointing at me and whispering that I was a snob for going to boarding school. I was perplexed about this because I had been really making an effort to keep up with my old friends. At the party, I was so fried that I could feel my mind slide right out of my head. And then I saw Ms. O'Donnell and I thought, *This is it. I'm screwed.* Ms. O'Donnell could spot someone high on anything a mile away. I ran out of the party and drove home. On that day, I felt something inside of my mind snap. After that incident, I worried that Ms. O'Donnell would say something to my parents or my new teachers. So I was more careful than ever to sidestep or deal with trouble before it happened.

At Monticello, students really looked out for each other. No one wanted friends to get in trouble. For example, I once went to a student government meeting after having smoked a bowl up in Bob's Bunker. When I walked into the classroom, where the meeting was being held, about ten minutes early, Wolfgang, a Dead Head who was in student government, said, "You'd better get out of here. You reek like buds." I ran up to my dorm and sprayed myself with an aerosol deodorant and put some eye drops in. I seldom skipped a class to do coke, but I did one day when I had just gotten some in the mail from home. I asked a friend to take me off the absent list when teachers weren't looking. Having this kind of back-up protection came in handy, on occasion.

Staying a few steps ahead of the teachers was an easy thing to do. I'd been doing it my whole life in school. Students always agreed that students come first and we were always helping each other out. Once at a school dance, word was out that John, my dorm head, wanted to speak with Dexter. Zack and I knew that Dexter was totally drunk, so Zack went out onto the dance floor and attracted attention to himself by dancing wildly while I took Dexter out the back door. The music was really loud and he couldn't figure out what I was doing. But once we got outside and I told him that John was coming towards us, he knew what was up and took off. I delayed John long enough for Dexter to get away.

Another time, Zack and I happened to be in the faculty room getting an extra chair to bring to a student government meeting. I saw a folder lying on a coffee table; I opened it and saw a letter from the headmaster to all resident faculty about Monticello's "Party Problem." Monticello would be instituting a faculty patrol effort; each morning, afternoon and evening different teachers were scheduled to walk around the campus and through the dorms. Attached to the letter was the patrol schedule. Zack quickly made a copy of the letter and stuffed it in his jacket before we returned to the meeting. Later that night, Zack made fifty copies of the letter and schedule on the library photocopy machine. We then went around to all the dorms distributing them to our friends.

Now and then, though, the faculty managed to take us by surprise, like the night in November when they decided to hold a fire check—scouting around to see if there were any heaters, coffee makers, drugs or other illegal things in the dorm rooms. Fire checks weren't out of the ordinary, but this one caught me off guard. The Monticello grapevine usually worked fast and efficiently; in the past, I always knew when there was going to be a surprise check because members of the student government were notified in advance and often asked to help.

On the night of the fire check—just a couple of weeks after we had that conversation about LSD—Carol's dog, Scooter, came into my room before she did. I wasn't that concerned until the dog went over to a shoe box and started sniffing. I had been holding a few ounces of pot in my room for the past couple of weeks and every few days, I'd hide it in a different place in my room so that it wouldn't get stolen. (I had learned that not everyone at Monticello was honest.) Scooter seemed to be trained. He went directly to the spot where I had last stored the buds. Within a minute, the dog had picked out every hiding place I had the pot in during the last week.

When I heard Carol coming, I took Scooter by the collar and led him out of the room. He went reluctantly, and then returned when Carol came around the corner. I thought, *Shit, my room is next.* Then I said to Carol, "Scooter is going to have to stay outside because I'm allergic to dogs, okay?" She laughed, kept the dog out in the hall, and stepped into my room. "I'm sure there's no problem with your room," she said. I laughed as if she'd made a joke between friends. I told her the only problem was that there needed to be a little more heat in the rooms, they were often cold as a tomb. I did have a heater, but it was hidden under my bed. We talked about volleyball for a few minutes and when she left I breathed a sigh of relief. Because in addition to the pot, I'd left a bottle of whiskey in the refrigerator. I was glad she hadn't asked me for a soda.

Oftentimes, I was forced to make up a lie on the spot—this came naturally to me. I remember, one time J.T. and I had just come back from Burger King where we got really baked and munched out. Don, who was both dean of students and my academic advisor, saw us walking into the main hall; he looked at us seriously and exclaimed, "Your eyes look wasted." Matter of factly I agreed and told him that we had just ridden my scooter without helmets from town and that was why our eyes were red. He was suspicious of us, but had to buy our story as I still had my motorcycle gloves on. J.T. and I went straight back to my room and used eye drops.

One night, I had to face my dad when I was even more stoned than usual and totally unprepared to see him, or any adult for that matter. I had been up in the hills with my good friend, Kelly, talking to her because she was depressed about her boyfriend. Kelly and I had dusted (smoked) two green bomber joints and we were totally baked. When I came back into the dorm, Brad told me my dad had just dropped off my scooter for me and that he was out in the parking lot. I went outside and jogged up to the window of my dad's truck and said, "Hi, Dad, thanks for bringing the scooter." I will never forget the look he gave he, it scared me, and for the first time made me feel guilty. He looked at me as if he had never seen me before and said, "Craig, are you all right?" I told him that I was getting over a cold and that the nurse had given me some strange medication. He turned off the truck and walked back to my room with me. While we walked, I could sense that he knew something was up and he even asked me if I was "on something." I coughed a few times and sniffled to show him how sick I was. The worried look on his face made me very nervous. I'd never seen him look worried about me before. To add power to my alibi, I showed my dad that the heater wasn't working in my room and told him that everyone in the dorm was getting sick. He called me later that night to see how I was and I thanked him again. He had taken the time and gone far out of his way to bring back my scooter and spend some time with me and I was too messed up to talk with him. I actually cried a bit as I fell asleep, sad that I had let him down.

It wasn't long before I began to lose control.

It started in November, when a group of my friends and I decided to pool our money and buy as much coke as possible for a "White Christmas." In on the deal were Eric, Todd, Sharon, and myself. Eric and Todd, both day students, were big partyers; I'd gotten baked with them on many occasions, but I wanted to get to know them better. I believed that doing a coke deal together was the perfect way of becoming better friends. Sharon, a boarder, from San Diego, was different. We were already friends. Sharon lived in the dorm next to mine and kept a horse at school. Because she always had so much money, Sharon was a good person to bring in on the deal. Her parents were divorced, and both sent her checks regularly for "living expenses."

The four of us agreed to raise the funds to purchase a half ounce of coke, 16 grams. The street value of coke was about $100 to $150 a gram depending on the dealer and quality of the blow. Buying half an ounce in bulk would cost us $2,000, bringing the price down to $50 a gram. We would all contribute money to pay for the amount of coke we wanted; I'd received a one-time gift from my grandmother on my dad's side, of $500 that year. I was contributing over half the money to the deal, the others gave me their share before I went home on Christmas break. Since Eric and Todd were day students, I arranged to deliver the coke to them after the school had closed. Sharon would get her coke in the mail or after vacation.

I raised the rest of the money by trading my leather motorcycle jacket to Dexter for 2 ounces of pot which I, in turn, sold to other students at school. Boarding students are required to leave $500 with the bursar's office for incidentals or emergencies. I managed to get $200 from the $500 by calling my parents and telling them that I needed to purchase hiking boots for a trip to Death Valley that I was scheduled to take in the spring. I told my mom that the phys. ed. department recommended that students buy their boots early in order to break them in. My mom forgot that I had already bought boots at the end of the summer for the coming trip.

I got the rest of the money by selling oversized candy bars to other students. A friend from home had stolen a box of these deluxe bars from a delivery truck parked behind the supermarket downtown. The candy bars were his payment of a debt of $65 for some cocaine I fronted him. Instead of selling the candy bars at the $3 most stores charged, I displayed them on my stereo for the dorm to see, and sold them for $2, making a quick $100. I remember showing Brad the stack of $100 bills. His jaw dropped. Brad ended up helping me by selling the candy bars on campus and I promised to line him up after I scored. He was pleased with this exchange; Brad had become one of the regular partiers on campus.

Sharon had no problem pulling together the money, but Eric and Todd had to sell VCRs and a TV to other students cheap. These items came from public school friends who had stolen them.

Putting this deal together was really exciting. I liked being in charge of organizing the details. Eric, Todd, Sharon, and I would get together in my room at night and go over the plan. We'd talk about who was getting what and how much more money we had to come up with. Since we had been talking about the score for over a month, a lot of people had heard about what we were up to and were expecting to be lined up or sold a quad—quarter gram.

On my first day back home in the Napa Valley, I called Mike, who was supposed to pick up the half-ounce for me. He came over to my house, took the money, and told me that we needed another $150. Even though that wasn't our original arrangement, I didn't argue with him. I just wanted to get the cocaine in my possession. So Mike called another friend of ours who was always looking for coke and came up with the $150 from him. About a half hour later, he came back with the blow in a giant bindle made from a sheet of newspaper. Since both my parents were out, he opened it up on the kitchen table and dumped it onto a mirror I had taken off the wall. The first thing I noticed was that it wasn't rock-meaning that it had been sifted. I told him that I thought it looked "short" and that I "wanted rocks."

He kept telling me that the deal was done, there was no way he could take it back. He argued that we had to keep it and that if I wasn't satisfied he would sell enough to make my share break even. Strangely, Mike instantly urged me to do some of the coke. I should have weighed it out first; after all, a lot of money was changing hands, but something stopped me. For some reason I just didn't make the effort to borrow a scale. Once I had done a few lines, I figured that I'd keep the coke, even if it wasn't that good. I had started using it and there was no stopping me.

I called up Eric and Todd and told them that I wasn't satisfied with the coke, that it wasn't rock. They wanted it anyway. I told them that I wanted to give them their money back. They kept telling me to "bring it, bring it." When I drove up to school, they got into my car and both did a line. Eric said it was good and they left with their share, one eightball. I had fewer than three eight-balls left. This included the two eightballs I'd paid for, plus Sharon's eightball. But Sharon had left school early to go to Mexico with her mother, and she hadn't called me yet. I didn't know what she wanted to do about her share.

With all this coke in my possession, I felt like a little kid who can't wait to open his presents on Christmas Eve. That weekend, I did an enormous amount of blow with my old friend Ben. That night was a blur. I think that I did well over an eightball—3.5 grams—by myself. I might have done more. I started out the night by snorting lines that were about a foot long. Even though I kept telling Ben to make me stop, I wouldn't. At one point, I fell back on the couch and the entire living room went white, then black. Unlike my earlier whiteouts, this one felt like it was going to last forever. I couldn't think or feel for a long time. I could hear Ben saying something, he sounded as if he was a long ways away. I was sure I was dying. Then I heard a voice in my head say, "Breath slowly, slowly." I finally started to breathe again and my heart, although beating fast was once again beating evenly.

I opened my eyes and Ben was sitting across from me, staring in awe. "Dude, I thought you were gone for sure!" I sat up and looked at the pile of coke left on the table. Ben lined another big one up and handed me the straw. Without hesitating I did the line, but not all of it. What had just happened really scared me, but my body's craving for the coke was stronger than my will to stop doing it.

Ben and I left the house to go for a walk, doing two grams worth of bullet shots from a pocket-sized contraption that shoots cocaine into your nose. Afterwards, we sat down on a little bridge by my house and smoked a joint to come down. I was so fried that I could barely walk. My heart was going a mile a minute; I thought I was going to "stroke out," to have a heart attack. All of a sudden I whited out again and I thought, *I'm going to die, how strange, I never thought I would.* My mind had finally split. I was no longer the same and I was balancing on the beam of insanity and life. However, insanity had the stronger hold of me. I tried to deny it, but there was no escaping.

By the time Christmas rolled around, I only had about half a gram left. So I took it with me to Portland, where I went with my parents to visit my sister, Amy, and my aunt, Pat. I hadn't seen Amy in about six months. The first afternoon that we were there, I put out the last of my cocaine to share with her. Lining her up seemed like the best Christmas present I could give to both of us. I thought I was giving us a chance to finally connect and create a time where we could be "real" with each other. But Amy didn't want to do any coke and was surprised at the size of the lines that I laid out for us. To me, though, both lines seemed small. I tried to convince her to do some coke with me because I really wanted to have a better relationship with her, and I knew coke was the only way to do it.

Amy was the first person who ever turned my drugs down.

Since Amy didn't want the lines, I did them both. The coke helped put me in a talkative mood and I asked Amy what was going on and whether she was happy—things like that. Then Amy really freaked me out and told me some things I wasn't prepared to hear. She said that our parents had been unhappy for years and that they didn't even like each other. I was dumbfounded and shocked. I felt like I had been lied to all my life. And the last thing I wanted was divorced parents. When I asked Amy how she knew mom and dad were having problems, she said that mom had told her. I wondered why I hadn't been told they weren't happy. At the same time, I couldn't understand why I hadn't been able to figure it out myself. I had no idea that my parents weren't happy, and I was furious at the idea that things weren't as they seemed.

Later that day, I approached my mom and asked her in a subtle way how she and dad were doing. I didn't know how to ask a direct question when it was about something personal, so I asked "How are you and dad getting along?" She gave me a panicked look as if to say, "Why are you asking me that?" but she said, "We're doing fine." I looked at her seriously and said, "Really, are you sure?" My mom told me she didn't want to talk about it and then walked away. This was the way in which most problems were dealt with in my family, just walk away.

I was angry both because I didn't like the idea that she and my dad were having problems and because she wouldn't tell me what was going on. Later that afternoon, when I was sitting by myself drawing, my aunt, with whom we were staying, came up to me and said sternly, "Craig, problems are part of life." She didn't mention my parents, but I knew that's who she was referring to. Judging from her tone of voice, I also got the impression that the topic of my parents' marriage was off-limits, so I went back to my abstract drawings of eyes, faces and heads. But I couldn't stop thinking about what happened and what I should do.

One side of me wanted to talk to my dad because I felt that he was getting the short end of the stick and that my mom wasn't giving him a chance. But my sister had told me not to say anything, and it was the first time she had ever confided in me. I decided it was probably best to shut up and not ruin my father's vacation. Instead, I got drunk in front of the TV every night on eggnog and rum.

Things didn't go much better back at school after vacation. Sharon, who decided at the last minute to transfer to a day school in San Diego, kept calling the dorm looking for me. I knew she wanted her share of the coke or her money back, but I didn't know how to explain to her that I had used it all. She sent one of her friends, a senior from Boys' Dorm B, to come talk to me. Then Sharon's father called me, wanting to "set everything straight." I didn't want to have to deal with a parent, so I pulled together $250 by selling my stereo cd-player and sent the money to Sharon. I felt like hell for having disappointed her. It wasn't like me to rip anyone off or to avoid them. I felt out of control, as if something inside me had changed for the worse and wasn't going to get better. I was shaky inside, I could no longer think clearly, even when I wasn't stoned.

On top of this, Eric and Todd were giving me the cold shoulder. When I asked them what was wrong, they told me that they had weighed the coke I sold them and that it had been a half gram shy. I apologized and told Eric and Todd that friendship was more important to me than money and I asked if there was any way that I could make this up to them. I ended up giving them $50 to cover the half gram, but they were still cold to me for quite awhile afterward. Even though friends from the dorm said that Eric and Todd deserved whatever came to them because they were always shorting people deliberately, I didn't feel much better. I hadn't shorted Eric and Todd to "get" them. I was haunted by the feeling that my reputation at Monticello was ruined, that my credibility was shot.

A week later in mid-January, I got an unexpected and very unwelcome surprise. I was in my room lying in bed because I had convinced the nurse to let me stay in my room for the day. I had showed her my report cards and that I was in fact an A student and that I needed a day off because I didn't feel all that well. She knew me and agreed that it was okay but not to make a habit of it. I thanked her and went back to sleep. I awoke to keys at my door, I pulled the covers over my head to go back to sleep. Thinking that it was the nurse, I turned over to say something and my heart did a free fall. Standing in my room was the school psychologist, Mary Kay, and the dean of students, Don. My first thought was, *They found out you sold coke,* but all I said was a groggy "Hi" to show them that they'd woken me up.

Don pulled a chair up to my bed and said gently, "We've received reports from students that you are using a lot of cocaine."

I drew back as if someone had slapped me. My first thought was that Eric and Todd had narced on me as a way to get revenge for the coke deal. But I knew that going to the teachers wasn't their style. Don interrupted my thoughts to say that the school wanted me to spend time away from campus. He said I wasn't being suspended but that the school wanted me to go home and discuss this matter with my family. He said I was technically being given a sick leave.

This shocked and scared me. I argued my head off, but Don wouldn't listen to me. Instead, he said that I could call my parents before he did and tell them what had happened. As soon as the teachers left, I went right to the dorm phone and called my dad at his office. I told him that there had been a big mix-up at school and that certain people who didn't like me were spreading lies. I told him that I once snorted No Doze to stay up for an exam and that maybe someone saw me do this and thought it was cocaine.

After my parents came to get me, I thought we were driving directly home. I got my second surprise of the day when my dad said that they were taking me to get a checkup. I told him I didn't need to see a doctor. But he said I didn't have much of a choice in the matter. I told my parents that I hated them and that by choosing to believe rumors, they were abandoning me as their son. I told them it would be a cold day in hell before I ever forgave them. Even though I was crying pretty hard, they didn't say much during the car ride.

In the waiting room at the doctor's office, I tried to get a grip on myself. I figured that my best strategy at this point was to cut the crap and tell the partial truth. So I told my parents that I had tried coke a few times and a few other drugs in moderation, but that the drugs didn't affect my performance and none of the teachers suspected me. I explained to them that I knew both the short- and long-term effects of each drug I'd taken. I told them about Ms. O'Donnell's health class and all the outside reading I'd done about drugs. I thought to myself, *Tell the truth. Let them see how in control you are. Show them there is no problem.* Then I gave the example of knowing how to tell if LSD is cut with strychnine. This really upset my mother, who said, "Strychnine? Isn't that poison?"

Both my parents wanted to know why and to what extent I used drugs. I tried to explain how drugs sometimes added a new twist to life and that I only did them now and then. I explained how cocaine in particular would let me really open up to others and helped me share my true feelings. I also tried to explain to them that LSD was harmless and that it was something I only did once or twice a year. I tried to describe the bond I felt after having tripped with a friend and how much more fun it was to laugh for hours on end about nothing in particular. I compared myself to my dad, saying that like him, I was high-strung and occasionally I needed to relax by smoking pot.

The doctor checked me over and asked me a few questions. He wasn't very sharp and it was easy to fool him. He tried to be sneaky and pretend as if we were checking my arms for strength when he was looking for needle tracks. I told him point blank, "I don't shoot drugs." A bit shocked at my bluntness, he denied that he was looking for "tracks." He then asked me, "Exactly why is it that you are here then?" I thought for a minute about how I should explain this, to put myself in the best light possible, "I tried cocaine over Christmas break, I didn't even like it but someone told my school that I had a 'drug' problem, so now I'm here." He looked at me and in a fatherly and caring tone and asked, "Do you have a drug problem Craig?" I looked him straight in the eyes and said, "No, I think that there has just been a series of miscommunications and now I'm here wasting your time." He gave me a thorough exam and since it was 6 P.M. and the labs were closed, he didn't give me a blood or urine test. Out in the lobby, he told my parents that he didn't see any signs of extensive use or damage. My dad was giving me strange looks, though, and inside I felt a little out of control.

Denial

After my checkup, I convinced my parents to keep everything I had told them about my drug use between the three of us. I told them how hard I had worked to build a good reputation among the faculty and explained that I didn't want my teachers to get a negative impression of me. I didn't want to be labeled as a drug user. My parents agreed not to tell the school what I told them. On my end of the bargain, I agreed not to do drugs anymore.

I really thought I could stop using drugs. Part of me even wanted to. I wanted my parents to be proud of me. After a week in which I drank instead of using drugs, I got right back into partying—only I wasn't as blatant. I was a little nervous about getting caught red-handed. Even though I hadn't been formally suspended and had no major infractions on my record, I suspected that I was being watched. The dean of students had even told me that if I were caught with drugs, I'd be expelled. I didn't believe that he was really serious, however, because no one with a record as clean as mine ever got expelled. Nonetheless, I made sure that I steered clear of big party rooms and took precautions when I did get high. I stopped doing bong hits in the bathroom and I no longer baked pot brownies in Zack's toaster oven. I didn't go home for six weeks. When I called my parents to check in or ask for money, I never stayed on the phone for more than five minutes. We never talked about whether or not I was using drugs.

All in all, the new year had not gotten off to a good start. I was still freaked out over the "White Christmas" deal and thought that people were talking about me. Then, to make matters worse, two close friends, Kelly and Lisa, took me aside and said that I shouldn't spend so much time with Zack. This surprised me because I thought they liked Zack. But Kelly said that liking Zack had nothing to do with it; I was idolizing him. Idolizing Zack? This really worried me. I admired Zack, but I hadn't realized that my admiration was so obvious. Since the last thing I wanted was to be a clone of someone else, I took their advice and began spending less time with him.

Zack didn't understand why I didn't want to be around him so much any more and I didn't know how to tell him what Kelly and Lisa had told me. Instead, I spent more and more time doing other things. If he stopped by my room and asked me if I wanted to go to dinner, I'd say that I was studying or had other plans, then show up a half hour later with someone else. But, if he asked me to go get high, I'd go—that wasn't something I was going to turn down.

I felt really guilty for disassociating myself from Zack. When I wasn't high, I felt bad the way I was ignoring him. I would think back to the times my sister tried to tell me who to hang out with. But once high, I was no longer able to make those decisions and it was easy to forget about that problem and the rumors Eric and Todd were spreading about me ripping them off.

These isolated worries were just part of my problem. In February, I felt a wave of paranoia enter into my head and stay. Even though my grades were great and I had just made the volleyball team, I knew I was falling apart and I couldn't figure out why. Each morning, I'd wake up feeling totally out of kilter and unsure of myself. I didn't know how to act anymore. I didn't know where to turn. I began to doubt myself. My nothing-fazed-me poker face felt more like a teeth-clenched blank expression. The worst episode occurred during the last week in February, when a beautiful day turned into an unstoppable drug-induced nightmare.

It all started out innocently enough. I'd gotten up early on a Saturday and, as usual, did one hundred push-ups and a few bong hits by myself before brunch. The campus was pretty quiet because half the student body had gone to the Grateful Dead concert in Oakland. At the dining hall, I hooked up with several seniors, most of them day students who'd spent the night at school. Since everyone thought I was a certified lifeguard, we decided to hang out at the pool. I had always wanted to get to know these people better, so we spent the rest of the day, swimming and sitting in the sun, leaving the pool every once in awhile to take some bong hits or drink a beer back in my room.

Then Adam, one of the seniors, invited all of us to spend the night at his grandmother's house in Berkeley. We agreed that leaving school was a great idea, and the first thought that ran through my mind when I heard him say Berkeley was, *Great. Maybe we can blaze.* Berkeley, located just outside of San Francisco, is known for having good drugs.

At this point, I hadn't done LSD in about a month because I'd had two bad trips—the first at school when I thought Zack was gay, the second at home when I ran into my old teacher, Ms. O'Donnell. So I wanted to have a good trip. On top of that, I felt that this group of seniors would like me more and that we could be much better friends if we blazed together. I wanted to show them how I was able to take more than them and act as if it didn't affect me. That way I'd regain some of the credibility that I'd lost with the Christmas coke deal. I had an LSD reputation to uphold because I had sold them LSD throughout the semester. Although I'd never tripped with them, I often told them how much I liked to fry and boasted about the number of hits I'd done with my old friends in the Napa Valley. What I didn't take into account was that my tolerance from not doing it in so long was way down.

That afternoon, we all signed out, saying that we were going to Berkeley for the night. Signing out was a rule at Monticello. Everyone took cars, except J.T., a junior from my dorm, and me. Since it was a beautiful afternoon and I didn't have a car, I decided to take J.T. on my scooter. This was dangerous for a couple of reasons. First, our combined weight was too heavy for the scooter, and second, the scooter didn't meet the minimum two-wheel vehicle weight or power requirements for freeway driving. In other words, it could be blown over by a heavy gust of wind. But I really didn't care about the law or what was considered safe; I had been driving motorcycles and minibikes since I was seven years old and trusted my ability. The fact that I was stoned mattered even less. I always drove stoned, or amped or on acid.

I was glad that J.T. was going to the party, I knew him really well. Nothing ever seemed to phase him, a quality I really admired. During the semester, J.T. and I spent a lot of time doing homework, listening to music and getting stoned. He was one of the few students at Monticello who was into jazz; he even played the trumpet in the school jazz band. I always learned a lot when we hung out. We didn't just sit around and bullshit. Also, like me, J.T. had recently made the varsity volleyball team. In fact, he was probably the best player on the team.

After more than three hours on the road, J.T. and I rolled into Berkeley. We drove past the University and parked in front of Rasputin's record store on Telegraph Avenue, the street where all the action was. We tried calling Adam at his grandmother's; since no one was at his house yet, we got some pizza at Blondies and walked around. On the street corner, there were all kinds of people—students, punks, rockers, burn-outs, hippies who looked like relics from the sixties. People were selling tie-dyed shirts and crystals, silver earrings, and "No Nuke" signs from the backs of vans and on the streets. One guy was giving away pet lizards. Another was singing Neil Young songs and playing the guitar. It looked like a carnival or the parking lot at a Grateful Dead concert.

As we walked around eating our pizza, we heard burned-out hippies sitting in doorways, whispering to us, "Big green buds." One pimpish-looking guy dressed in a pink polyester suit came right up to my shoulder, walked tightly against me, and quietly said, "You got acid?" What he really meant was, "Do you want acid?" But by asking us first, he was making sure that J.T. and I weren't a bust—narc. I could tell by looking at him that he just wanted to rip us off, so we ignored him. We called and got directions and drove a couple of miles, further into the Berkeley Hills.

Adam's grandmother's house, a huge split-level, was located on a steep incline and surrounded by carefully manicured hedges. No one answered the front door, so J.T. and I walked around to the side of the house, where we heard voices and music. In a room off the porch was the group from school, sitting around drinking beer and smoking pot out of the biggest bong I'd ever seen.

I said, "What's up?"—the standard greeting—and everyone else said, "Not much," the standard reply. Adam loaded up another bowl and said, "Sit down and meet Mr. Hookah,"—a giant Egyptian tobacco water pipe that six people could use at the same time by inhaling from any one of the multi-colored hoses coming from its sides. I thought this was a great idea because I was stressed from the long drive. I sat down on a beat-up couch to take my turn with "Mr. Hookah." Adam and I both had reputations as big smokers so we both took three tubes for ourselves and competed for the biggest hit.

After loading a few more bowls, we barbecued chicken out on the porch. While we were eating dinner, we heard voices shouting, "Adam," really loud. Then a whole new carload of people from school—all guys—came around to the back of the porch. With this group were Eric and Todd; I was uncomfortable about seeing them because I thought they were still mad at me over the coke deal.

After dinner we ate some ice-cream and cake that Adam's grandmother had left for us. As I sat on the couch, I looked around thinking, *What a scene.* Out of the ten people that were there, one had already been expelled from Monticello for stealing liquor from the local Safeway. Five of the people, myself included, dealt drugs. Three of these dealers had two major infractions and were being watched carefully by the administration. I'd recently been sent home, but not suspended. As for the rest of the group? Well, like J.T. who came on the scooter with me, they were just big partyers. We lit up the bong once again and Lucky, a senior from Seattle, passed out a handful of concentrated caffeine pills that he had ordered from an advertisement in *High Times.* I didn't want to trash my stomach so I only took one, but everyone else took a couple of pills and washed them down with beer.

While the rest of the party was inside listening to Zepplin, I took Blake, a senior who was a peer counselor, out on the porch and asked him if he knew where to score some fry—LSD. Blake, who was a punker, had grown up in Berkeley and knew the people downtown. When he said he knew where to score I went back inside and starting with J.T., I asked the others if they wanted to blaze. They all got excited and said that it sounded like a great idea. We pooled $40 and I offered to drive Blake to get it.

The ride back down the Berkeley hills was hairy. While I drove, Blake sat backwards on my scooter's trunk, screaming and yelling. On the way into town, I thought about how much I wanted to trip with this group of people and show them that I was in control and that I deserved to be one of them. Being able to take a lot of acid and then act normal was a way to prove to myself that I was in control of my life.

On a street off Telegraph Avenue, we saw some hard-core punks with spiked dyed hair and engineer boots. They all had their noses, tongues and cheeks pierced. Blake looked like he was part of their group so he jumped off the scooter to go talk to them. Before he left I handed him an additional $16 from my wallet and said, "Score me some extra." I drove around the block and parked. Within five minutes, Blake came back and said, "Let's go."

"You got it?" I asked.

He said, "Yep, it's killer too."

"What kind," I asked

"Blotter," he replied happily then yelled out in triumph.

"How much?"

"Three fifty a hit."

When I asked him what it looked like, Blake said we should eye it up in the hills. I liked this idea so I could get a look at the fry before anyone else did. I also wanted to take my extra hits out. Among big partyers, it's an unspoken rule not to seem too eager.

On the way back to Adam's house, a cop car flashed its search-light on us and I thought, *Oh shit I'd better jam.* Blake who was still sitting backward on the scooter motioned for me to drive down a dirt path off the road. I did, squeezing the scooter right through a partially open gate. Then I turned the lights off so that the cop wouldn't be able to find us, and coasted blindly down a path. The cop car drove by and Blake patted me on the back, "Good driving man, I thought we were gone for sure." I packed a bowl both to celebrate our escape from the cop and to let the conversation flow into "eyeing the fry." Blake picked up my cue and we examined the acid. I asked him if he knew the "punks" that sold it to him. He said, "Sort of, they go to Berkeley High."

He handed me the rectangle of hits, which I held at the edges like a photograph so as not to get my fingers on it. I told Blake that I wanted to cut my extra hits out then but he said, "I want to wait until we get back. Okay?" It wasn't okay because I wanted my hits, but I pretended that it was fine. After smoking one more bowl for the road, we drove to Adam's.

The once-mellow scene at the house had changed. While we were gone Todd and Shane, a senior day student at Monticello, had been wrestling and Shane had stuck Todd in the arm with a skewer. Everyone was talking about "all the blood." Eric and Todd went to the hospital because wherever Todd went Eric followed. I was sorry to hear that Todd had gotten stabbed but I was glad they'd left the party.

While they were gone, I took out the little gold scissors that I had and gave them to Blake to divide the acid. Blake cut out eight hits for me. I gave two of mine to J.T., who didn't have any money with him, set aside four for myself, and I put the remaining hits in my wallet for use later. Once everyone got his share and all the money matters were straightened out, we all sat around the coffee table and grinned at each other. The next step was understood; we each put the little serrated squares on our tongue.

Most everyone swallowed their hits. Blake sucked on his and then spit them out. I chewed on my four hits, a ritual I'd started with my friends at home. J.T., who'd never done LSD before, looked around the room to make sure that he was doing the right thing. The acid had a bitter taste, so I knew immediately that it had been dried with strychnine or speed. Then Blake said, "Everyone write their names down and how many hits they bought so that if it's bunk I can get your money back." J.T. nodded, pretending that he knew the difference between good and bad acid. I started feeling a vague uneasiness creep over my shoulder and into my head. The last thing I wanted was bunk acid. While waiting for the acid to kick in, we smoked a lot of shake—pot clippings—probably more than an ounce. For a long time, I thought that I was just really stoned—then all of a sudden, my body went "floppy,"—floppy is the feeling right before you get pins and needles in your leg or arm, only with acid, your whole body is affected.

As I was looking around at everyone, wondering what they were thinking about, a voice inside my head whispered, *They don't like you, Craig.* Where this strange voice came from I'll never know, but it disturbed me. I looked around the room: everyone but J.T. was laughing and joking around. They seemed perfectly normal and relaxed. J.T., though, looked distressed and a little pale. I could tell he was wondering what the hell was going on; after all, it was his first trip. Seeing J.T. comforted me. I knew I wasn't alone in feeling uneasy.

Bowl upon bowl was sparked in the big pipe. The tubes rotated to me, but I declined. Everyone started coaxing me to take another hit. They urged me not to break the pattern. After I took another hit and passed it on, the inner voice said to me, *They're trying to get you real stoned, Craig, so they can kick you out of the house.* The idea really worried me because I didn't know Berkeley well at all and wouldn't know how to get home—especially in the dark and on acid. I told the voice to shut up.

After a couple of hours, the party moved out to the porch— bong, beers, and all. I sat down by myself on the porch steps and looked out into the fuzzy darkness. The inner voice then said, *That's where they are going to send you.* Again, I told the voice to "Shut the fuck up," but it ignored me. I was beginning to feel over- whelmed with despair. I felt that I had better do something to be accepted or I'd have to leave.

A song on the Led Zepplin tape ended and a new one began. Everyone knew the words by heart and they all stood in a circle singing. *The voice said, Sing if you want to be accepted. THIS is what you must do!* I felt as if everyone was looking at me thinking, *He doesn't belong here. He's not one of us. He doesn't even know the song.* I decided that I'd better start singing along even though I'd never heard the song before. I thought I could wing it. So I started to sing, but I could barely get the words out of my mouth. I kept try- ing and trying and then Cam, a senior and a big coke dealer on campus, looked at me and laughed. Then everybody started to laugh.

They are laughing at you. They hate what you are. They really hate you, the voice said. At this point, I wasn't sure what to do so I blurted out, "I have to go to the bathroom." When Cam said, "Go ahead," I took his words to mean, *Go ahead. Get out of here. We don't want you.* So I slowly walked inside to the bathroom and shut the door. I looked at my face in the mirror. My skin was bright red, as if I'd just been really embarrassed, and my pupils were huge. I took a piss and noticed that my urine was white, a sign that the acid had been dried with speed. My testicles were contracted and they ached.

I sat down at the edge of the porcelain bathtub and tried to get a grip on myself, but this proved to be an impossible task. Up to this point, fighting the bad trip and regaining some control was a battle I thought I had a chance of winning. But the voice was now stronger than I was. It was starting to talk faster and faster, like those "speed talkers" on TV and radio auctions. I couldn't keep up with what the voice was telling me. But I knew that everything it said was bad. I believed it when it told me, *They're outside talking about you right now.*

While I was in the bathroom, I decided to roll a joint. My inner voice added, *If you do, they won't make you leave.* So I got out my pot and rice papers, but for the life of me I couldn't roll a joint. The harder I tried the worse it got. I assumed everyone would be angry with me because I couldn't roll the joint. I had convinced myself that they were outside waiting to smoke it.

I walked out of the bathroom not knowing what to expect. When I passed the doorway leading into the family room, I thought the beads were laughing at me. The swishing noise they made seemed to be filled with evil voices.

Then I came to a dead halt. The family room looked different. It was dark, yet it seemed to be glowing—someone had turned on a florescent light. I thought I was all alone, except for Adam who was passed out on the floor next to the couch. The first thing I assumed was that everyone was trying to freak me out and make me leave. Then I looked at my sweatshirt; it was glowing like a lighthouse.

Wall posters of psychedelic skeletons playing guitars and corpses coming out of the earth totally unnerved me. They seemed so negative and death-oriented that I didn't know what to think, and my head turned quickly from poster to poster. I had trouble focusing my eyes. Then Peter, one of the senior day students sitting on a couch, said, "Dude, sit over here." Hearing his voice made me feel better, even though I knew he only wanted someone to do a bong hit with. Although I didn't feel like smoking any more pot, I took a hit anyway and felt myself sink into the couch.

Soon, everyone came back in the room and sat down. The one good thing about the darkness was that no one could see my eyes. I liked this until the voice told me that everyone else could see each others' eyes. I was the only one who lacked this ability. The voice said, *They are all looking at you, can't you even see that, they are looking at YOU.*

What I could see in the darkness were teeth. When people smiled or laughed, their teeth looked hungry for my defeat. I tried to tell myself to calm down, to get a hold on myself and that this would be over in a few hours. But the voice intruded into my thoughts and said, *You may get over the trip, but they won't forget it. Everyone knows you are a liar and a cheat. They think that you've lied about all your trips, it's obvious you have, you can't even handle this one.*

I remembered that I had brought my neon orange and yellow hackey sack with me to the party. I took it out, but playing hackey sack was like rolling the joint: I simply couldn't do it. When the hackey sack was passed to me, I missed it entirely; there were so many tracers coming off the sack that it was difficult to follow. In a very calm and controlled voice, I said, "These lights are a trip. It's hard to follow the sack." I tried to keep a straight face because I didn't want anyone to know that anything was wrong. Normally I was a great hackey sacker. But inside I was crying, screaming, and exploding with confusion and fear.

I sat down on the couch and thought about what a fool I'd made of myself at hackey sack. The room started to look very fuzzy. The jeering, hovering teeth seemed to move in slow motion. Blake's voice suddenly said, "Let's go to the rock." Then someone opened a door and we all went outside. I'd never heard of the rock. I was just glad to get out of the dark room with all its weird lights and teeth and trippy posters.

Out on the street, a heavy, thick fog was coming in. It swirled under the street lamps and seemed to creep up the streets. We all started walking down the steep hill. J.T. and I lagged behind the rest of the group. J.T. said, "I don't think I'm gonna come down." This is a classic first time/bad trip symptom, so even though I was scared, I told him not to worry and that it would be over in a few hours. I felt bad for J.T., but also glad to be around someone who wasn't about to exclude me.

I looked ahead and saw everyone in front of us put their arms on each others' shoulders and start walking in syncopated giant steps. The inner voice told me, *They're blocking you out, Craig. Get in now or be lost.* Without speaking, J.T. and I walked to the opposite sides of the road and hooked up onto the people at either end of the group. For a few seconds, I felt included, so I tried to grab onto that good feeling and make it into some sort of reality.

The group came to a stop in front of an enormous rock. The rock must have been 35 feet wide and 50 feet high. Several of the guys started climbing up some stairs that seemed to have been cut into the side of it. Again, J.T. and I dropped to the back of the group. Everyone except the two of us was laughing and shouting. I was trying hard to concentrate on climbing, when I head Lucky say, "Where's my Coke?", referring to the drink he'd brought with him. Then everyone burst out laughing.

At that moment, my mind split and fizzled. I was so freaked out. I thought they were talking about the coke I'd sold Eric and Todd over Christmas vacation. I was sure that they were making fun of me even though neither Eric nor Todd were there. I started to get more scared than ever, and the inner voice said, *See, I told you. They hate you.* Looking at the rock, I thought, *If I go up any further I'm never going to get down.*

Ahead of me in line, I heard more laughter and was sure that I was the source of the joke. Behind me, J.T. was having trouble climbing. I was grateful when he asked if I wanted to go back down. Once J.T. and I made our way back down to the ground, I took a good long look at the rock. I saw a much better set of steps built into the face of the rock that I hadn't noticed before. My inner voice said, *How could you have missed these? Take this obvious way to the top.*

For several minutes I stood below the rock trying to talk to J.T., when all I could really concentrate on was the dialogue in my head. The voice was coaxing me to climb; *Just go up it, it's easy, if you do they will accept you and you will be part of the group. If you don't then you will always be a loner, like at your old school.* I heard some more laughter from the top, my inner voice continued to coax me up the rock; *Go ahead what are you afraid of? There are stairs right there for you.* I could see the stairs, they went right to the top, where I was supposed to be. My inner voice said, *They're laughing at you because you can't climb the rock.* At this point, I couldn't take it any longer and decided that I wanted to climb the rock and show them I could do it.

I walked over to the rock and showed J.T. my new way of getting to the top. J.T. couldn't see the stairs and said, "I'm not going." He walked back to where the others had climbed up to give it another shot. More laughter came from the top, the pressure was too great, I started to climb. There were no stairs after the first couple steps, I began to free climb. I was about twenty feet from the ground when I had a "moment of clarity," a completely different voice spoke in my head. It said in a confident and comforting tone, "Craig, go back down, go back home." Without questioning it, I descended from the rock. As I stepped away and looked to the top I realized that there had been no stairs, just a near vertical face.

J.T. came back around still looking distressed. I saw him and repeated what the voice had said to me; We need to go back home. But we didn't know the way and a heavy fog from the bay was coming in. As we sat there, we lost sight of the others on the top of the rock due to the fog.

Just then Shane, the day student senior who had stabbed Todd, came from behind the rock. I looked at him with yearning, my eyes begging him to take us back. My expression must have made it clear that I needed to go back. He said he'd show us the way to Adam's. By this time it was close to midnight and the fog was heavier than ever. It swirled in what looked like orange, misty circles. The black night that surrounded us seemed dark and evil to the core. When I asked Shane if he knew where he was going, he said, "I'm not sure. I'm just wandering."

J.T. and I looked at each other in desperation—the thought of getting lost was just too overwhelming. I tried to remember the way we came but every road looked like a wrong turn and all the homes tucked into the hills looked the same. I was certain we were lost, that we'd never get back. The negative inner voice threatened again, *See, Craig. This is part of the plan. They just want to lose you in the fog because they hate you.* Just when I thought that at least I had J.T. as a friend, the voice muttered, *J.T. hates you too.* I was feeling completely helpless and on the verge of tears when Shane said, "We're here."

I looked up and, sure enough, there was my scooter parked right where I left it. The scooter represented salvation to me. I quickly ran over to it and tried to start the engine. But I was so fucked-up that I couldn't put the keys in the ignition. My inner voice kept urging me, *Get out of here, Craig. You've got to get out of here.*

When it looked like I wasn't going anywhere, I reluctantly followed J.T. inside and we sat down on the couch. Shane put on AC/DC, *Highway to Hell.* At this point, the traces were worse than ever and I was beginning to have intense hallucinations. The posters seemed to beckon me to join them and whenever I turned my head, everything was a blur of jumbled figures and noise. I wasn't able to say anything to Shane or J.T. All three of us just sat there in silence staring around the room.

Once again, the voice began telling me I was terrible and that I had no friends. Then Peter burst into the room panting and screaming, "Oh, fuck man! Oh, fuck!. You are not going to believe what happened." Startled, I asked what was wrong. He said that while they were all up on top a police helicopter had spotted them and had told them to "Stay right there." Then a few cop cars pulled up and while they were spotlighted on top the cops came up and pulled them off one by one and booked them. Supposedly there had just been a murder in the hills and they were doing a "round-up." Peter said that the only reason he didn't get hauled in with the others was that he'd hidden in a crevice of the rock and the police didn't see him.

I was very confused by this news because the inner voice kept saying, *It's all a lie. What they mean is that they called the police on you, Craig, and they are going to take you to the station.* Since I believed that everyone had plotted against me, I decided to call their bluff by not saying a word. I stayed motionless on the couch. I watched and waited.

Peter woke up Adam, who was still passed out on the floor, and told him to go wake up his grandmother's housekeeper so she could claim legal custody of the others. After a couple of hours, the rest of the group came bouncing in through the beaded entrance-way. They started talking wildly about "jail." I was petrified because I thought they wanted me to go home. I had the feeling that I didn't belong but at the same time, I felt I couldn't leave if I wanted to. I sat there very quietly in the purple hazy light. Then my inner voice began to tell me what each person was thinking.

I looked at J.T. *Can you ride your scooter now, loser?*

I looked at Dexter. *You are so fucked-up. You lied about all the times you blazed.*

I looked at Blake. *You liar.* This went on and on. The inner voice was like a cassette tape on fast forward.

I sat back and closed my eyes so I wouldn't have to look at anyone and hear the voice tell what they were thinking. Inside, I was screaming and pleading for the trip to be over. But it didn't stop; it went on and on. At about five o'clock in the morning I heard a blood-curdling scream. I opened my eyes and looked at Blake, who was sprawled out on a chair. "That's Shane," he said, still half asleep. "Don't worry. He's crazy."

After the scream, I fell asleep on the couch for half an hour and dreamed that I had jumped off the rock. I woke up and saw that everyone was asleep on the floor except J.T., who was sitting against the wall, holding his knees against his chest, and staring into space. He looked at me and tried to smile.

I said, "Let's go back to school."

The ride back to Monticello was long and cold. My hands were stone white from the freezing wind, and I was tired from not sleeping. The more I drove, the more depressed I became. I said to myself, *You almost lost it completely last night. What are people going to think of you now? You couldn't even handle a few hits of acid.*

I convinced myself that the one thing I needed to do in order to feel better and prove to myself that I was okay, was to trip again as soon as possible. I knew doing this would also show the others that Berkeley was just a mistake and that I really could handle blazing. When I got back to campus at around 8:30, I dropped J.T. off at his dorm; he was looking very burned-out. Then, I went right over to Boys' Dorm B, where Brad lived.

I walked into Brad's room, sneaked up to his bed and looked right into his face as he slept. He must have felt something because he opened his eyes only to find me staring into them. He jerked back and yelled, "Dude! What are you doing?"

Stepping back I said, "I brought you back a present from Berkeley, you want it?" I asked knowing full well that he had never done fry and had asked me many times to get him some. I held up my wallet and showed him the hits. "Is that?" he paused and waited for my response.

"Yep, let's go." He jumped out of bed and put on random clothes from his floor. In less than a minute he was standing there dressed and saying, "I'm ready, let's go."

We went back to my dorm and I grabbed a pair of shorts and a T-shirt for later, and packed a knapsack with pot, a pipe, and some Chinese cracker snacks my father had sent to me from Asia. I put on my leather hiking boots in order to break them in for the upcoming school trip to Death Valley.

Brad and I took my scooter about two miles up into the hills behind the school and the nearby valley. From this perspective, Monticello seemed small and unimportant. My problems seemed far away. I was confident that I was going to have the good trip I needed. I cut the hits carefully with my little gold scissors—stolen from the hospital back home, and handed Brad his hit. We looked at each other, smiled, and then dropped our hits. Though I'd been up for over twenty-four hours, I felt I was getting my second wind.

We smoked pot until the new acid started to kick in, my head felt lighter, less crazed. I knew that I'd made the right decision and told myself that the reason I'd had a bad trip the night before had to do with the people and circumstances, not with me.

Being with Brad made all the difference. I felt no pressure, it was like being with my long-time friend Dirk back home. I knew that Brad really looked up to me. After all, he was my "Little brother," and I taught him pretty much everything he knew about drugs. With the others in Berkeley, I felt like I had a reputation for LSD that I had to live up to. But with Brad, I could do no wrong.

For most of the morning, we hiked around in the hills. We laughed and joked and talked about our friends at school. Since I'd only taken one hit, my trip was not intense—nothing like the one the night before. The inner voice that had haunted me all night was now gone and began to feel like it had never really existed. I felt back in control.

Acid can't help but make you think a lot, especially during the day, because you tend not to hallucinate. Instead, you turn inwards and contemplate things, mostly from the past. Brad and I were in the mood for reminiscing. We decided to drive to the top of the mountain, where orientation for new students was held in September. We wanted to see if it still looked the same.

The campsite didn't look much different than I remembered. The circle of big oak trees, the fire pit, the picnic tables—it was still the same. We sat down on the picnic table, and I asked Brad what he thought of me. I had learned to do this in Est, it was a way of perceiving people differently and learning how I was perceived. This was a low-risk question because I thought I knew what the answer was going to be. Brad said that he liked me a lot and thought I was smart. Hearing this made me feel good. I told him how far I thought he had come. To memorialize our trip, we took out our Swiss Army knives and etched the sign for acid—a capital A with a circle around it—plus the initials of our first names onto the picnic table. The symbol read BAC. For us, these initials had a double meaning. Since the circle with the A represented acid, having our initials there meant that we fried together. BAC was also short for "We'll be back." In fact, I told Brad I was going to be on the orientation committee next year and that I wanted him to volunteer for it, too.

At the end of the day, we sat in a meadow watching the sun go down and I gave Brad a "wall hit" to trip him out. A wall hit consists of pressing someones jugular veins in order to stop the blood flow to their heads until they pass out. (For a couple of months at Monticello, wall hits were a big craze. Brad used to do them to himself in the middle of class just to get excused.) As was usual, when I gave one to Brad, his whole body started jerking as if he were having a seizure and his eyes rolled backward in their sockets. I helped him to the ground so that he wouldn't hit his head on the rocks; as usual his whole body went into convulsions and drool came out of his mouth. A few seconds later he woke up, very confused. When Brad realized where he was, we burst into hysterical laughter for several minutes.

Brad begged to give me a wall hit. Although I really didn't want one, I agreed as a show of trust. But as I passed out, high-speed dreams went flashing through my mind. I felt like I was back in Berkeley during the worst moments of my trip. I woke up and looked at Brad in desperation. I asked him, "What's going on? Where am I" What happened?" For some strange reason, I was convinced that it was time for dorm check, that I had to be ready to face John, my dorm head. I started to panic. I thought *Oh, my God, I'm freaking out. This is it. I've lost control and I'm not coming back!* Luckily, after a few seconds, I realized where I was. And although the feeling that I was having a bad trip quickly passed, the experience confused me. It made Berkeley seem too close.

While we recovered from our wall hits, Brad and I watched the sunset. We waited for the last possible moment to drive back down to campus because I didn't want the day to end. Except for the wall hit, I was having a great time. Once we got back to school, Brad said he'd come back to my room later to hang out. I parked my scooter.

In the parking lot, the first person I ran into was Wolfgang. Instead of saying the standard, "What's up?" he said, "How are you doing?" in an unusually concerned tone. I knew from this that Wolfgang had heard about what happened at Berkeley, that everyone was back from the party at Adam's and that, no doubt, they were all talking about it. Before Wolfgang could even start asking me questions, I told him that I'd just spent the day blazing with Brad in the hills, and that we had a great time. Wolfgang just looked at me strangely.

Later that evening, my worst suspicions were confirmed when Blake stopped by my room. He had a serious expression on his face and started the conversation by saying, "Are you all right?" He said that everyone was really worried about me and that he was sorry that he didn't help me out at Berkeley. But inside I had a lot of conflicting feelings. I wished someone would have helped me at Berkeley, but at the same time, I didn't want to admit that I needed help. Brad was in my room at this point, playing computer games, and he told Blake about the great trip we had just had. I just thought, *Thank you, Brad, for saying that.*

Blake looked at me with surprise and awe. I told him that the reason I had bad-tripped in Berkeley was because I was in a tripping rut and by tripping with Brad, I pulled myself out of it.

My main concern, though was still that no one hated me. Blake assured me that everyone was my friend and that I shouldn't worry about what happened at Berkeley. When he said that I wasn't the only one tripping-out that night, I felt better.

After Blake left my room, Brad and I put on a Pink Floyd CD and talked some more. I suggested that we trip again next weekend, but Brad said he didn't want to, that he was burned-out. I wrote off Brad's reaction to inexperience. After all, tripping is usually pretty draining. Then Brad said that he wanted to lay off drugs for awhile. I thought about this for a second—cleaning out my system didn't sound like a bad idea. I needed to get in shape for volleyball and could probably use the break.

Brad and I shook hands. We agreed not to do any drugs for a week.

Residential Treatment

Within twenty-four hours, I had broken the pact I made with Brad by doing half a gram of coke before volleyball practice and polishing off the rest of an eighth of Sonoma Coma (pot grown in Sonoma County) afterwards with a friend. The next day, Tuesday, I was in route to history class when Mary Kay, the school psychologist, took me aside and asked me to come to her office after class. This wasn't out of the ordinary because Mary Kay ran Peer Counseling and Peer Counseling was one of my main activities. Nevertheless, all throughout history class, I had a premonition that something was really wrong.

After class, I walked over to Mary Kay's office. Sitting inside with her was Fred Jacobsen, another teacher. I couldn't figure out what Fred was doing there; I didn't have him for any classes. But I knew that whatever was going on had to be serious because both of them looked very grave.

Mary Kay was the first to speak. "We understand that you've been abusing LSD and we are very concerned," she said. I couldn't believe what I was hearing and immediately started to argue with her. I denied that I had ever even tried LSD. Mary Kay went on, "One of your friends went to Fred and told him that you had a bad trip this weekend."

Someone from the Berkeley party betrayed me, they will pay dearly, I thought. Being pulled aside by Mary Kay confirmed what I was feeling over the weekend—that I really was hated. Mary Kay said how the administration couldn't ignore this kind of information, and that this was the third time that something had come up about me and drugs. Even though I tried to look as though I was paying close attention to what she was saying, I wasn't. At this point I could only think about two things—who had narced on me and how I was going to get out of this mess.

Then Fred dropped the bomb. He told me that my parents were coming to school to take me to a treatment center to be evaluated. "There is no way I'm going to a treatment center," I said. Then I began shouting. I pointed out that I was in student government and Peer Counseling. I played volleyball. I got excellent grades. I asked them if these were the signs of a drug abuser. I dared them to get out my last report card. I told them that I wanted some answers.

Fred tried to calm me down. "We're not saying that you definitely have a problem. You're just going to be evaluated." Mary Kay kept asking me how I felt, and I told her that I wanted to kill myself and that she was ruining my chances of getting into a good college. I demanded that they call my parents and tell them to stay at home. They refused. This really set me off and I yelled at them some more. But Mary Kay and Fred wouldn't budge. I started to cry.

By the time my parents arrived at school, I was feeling really trapped. I had managed to stop crying before they arrived but the minute I saw my mom, I broke down again. I was really upset. I don't remember what I said to my mom and dad except that I kept apologizing over and over again. I was sorry that they had to take the time out of their schedules to come and see me like this; that they sent me to this expensive boarding school and were now being forced to listen to a story about a drug problem that I supposedly had. Although I didn't say anything about it, I knew there were plenty of other people at school who did more drugs than I did. None of these people got the grades I did or participated in as many activities as I did. I was furious at myself for somehow letting this mess happen.

Once I stopped crying, my parents took me back to my dorm to get some clothes and the rest of my books. Since there was no one around, I went over to Boys' Dorm B and slapped a note on Brad's door: "Someone narced me off—find out who."

The ride to the hospital was long and emotional. I tried to explain to my parents that I only used drugs recreationally and that I didn't need to be evaluated. But like Fred and Mary Kay, my parents wouldn't change their minds. My mom kept telling me that everything was going to be all right. She kept saying, "We'll see. We'll see what they say." I told her that I already knew the answer—that I didn't have a problem and that this evaluation was going to be a waste of everyone's time. My dad seemed to understand my point of view. In fact, he said, "We'll show 'em."

At least my dad believes me, I thought. I knew what I had to do was "show" those doctors, or whoever was in charge of the evaluation, that I didn't have a problem and that this whole thing was one big mistake.

The hospital was in Sonoma county, in a town about three hours away from school and about half an hour away from my home. When we finally arrived, my parents seemed to know exactly where they were going. In the main reception area of the hospital, a nurse nodded as if she were expecting to see them and buzzed us through a set of doors that opened into a separate wing. We walked down a short narrow hallway toward another reception desk. There were doors on either side of us. One of the doors was open, revealing an ordinary-looking hospital room. Inside, a girl was packing a bag and telling a man—who I assumed to be a doctor or counselor—that she was going to "get the fuck out."

Although I was very upset about what was happening, I was thinking to myself, *No problem. This is going to be a short vacation from the pressures of school.* I tried to think about what the good side of my situation might be. I told myself that I'd probably get the chance to work out in the hospital gym to get in better shape for volleyball, and that maybe during my short stay I'd catch up on the reading for my American Civilization class. Most of all, I was confident that the people at school were going to have to do some serious apologizing to me when I got back—particularly Mary Kay and Fred. And whoever had narced me off would pay dearly. I believed that they were personally screwing up my education by putting me someplace I clearly didn't belong.

A very tall man with a short cropped beard greeted us and said his name was Ken. He sort of reminded me of a GI-Joe doll. I didn't like this guy because of the hungry look in his eyes; he looked like he wanted to devour me. His smile, too, seemed prefabricated. When I shook his hand and said, "Hi, my name is Craig Fraser," he did a double take. My parents and I sat down in his office, and Ken asked me if I knew why I was at the hospital. I told him that yes, of course I did; I was there to be evaluated to see if I had a drug problem. Then, he looked at me in a really condescending way and said, "Now, what do you think, Craig?" Do you think you have a drug problem?"

I looked him directly in the eye and said, "No. I'm sure I don't. I'll be going back to school in a couple of days." When I said this, his pre-fab smile faded quickly.

Ken explained to my parents, as if I wasn't even there, that the treatment at the hospital was called the Pegasus Program and that it was divided into three parts—Phase One, Phase Two, and Aftercare. During Phase One, the staff determines whether or not the patient is chemically dependent. The evaluation begins with a twenty-four hour "detox" period and then, depending on the patient, a follow-up observation that could last anywhere from three to six days. After that comes Phase Two, the treatment part of the program, which usually lasts four weeks. Aftercare consists of anywhere from three to six months and involves follow-up, outpatient meetings, and treatment. He then looked over at me and smiled that fake smile. I told him not to worry and that I'd be leaving in three days. My father looked at me and nodded with approval.

Ken told me to go wait in a room called the "Fishbowl" while he talked to my parents. I asked my dad to bring me my school books and clothes from the car. I wanted to get to work on a paper that was due on Monday.

The Fishbowl room was located a couple of doors away from Ken's office. There was no doubt how the room got its name: there was a big glass window cut into the wall so that nurses sitting at the desk at the end of the hall could look in on its occupants. To make matters worse, the room was pale blue and ugly as hell. On the walls were posters of a hang glider and a sailboat. I wondered if these decorations were meant to soothe the patients. The air smelled synthetic, so I tried to open the window to the outside. But it was bolted shut. There were two bulky hospital beds in the room, but the wires to make them go up and down had been pulled out. When I saw the rubber sheet on the beds, I thought, *This is getting to be too much.*

A group of kids walked by the room. They were making a lot of noise and pushing each other around. A guy who had long hair and was wearing a Iron Maiden concert T-shirt poked his head in the door and said, "Dude, you'll love it here. It's like Club Med." Ken heard the commotion and came out of his office. He shut the door to my room and told me to stay inside. I asked him about my parents, and he told me that they had left. This made me furious; I felt they had betrayed me.

Even though I was fuming, I decided to relax and lie down since it looked like I wasn't going anywhere. I was just about to fall asleep when someone knocked on my door. Before I could answer, a very short and chubby Hawaiian woman wearing little white nurse's shoes walked in. She introduced herself as Anna and said that she was a nurse's aid and a recovering addict. Anna told me that she had to take my vital signs and ask me a few questions. I felt comfortable with her right away because she seemed really friendly and sort of spacey—as if she wasn't all there.

Anna began asking me questions about how much and how often I used drugs, noting the answers on a clipboard. I decided to be honest with her about "how much" I took, but to minimize the "how often" parts. I wanted to show her and myself that I didn't have a problem and that I could handle drugs. I made a point of looking her directly in the eye. As often as I could, I'd steer the conversation toward Anna's personal experiences and ask her questions about herself. We'd get way off track and then she'd stop and say, "Enough about me. Let's get back to the questions."

I really enjoyed our conversation: talking about drugs was one of my favorite pastimes. I was certain that after our interview was over, Anna would see that I didn't belong in a treatment center. When she left, I lay down on one of the beds and fell asleep. Although I rarely napped in the afternoon, I was still pretty exhausted from all the partying I'd done the weekend before.

A couple of hours later, a doctor came into the room and woke me up. He said that he had to give me a physical. This was something I had been dreading since I'd first arrived because I knew that the issue of blood and urine tests was going to come up. When he asked me for a urine sample, I simply told him that I didn't have to go to the bathroom. As for the blood test, I made up a horror story on the spot, saying that last time I'd had a blood test the nurse was new and had pulled the stopper to the syringe out at the wrong time, causing blood to spray all over me. I described how I threw up and passed out at the sight of myself covered in my own blood. I told the story with such conviction that I almost believed it myself. Then I gave the doctor a terrified look as if I were reliving the traumatic experience. I followed it by having my eyes well up with tears to show how affected I had been from the experience. I think the doctor was pretty upset by my story. He said he'd see if there was something he could do and left the room.

Ten minutes later he came back with a glass of water, which he insisted I drink. As for the blood test, he said someone would be in to talk to me about it later. Like Anna, this doctor began to ask me questions about my drug use, only he did it in a different way and asked the questions in a different order. This really worried me. I couldn't remember if I told Anna that the last time I did coke was Christmas or Halloween. Had I or hadn't I admitted to using opium? I knew if they compared notes, my answers weren't going to be consistent. After the doctor left, a different nurse came in and handed me a cup for my urine sample. I thanked her and told her that I wouldn't be needing the cup for awhile, even though I was in pain I had to go so bad. She said, "We'll see about that," and I said, "Yes, you certainly will."

I fell asleep again only to be awakened by another nurse. I knew something was going on because while she took my vital signs, she asked me a lot of stupid questions about my hobbies and school. The topic of drugs never came up. Then right after asking me how long I'd been playing volleyball, she said, "Now, I hear you don't want to get a blood test." I couldn't very well say, "I don't want a blood test because you'll see THC, LSD, Speed and traces of cocaine," so I told her my horror story about my last blood test. It was becoming more and more real each time I told it.

When the nurse didn't react sympathetically, I told her flat out that I would not give blood and that being a minor they had to have parental consent and I wanted to see written proof. She left the room very upset. I was glad I had won more time for my body to process out all the drugs I had in me. No matter what, I knew they would detect THC. An hour later I was called out by Ken. He had to come back from home to get the parent consent form out of his office and show it to me. He was furious. I looked at it and read it very, very slowly. He told me to "Hurry up!" and I explained that I had dyslexia and it took me a long time to read things. Once I was done I looked up at him happily and smiled. Since I had already lost the blood battle, I knew at least I could piss him off a bit more by being nice. I sat down and held out my arm for the nurse.

A few minutes later, an orderly brought in a tray of food that made the stuff at school seem like fine dining. I barely touched it.

Then another nurse came in and handed me a pair of light blue pajamas. She told me to put them on and to give her my clothes. I told her that I was very sorry but that there was no way that I was going to wear what I called "Smurf pants from hell." She left the room in a huff and returned with GI-Joe doll program director, Ken. From a folder, he pulled out the contract my parents signed on my behalf, the same document I'd seen a few minutes before. I complained about my rights and Ken said, "You're a minor, and it doesn't matter what you think."

Ken threatened to call my parents and tell them that I was being a pain in the ass. I didn't want to cause my mom and dad any more trouble, so I agreed to put on the scrubs—but only if they would get me a smaller size. The ones she wanted me to put on were way too large. It was just my luck that there were no more in my size and that they had to do a wash just for me. I liked inconveniencing them. When the nurse came back with the scrubs, she also brought in my overnight kit which my parents had left for me, and asked me to dump it out. She took my deodorant, my hair spray and even my wart medicine. When I asked why I wasn't allowed to have these items, she said that I'd use them to get high. I argued that I wasn't even an addict. She said, "I hope you're right. Now give me your shoes." This was a bit much because I needed my shoes to play hackey sack. But I gave them to her anyway because I'd had it with hassling over stupid issues. The nurse said that patients in treatment are allowed socks but not shoes, so they won't run away.

I was drifting off to sleep, when I heard some kids outside in the hall swearing at one of the staff members. I had never heard anyone speak that way to an adult. While all this commotion was going on, I quickly slipped out of my room and into the room next door and said "What's up?" to two guys who were playing cards. Before we could start talking, Ken escorted me by the arm back to the Fishbowl and told me if I violated the rules again I would be put through another twenty-four hour observation. I didn't like the idea of having to spend another day by myself so I went to bed.

During the night, I was awakened several times by a nurse who wanted to take my vital signs. This annoyed me because I was very tired. I was half asleep when she wrapped the blood pressure thing around my arm and put the thermometer in my mouth. I remember telling her to "Leave me alone."

The next morning, I woke up with a start, wondering where I was. Then I remembered that I was in a hospital, not at school. I wanted to take a shower and walked up to the front desk where a nurse handed me a towel and a basket with some shampoo and soap in it. She also gave me a pair of thin Styrofoam slippers with smiley faces on the toes. She suggested that I wear them because there was a fungus going around.

In the shower, I forced myself to cough. This was a morning ritual of mine, just like brushing my teeth. After several gut-wrenching coughs, black chunks of what I always assumed was tar and resin from the pot I smoked came up. That morning only two black chunks came up, not my regular three or four, because I hadn't gotten high the night before. Then, I went back to my room, got dressed and took a good look at myself in the mirror. With the Styrofoam shoes and the blue scrubs, I looked like a Smurf from the Saturday morning cartoon. I wasn't pleased at all.

That morning, one of the assistant program directors, a tall black woman named Pat, stopped by my room and gave me a booklet called *The Chemical Assessment Workbook for Adolescents.* Pat refused to bring me my books or give me my Walkman, telling me to "concentrate on why I was here." Even though I thought it was a waste of time, I began to fill the workbook out. Doing this was like taking a test at school—only easier. There were charts and essay questions. I had to list the grades I'd gotten from sixth grade to present. The first question in this section was, "How have your grades changed since you began using drugs?" I knew my answer was a complete burn because my excellent grades contradicted the profile of the stereotypical drug user who did badly in school. In the section, entitled "Feelings," some of the questions were, "How do chemicals affect your ability to have fun?" "How has using chemicals affected your relationship with your parents?" Other parts of the workbook dealt with spirituality, drug history, and signs of abuse. I actually didn't mind filling out the work-book; it was kind of fun and I figured that the faster I finished it the sooner I could go back to school.

My approach didn't go over very well. When Pat came to my room a half-hour later to see how I was doing and found me play-ing hackey sack, she skimmed my workbook and told me that I was taking the evaluation process much too lightly. I told her that I was sorry if I didn't live up to her expectations of a perfect patient; she'd made a mistake even admitting me to this program. A few minutes later her backup squad, Ken, came into the Fishbowl; he was furious with me as usual. He said, "I've had about enough of your shit, punk. Now work on the book." He sort of scared me but I didn't show it. I just asked him if he had a waiver from my parents to be verbally abusive. He stormed out of the room defeated again. I spent the rest of the morning adding some additional information to the workbook and drawing pic-tures in the margins.

In the afternoon, Pat came in and told me that the kids in Phase One needed to use the Fishbowl to watch a movie on alcoholism. She asked me to go to the kitchen. After I got there, she brought another patient into the kitchen. I was glad to have the chance to meet someone my own age. The other patient's name was Scott. He was short and wiry, maybe fifteen-years old. He had long blond hair and looked like a surfer. Pat asked him if he minded that I was in the room while she asked him some personal ques-tions. Scott said, "No problem." As Pat got out her note pad and reviewed what was on her clipboard, I looked at Scott and tapped my nose with my index finger. This signal meant, "Are you in here for blow?" He shook his head and pinched his thumb and index finger together. He quickly drew his fingers to his lips as if smoking a joint. Then he raised his eyebrow, which meant, "What are you in for?" I tapped my nose to signal coke and then tapped my tongue, which indicated acid.

Pat started asking Scott questions similar to the ones I had been asked the day before. Scott claimed that he got high when he surfed and drank on occasion, but that was it. Scott and I exchanged glances when it was obvious that he was lying. Then Pat asked him about his family and where he grew up, what his parents were like and whether he had any brothers or sisters. She reminded me of an impatient talk-show host.

I learned that Scott was from Santa Barbara. His parents were divorced and his dad, an airline pilot, had custody of him. He said his older brother had joined a cult and his sister, who was into coke, had just flunked out of junior college.

Throughout his interview, I gave Scott understanding nods and when he had trouble explaining something, I helped him find the word or phrase that he was looking for. My interruptions bothered Pat and she gave me several "drop dead" looks. I offered to leave but she said, "There are no secrets in the Pegasus Program." Her smugness made me sick. I asked her if she were an addict and when she said no, I snickered and asked her, "Then who in the hell are you to decide what we are?" Scott thought this was really funny. Pat was furious but she couldn't send me back to the Fishbowl since it was occupied.

About an hour later, Mitchell, one of the counselors, came to my room to drop off my lunch and said, "You've got a bad attitude, mister." I didn't like his attitude, either, and asked him in an innocent-sounding voice if his main job around the hospital was delivering food to patients. He handed me a booklet entitled *Pegasus Guidelines* and stormed out of the room. The booklet was just what I had been looking for, so I sat on my bed reading about my rights and the rules of the program. A few minutes later, a nurse popped her head in my room and asked, "Are you ready for Phase One, Craig?"

I was glad that I was finally being allowed to join the others. They weren't hard to recognize. Like Scott and me, the three of them were dressed in blue scrubs. They were all standing around the nurses' station at the end of the hall, furiously taking "power drags" off their cigarettes. In between puffs, two girls, Jan and Monica, said "Hi" to me. I said "What's up?" and introduced myself. Jan had big brown eyes and reminded me of a puppy dog. Monica looked like a tomboy. I already knew Scott from the meeting in the kitchen. Standing next to Scott was a guy named Dan, who was overweight and needed to shave. I thought I must be the youngest since everybody looked so old.

The counselor directed us to a place she called the community room and announced that it was exercise time. She told us to sit on our butts and roll a ball back and forth. I refused to play. The counselor said that just because I didn't like the game didn't mean that the others didn't. I said to the group, "Whoever likes this game raise their hands." No hands went up. Then I asked, "Who wants to play something different?" Everyone raised their hands. I suggested that we play hackey sack. Everyone liked that idea, particularly the two guys.

When I told the counselor that we needed our shoes for hackey sack, she said that wearing shoes during Phase One was against the rules and that we weren't allowed to wear personal clothing until Phase Two. I saw my second chance to upset the counselor and told her that the rule book said that all patients could wear their own clothes after the first twenty-four hour observation period. Her face began to turn red and Scott said, "Yeah, I want my shoes too." Then Jan, the girl who reminded me of a puppy dog, said, "Yeah. Give us our stuff." Soon everyone was yelling and GI-Joe Ken came running into the room, demanding to know what was going on. I quieted everyone down and told Ken to follow the rules and give us our clothes. He told me to shut up and that the rules had changed.

"You will remain in scrubs until Phase Two," he said. The fact that this guy, someone I didn't even know and who certainly didn't know me, just assumed that I'd be going to Phase Two seemed totally unfair. I felt that he was judging me without the facts so I flew off the handle and in the course of several sentences told him how to go fuck himself. The other kids in the group were completely silent as I yelled at him, but I could tell they were enjoying what I had to say. When Ken told me to go to my room, I laughed at him. The others laughed, too. They were promptly sent to their rooms as well.

After everyone had cooled off, I went with the rest of the group from Phase One to the kitchen for my first group therapy session. Pat, the woman who hadn't liked the way I filled out my workbook, was in charge of leading the discussion. She said that the group was going to ask me a series of questions because I was a new patient.

I sat in my chair and gave her my coldest stare. Pat looked up from her clipboard and said, "Why are you here, Craig?" Once again I calmly reminded her that I was there to prove to the people at my school that I didn't have a drug problem. I told her that I'd be leaving in three days. Pat tried to stare back at me and asked in an annoyed tone, "You don't have a problem?" I said no, never breaking eye contact with her. The main thought in my mind was, *I hate this bullshit.* While she continued to ask questions of Scott, the other new patient, I continued to stare at her. Uneasy, she kept looking away from me to glance at her clipboard or say something to the others. I loved staring her down.

After a bologna sandwich lunch and a period of writing in our workbooks, we had another group meeting with Pat. This one was held in the Fishbowl, with all six of the Phase One people squeezed onto one bed leaning their backs against the wall. Pat announced that she was going to talk about the "disease concept." I paid close attention—not out of respect, but because I was hoping she would make a mistake.

She began by asking what addictive drugs were. I spoke out immediately and said, "Any substance that changes your natural thought process." She asked us to name different types of addicts and people shouted out "speed freak" and "heroin addict." Then she wanted to know if drugs like these were psychologically or physiologically addictive, but no one seemed to understand what the terms meant. I spoke up and said that psychological addiction had to do with your mind craving the drug and physiological had to do with your body. The rest of the group nodded their heads to show that they understood what I meant.

Pat thanked me and said that she wanted other people to answer the questions. She asked Jan, "Now, Jan, what are your thoughts on addiction?" Jan said, "I agree with Craig." Pat then asked some more questions; when no one answered them and I started to open my mouth she gave me a look that said, "Let them have a chance."

Finally I couldn't take it any longer—no one was talking and I was getting bored. So I shouted out an answer. It didn't matter to me if Pat got mad; there was no place she could send me but the kitchen since we were all in my room to begin with. And, going to the kitchen would be like a reward because there was yogurt and fruit juice in the refrigerator.

The second part of Pat's discussion focused on the theory that drug addiction is a disease. She told us that it is not someone's fault if he is an addict, and that to overcome the disease the addict must abstain from all drugs. I thought that this was a crock and told her so. To me the idea that drug addiction was a disease seemed like a cop-out to help people justify the things they'd done. Pat also talked about the causes of chemical dependency. She went into the different factors that can contribute to the disease and said that it had been proven, for example, that children of alcoholics or drug addicts have a much greater chance of becoming addicts themselves.

Pat must have thought she was teaching a kindergarten class because when she asked the group to name some of the symptoms of addiction, no one answered her. Then, when she went around the group and asked each person individually, everyone said the same thing: "I don't know."

When she finally got around to me I listed some of the classic symptoms that I'd learned in health class, like loss of interest in family activities, withdrawals, poor grades, trouble with the police—none of which I showed. She wrote all these down on the board. The next subject she dealt with was dependency and how it is commonly denied, misunderstood, and misdiagnosed. She said that addicts who aren't in recovery will deny that they have a problem and make up excuses. By this time, Jan had fallen asleep; Dan kept nodding off. I did my best to stay awake and show Pat how much I knew about drugs. Even though I was angry and had no desire to be courteous, I thought that if I acted like a good student by contributing and paying attention, Pat would clearly see that I didn't have a drug problem and that putting me in the program had been a big mistake.

After the group meeting, Pat interviewed me alone, asking me some of the same questions she asked Scott earlier. I told her that my priorities were to get good grades and to get into a good college. Yes, I did get along with my parents; no, we didn't fight with each other. As for what drugs I did, I told her that I smoked pot on the weekends and occasionally at night to help me fall asleep—but only after my homework was done. She concluded the interview by asking, "If you don't think you have a problem, why do you think a fellow student would have told a teacher that they were concerned about your drug use?" I told her that the student probably did it for revenge. I explained to Pat that certain people at school were mad at me because of a misunderstanding over Christmas—the coke deal. She tried to ask me what this misunderstanding was, but I just told her that it didn't matter anymore.

Before dinner, we had yet another group meeting led by Ken. He gave us each a piece of paper and asked us to write down what we thought a perfect day would be like. "Who would like to read first?" he asked. No one volunteered. When he asked Jan to read hers, she said no. Scott also refused. I said, "I'll read mine." I told the group that my perfect day consisted of going to Hawaii with my girlfriend and spending the day swimming in the ocean and laying in the sun together until sunset. Ken gave me one of those, "You know that's not what I'm looking for," looks. Since no one else wanted to participate, Ken said that we should all sit in our seats until one of us decided to grow up. I asked the group why they didn't want to explain what their perfect day would be, and Scott said, "It's stupid." Everyone else nodded in agreement. I suggested that since it was Ken's idea to write them, it should be Ken's responsibility to read all of them. With that, everyone slid their papers across the table creating a small pile in front of Ken. He didn't like this, so he sent us all to our rooms.

Dinner was delivered to us from a kitchen located somewhere outside the unit. That night, it was Salisbury steak hidden in a gelatin-like gravy. The rule was that we were supposed to eat in our rooms, but I asked Anna, one of the nicer staff members, if we could all eat in the kitchen together. She said we could as long as we promised to be good for the rest of the night. So all of us from Phase One took our trays into the kitchen. During dinner, we talked about where we were from and how we ended up in "this lame place."

Monica, the girl who seemed like a tomboy, said she was twelve years old and that she really hated school. She said the reason her dad put her in the program was because he thought she acted "stoned." Jan, who was fifteen, was brought in because she had run away from home and stopped going to school so she could live with her boyfriend, Todd. She claimed her partying was limited to sometimes smoking pot and drinking beer. Throughout dinner, she played footsies with Scott and me. Dan, sixteen, said that he got high a couple of times from his dad's stash and that he had also "done paint twice." I told everyone that I was narced off by some kids at school for tripping. Scott, who I already knew a few things about, said that he "only smoked pot." Throughout this conversation, I got the impression that everyone was feeling everyone else out to make sure that no one was a bust. I was also stunned that I turned out to be the oldest. Then Jan told us that there was a new girl named Tracy in her room. Tracy hadn't been awake for more than half an hour in the past two days, and Jan had heard the counselors say that Tracy was in for shooting speed. Jan also said she heard that this new girl had been in the Pegasus program before.

After dinner came break time and everyone from Phase One, except Scott, rushed down to the nursing station to pick up their cigarettes which were kept in a drawer. The nurses had no idea that Scott was on room restriction so I went into his basket and took a couple of smokes for him. When Pat and Ken weren't looking I quickly ran into Scott's room and gave him the cigarettes. Like the others, Scott had matches hidden inside a wall outlet and other cigarettes hidden in the lights in the bathroom.

That night, the Phase Two people left the community room to go to group therapy session, so we spent the next part of the evening in there playing the game "Scruples" with one of the counselors. I saw this as the perfect chance to show the staff how together I was. Questions came: "Your father is having an affair. Your mother is unaware of it. Do you tell her?" "Would you lie to your psychiatrist?" "Your spouse and children want you to quit smoking. Do you?" Jan, Dan, Monica, and Scott all gave the expected answers like, "Fuck that. I wouldn't give up smoking for anyone," or "What does it matter? My parents are already divorced." I had played this game a lot at Monticello and really liked it, so I tried to give thoughtful answers that would make me look like a scrupulous person.

At nine that evening, Pat held a meeting for the Phase One members in the kitchen. The purpose, she said, was for us to reflect on what we had accomplished that day. Instead of a friendly discussion, though, it turned into a bitch session. Scott said that all he accomplished was getting put on room restriction. Jan said she got nothing out of the day. Dan glumly agreed with her. Monica said she didn't have an answer, and when Pat pressed her, she burst into tears and ran out of the room saying, "I hate it here. I want to go home." Then Pat looked at me doubtfully and said, "What about you, Craig?" I told her I learned a lot that day— that the program sucked and was a waste of my time.

Phase One

The next day was just more of the same, the only change being that it started a little earlier. The entire unit—people from both Phase One and Phase Two—had to wake up at 6:15 A.M. for a meeting. Still half asleep, I stumbled out of bed, splashed some cold water on my face, and then went with everyone else into the community room. Michael, one of the counselors, opened the meeting by suggesting that we say the Serenity Prayer. Everyone in Phase Two knew the prayer by heart. Some people from Phase One followed the words they saw on a poster on the wall. I had never heard it before and just listened:

> God grant me the serenity to accept the things
> I cannot change, the courage to change the
> things I can and the wisdom to know the difference.

After the prayer, Ken got up and said, "We had some trouble on the unit last night. Rod was found in Monica's room after lights out." After Ken gave a long talk about how important it was to follow the rules, Monica and Rod got the chance to explain their sides of the story to the group. I kept thinking "What is the big deal? I want to go back to bed." But to the staff, it was a huge deal. Since Rod was in Phase Two, he had to go back into scrubs and his free-time privileges, including smoking, were taken away. Monica, who was crying by this time, was put on room restriction. Both of them were told to sign a contract saying that they would stay out of the rooms of members of the opposite sex and stay more than an arm's length away from each other at all times.

After breakfast, we had room check; the staff claimed that people were stealing food from the community refrigerator and hoarding it. Ken searched my room and found a butter knife in my drawer, I'd kept it from my dinner tray the day before because it might come in handy for opening the window if I decided to run away. I told him that it was the first time I had ever seen it. "Hiding weapons," Ken said angrily, "was drug behavior." Of course, an argument started and then Ken asked me if I smoked. Knowing that smoking was like a lifeline for other patients, I said, "Yes, why?" He told me that my smoking privileges were suspended for the rest of the day. I pretended to act really upset, as if he were taking something really important away from me. But since I really hated smoking, on the inside I was laughing at him.

I was lying on my bed drawing pictures later that morning when I noticed a small girl walk by. I hadn't seen her before. Like the rest of us in Phase One, she was wearing scrubs, but she was so skinny that they were falling off her. This girl had long red hair bleached white at the ends. I knew she had to be Tracy, the girl that Monica had mentioned at dinner the night before.

I followed Tracy to the kitchen and sat down with her. She was skeptically looking over two yogurts and didn't directly acknowledge me, so I said, "Hi, I'm Craig." She checked me out from head to toe without any reaction. She looked really sick. Her eyes were sunken, her skin ghost white. Then she said, "Hi, I'm Tracy," sort of lethargically, as if talking was a supreme effort. I asked her what she was in for. She gave me a look that said, "I don't give a shit about anything" and said very slowly, in a deep, raspy voice, "I'm here for slamming."

When she told me she was from Napa, I asked if she knew Ron and Troy, the Napa LSD dealers and two of my best connections. At the mention of their names, she perked up a bit and a spark seemed to come into her eyes. Right away, Tracy said that Troy had the best fry around. Because she knew both of them, I figured that she wasn't a bust and it was okay to talk freely with her. I agreed and said that Troy was a good source for doubledip sheets. Tracy asked me how I knew Ron. I told her that I used to go score around the Napa town square over the summer. Then to show her that I wasn't bluffing about knowing Ron, I asked her if he still had his tongue pierced and a Mohawk.

While we talked, Tracy slowly tasted the yogurt as if it were some sort of bitter medicine. She cringed every time she swallowed some. I could sympathize; I remembered not being able to eat for a day or two after I had been on a coke or speed binge. I figured that Tracy was probably feeling that way because speed kills your appetite. I said. "Why don't you eat a raw egg?" But before I could finish the sentence, she said, "Fucking shut up or I'll puke." This was followed by some convulsions and gagging as she prevented herself from getting sick. She took one more bite of the yogurt and then threw the carton angrily into the garbage can. Still checking each other out, we sat at the kitchen table. I asked Tracy how long she'd been in the program. She gave me a baffled look as if I'd asked her a really hard question and when she asked what day it was, I told her that it was Friday. "Then I've been here for three days," she said. I asked her how long her "run" had been—how long she had been awake shooting speed. Tracy said she'd been up for five days shooting and snorting speed. Then she coughed and snorted. Her eyes opened wide and she looked at me with an expression of awe.

"I just swallowed a rock," she said, meaning that there was still some speed in her nasal passages. "What a trip." She laughed for a couple of seconds, then looked at me sort of curiously and asked how long I'd been here. I told her three days, but that I'd be leaving to go home. She told me not to hold my breath, and that I wouldn't be leaving.

When I asked her how she knew this, she told me that the counselors considered any drug use as abuse. She said that she knew this from experience; this was her second time through the program. "If you've admitted to using drugs once, you're fucked," she said. This upset me, and I tried to remember what exactly I'd told the counselors.

I was supposed to spend the rest of the morning working on answering the questions in the *Chemical Assessment Workbook* and "expanding on them," as Pat said. The rest of Phase One was meeting to discuss what they had written in their workbooks. By this time, it was clear to me that a lot of the program's activities centered around the workbooks.

I brought my "finished" workbook to a nurse at the nurses' station and asked her to give it to Pat because I was done. On my way back to the Fishbowl, I noticed that on the desk right by my door was a file with my name on it. I figured that one of the staff members must have left it there by accident. I quickly grabbed it and hid it under my scrubs. I brought it into my room when the nurse wasn't looking. I began leafing through the file and found out what each counselor thought of me. On a piece of scrap paper, I marked down some direct quotes and thought, *What a score.* I also found out that my blood sample had come back positive for THC, the active ingredient in marijuana, and was also positive for cocaine. When I was done, I put my file back exactly where I had found it and went back to my room. I was lying in bed staring at the pale blue ceiling when Pat came flying into my room a few minutes later demanding that I tell her where my file was. I asked her if she'd lost my file, knowing perfectly well that she was only five feet from it. She scanned the room, then walked outside to the desk by the door. She came back in with the file in her hand.

"This is highly confidential," she said. "I hope you haven't been reading it." I looked at her innocently as if to say "I don't understand what you mean," and thought, "You're not real bright and anyway it's my file, it's about me. If anyone should read it I should."

By the third day of treatment, I had been accepted as the leader of Phase One. Having the other patients on my side helped make life in the unit bearable. I missed all my friends from Monticello. I wanted to show the staff that everyone else would back me up if they tried to push me around; that they couldn't tell me what to do.

The only Phase One patient who didn't like what I had to say was Tracy, the new girl. All during the exercise period, she kept bragging about how she used to mainline speed. She also began bossing around the other two girls, Monica and Jan, giving them pointers on ping-pong. So I challenged her and beat her twenty-one to three. She stormed right out of the privilege room. Everyone else just snickered quietly.

At this point, the two people I liked best were Scott, the surfer, and Dan, his roommate. They were easy to talk to, like my friends back home, Dave and Ben. I also liked the fact that they asked me for help, which proved to me that I wasn't the one with the problem.

After lunch, we had another workbook session, which meant we all had to sit in our rooms by ourselves, and write answers to various questions. Pat told me that I wasn't done and should continue working on mine. The workbook was really beginning to bore me so I decided to sneak out of the Fishbowl and see what Scott and Dan were doing in their room.

Scott asked for my help with some of the answers because he was having a hard time understanding some of the questions. He asked me to explain the question, "How has using chemicals affected your performance at school or work?" I told him that it meant, "Have you ever skipped class or spaced going to work to get high?" Scott asked me what I put. I told him I wrote "no", and that I put in my notebook, "No, school and work are my priorities." Scott wanted to know how to spell priority. Even though I was flattered that he wanted my help, I told him he shouldn't copy me word for word. Then Dan said, "That's what I was trying to tell him before." Scott, who seemed confused and embarrassed, told Dan to "fuck off." He skipped ahead a few sections and pointed to another question, which dealt with "minimizing" drug use.

"Dude, what do I put for this one?" he asked. I asked him if he knew what "minimizing" meant. He said, "Yeah, but what should I put?" It was clear to me that he didn't really know how to, so to save him from further embarrassment, I said, "Think of minimizing as making a big problem seem like a small one." Then he wrote down, " I don't minimize nothing." We did a few more answers and made them all sound like Scott had written them so that Pat wouldn't figure out that I was helping him.

That afternoon, much to my pleasure, the afternoon group with Pat disintegrated into "non-group." We were all sitting around the kitchen table, and Pat asked us to discuss the section in our workbooks called "Family Relationships." As usual, no one would read what he or she had written, so I volunteered and told how both my parents knew that I smoked pot. Pat thanked me and asked for more volunteers. Still no one would read. Then she said, "This is group and you are required to do it." Hearing the word "required" set me off. I pointed out that the rule booklet said "If a patient doesn't want to participate in group then that patient will spend the remainder of the period in his or her room." Scott got up and said, "Later, I'm out of here." The rest of the group did the same thing, leaving Pat and me all by ourselves. I stayed in the room and stared her down just to fry her mind.

Pat wasn't the only counselor I continued to upset. That day I also scared the shit out of Ken after we'd watched a movie called, *The Boy Who Drank Too Much*. The movie was about a kid whose dad was a pro hockey player and an alcoholic. The kid played hockey, too, and brought alcohol to school and got bad grades. I thought it was a dumb movie and didn't like it at all. But during the discussion group afterwards, I said that the movie was good because it made a "strong statement about priorities." Scott, on the other hand, said it was "lame" and Dan said it was "stupid." None of the girls would talk, so I asked Ken, who was leading the group, what he had thought of it.

Ken said that he thought it was an excellent example of the progressive nature of alcoholism. He went on for a few minutes about what he thought we should have gotten out of the movie. Then Scott asked if we could take a cigarette break. Ken agreed to a break—but only if the group put more effort into the discussion. So Jan raised her hand and said that the kid became an alcoholic because his dad was one. This is just what Ken wanted to hear; he began talking about children of alcoholics being at a higher risk for addiction. After about twenty minutes of talking, he announced that it was time to go to the kitchen for group.

Everyone wanted to know what happened to the cigarette break. Ken said, "I told you I would consider it, but we used up all our time discussing the movie." I thought that this was completely unfair and manipulative. I pretended to lunge at Ken with my pen, but stopped before the pen hit him in the chest. Then I looked him coldly in the eyes and said, "I hope I see you on the outside someday."

Ken freaked out. He thought I was seriously trying to stab him and started yelling at me. Everyone else started yelling back at him. Scott, my ally by then, told Ken to "fuck off." Ken, in turn sent both of us to our rooms.

I continued my efforts at upsetting the staff right through the afternoon because I was feeling really frustrated and was convinced that they had no right to keep me there. I wanted to see how far I could push their stupid rules. For example, Phase One patients were not allowed to have any contact with the patients in

Phase Two. I thought this was ridiculous and during free time, I slipped right into the community room where they were playing ping-pong and sat down on one of the couches. A beautiful blond smiled at me and I smiled back. Seeing her made the visit worth any trouble I could possibly get into. I managed to play a couple of games of ping-pong before I heard yelling in the hall. Then I jumped behind the couch.

Ken and Pat came into the room saying that a Phase One patient was missing and did anyone know anything about it? No one said anything and the blond leaned behind the couch and said, "Hi. My name is Nicole. You'd better get out of here. They're looking for you." I thanked her, told her my name was Craig, and scooted down the hall toward Scott and Dan's room. They said, "Dude. Busted. Where've you been? Everyone is looking for you." I sat down on one of the beds and said, "I've been here the whole time, right?" They nodded in agreement. A few seconds later, Pat came storming into the room wanting to know where I'd been. Scott looked at her and said sarcastically, "He was in the bathroom."

Pat sneered at us and started in on Scott. Before she could say much I said very loudly, "Excuse me, you lost me, here I am, you don't need to use Scott for your scapegoat, Pat." She just stood there looking at me for a few seconds and then left the room.

That night after dinner, while everyone else was smoking cigarettes and talking, I noticed a sharply dressed guy in an Italian suit walk into the unit. He reminded me of someone from *Miami Vice*, and I was immediately suspicious of him. He spoke really fast as if he were on coke and his eyes didn't stop darting from one place to the next. I heard him talking to the nurse about having just come in from "an intense Narcotics Anonymous meeting." When I heard the word "narcotics," I thought that he was a narc, a narcotics officer, like the one who had given the talk at my public high school. I asked him whether he was a narc; I wanted to remember what he looked like for future reference in case he was a narc. He laughed and said he wasn't a narc but a recovering addict who had wasted five years of his life doing cocaine. He said his name was Will and that the Narcotics Anonymous, or N.A., was an organization composed of recovering addicts. We talked some more and he told me that he used to be in the movie business and that while he was in college, he took a year off and traveled around South America. Will said that he was now a counselor in our program. Then he tried to sack it up with me, which I thought was pretty cool of him, but he had a hard time of it in his lizard-skin shoes.

Will's words really shocked me. After all, I knew plenty of people who did drugs, but I'd never met someone so cool who called himself a "recovering addict." Will was the first counselor that I could relate to.

The topic for group that night was "values." Will passed around a handout sheet that listed seventy-two incomplete statements. We were told to complete them and then read them aloud. Monica went first and read "If I had fifty dollars," and she filled in, "I would buy some new clothes." Jan went next with the "happiest day of my life was…when I first met my boyfriend." When asked what he'd like to be, Scott said, "a pro surfer." When my turn came, I said, "If I were five years older…I'd be finishing college at U.C. Berkeley and applying to law school." Tracy, the girl no one liked, announced that if she could be anywhere she'd be in an N.A. meeting. The others just stared at her in disgust and Scott called her a "kiss ass."

Before lights out, the Phase One group assembled in the kitchen for feedback and review. Ken led the group and told us what he thought of our participation that day. He said that a lot of us had "bad attitudes." He said that I needed to stop trying to control the group and to start listening more. Then I remembered something that he'd written in my folder, and asked him if he thought that my need for control indicated a lack of self-worth. He gave me a very surprised look.

That night before bed, Ken escorted a new patient into the Fishbowl. The new patient was about five-eight with black hair down to his shoulders. He wore a concert T-shirt, torn jeans, and old sneakers. He looked like a typical rocker. We exchanged the "hey" head nod as Ken searched the new patient's bag for drugs and paraphernalia.

The new patient said that his name was John. After Ken left the room, John told me that he was from Sonoma, and I made sure to say that I grew up in the Napa Valley. When meeting new people, I never said that I was from Monticello, or the town in which it was located, because I didn't want them to categorize me as a boarding-school type—rich, stuck-up, spoiled, etc....

While we were talking, John saw Jan walk by and recognized her. He ran out of the room to go say hi. Within five seconds, Ken was out of his office and had marched John right back to the room. John and I sat up late talking about the different hairy situations we each had encountered. He bragged about being a great burglar and told me that he'd broken into over fifteen houses, and once a friend of his was shot when they were running away from a house they had just ripped off. I told him about some of my cocaine and LSD adventures. I didn't sleep well that night because a male nurse came in several times to take John's vitals. Each time, John would yell, "Fuck you," and take a swing at the nurse.

By the next morning, my fourth day in the program, everyone in Phase One had come to agree that Tracy, the new girl, was definitely "the enemy"—no better than the staff. First, Tracy called Jan an ugly bitch during breakfast. Then Tracy told her that some people were just born ugly, causing Jan to cry. Although the rest of us tried to comfort her, she wouldn't believe that we thought she was very pretty and not ugly at all. Tracy turned on Scott during a morning community meeting at which people from both Phase One and Phase Two were discussing problems on the unit. Ken said that someone had been stealing food from the refrigerator again, and he wanted to know who was doing it.

When Tracy suggested in her bossy voice, "Why don't you ask Scott?" everyone, including the patients from Phase Two, stared her down—turning in another patient was the worst thing you could do. Ken, the program director, thanked her for being honest and for not exhibiting addictive behavior. I wanted to know what was so non-addictive about narcing on someone. Ken said that covering up for others is what street people do. "That's bullshit," I told him. Tracy loved it when he said this to me, "You might think it's bullshit because you are so impaired from your drug use." At that point, I got up and said, "Does it make you feel powerful to play God over a small group of kids, Ken?" Then I walked out of the meeting, while he tried to ridicule me further.

The next Tracy incident took place during a morning group meeting held in the Fishbowl. Everyone from Phase One was sitting in a circle on the floor. Will was leading the discussion. This time, Tracy attacked me. The purpose of this particular group was for us to get to know one another better, especially since two new people, my roommate John, and Tracy, had just joined the program. First, we all went around the circle and each said, "Hi, my name is so-and-so." The next question Will asked each of us to answer was, "How did you get here?"

Tracy went first and told us what we'd already heard many times before—that this was her second time through the program and that she'd been dragged back to it by her mother, a recovering alcoholic, after shooting speed for five straight days. She looked at Will very seriously and added something like, "This time I know I'm an addict and I thank God that I'm here." This sappy bullshit was too much for me to handle. I asked her what the hell she was doing in Phase One if she was an addict. Before Tracy could start to yell back, Will interrupted saying that it was the Pegasus Program's policy that each person has to spend at least three days in Phase One.

When Tracy gave me a look that said, "What are you, stupid?" I reminded her that she was the one who had fucked-up twice and ended up in this place. Tracy exploded and lunged towards me. I quickly moved out of the way and laughed at her, as she fell to the floor. She looked up and stared at me again. Will caught hold of her and told her to cool it. I nodded in sarcastic agreement. Then she told me to suck her left tit. I had heard her say this to Scott once before when they were fighting; she had even pulled up her shirt to show Scott that her left breast was smaller than her right one. So I said, "As soon as you start puberty and you grow your right one, little girl." After this little battle, it was my turn to talk. My reason for being in the program, I said, was that some kids in school didn't like me and narced me off. Will questioned whether I had a problem with drugs and I said, "Of course not." Then Will asked very directly why I had lied about my use. I started to feel very uncomfortable, although I said I had nothing to lie about.

"That's not what you said in the kitchen," Tracy said smiling at me. "You said that you knew Ron and Troy the LSD dealers in Napa. You told me that you scored sheets of LSD off of them." Will looked at me very seriously and asked me to explain the fact that my urinalysis turned up positive for coke and pot, when I claimed that I hadn't used coke for over a month.

"I forgot. It was a small line that someone owed me," I said, feeling more threatened by the second.

"Well, using when you don't want to is a sign of addiction," Tracy said.

I clenched my fists. I really wanted to shut Tracy up. "I think Will can do his own job," I said.

"It's obvious you're an addict," said Tracy. I felt that this little bitch was helping ruin my chances of getting out of this place.

"I don't think that you're in a position to judge anyone," I said to her in as calm a voice as I could muster.

"The records say that your friends turned you in because they were concerned," Will said firmly.

"That's wrong," I tried to explain. "They were mad because of some misunderstanding."

"What was the misunderstanding?" he asked.

"I don't really care to discuss it," I told him.

"Well, it seems to me you have a problem if you are forgetting when you did drugs and end up admitted to a rehabilitation program." Will looked at me and grinned.

I defended myself but he passed me by and said, "Okay Monica, why are you here?"

That afternoon there were a couple of minor uproars on the unit. After group, Monica tried to run away and had to be confined to her room, while Dan refused to come out of his room. John took a punch at one of the counselors. Tracy started a scene by calling Monica an ugly whore. The biggest problem of the day, however, occurred while everyone from Phase One was on a smoking break, standing around the nurses' station and puffing away. GI-Joe Ken came out of his office and announced that he wanted each of us to come individually into the community room because Phase Two had something to say to us. Scott, who was always getting into trouble, went first and came back looking totally harshed-out. He mumbled, "Jan, you're next"; and then explained to the rest of us that the people from Phase Two were really pissed because little boxes of cereal were missing off their trays at breakfast. Scott, Jan, and I were the culprits; I was happy that just stealing a few boxes of cereal caused so much of an uproar.

Then Jan came back from the community room and she was crying. When it was my turn, I was ready to argue. Ken was standing in the back of the room with his arms folded, and all members of Phase Two were seated on the couches looking very grave—except for Nicole, who smiled at me. I sat down in the only empty chair facing the group and asked, "What's the matter?" as if they were wasting my time. They asked me if I had stolen food from the breakfast trays and I said yes. Telling the truth seemed to surprise them, and no one seemed to know what to say next. One of the rockers wanted to know where I got off stealing food from other people's trays. I explained that I was tired of eating the crap that this hospital handed out. Another patient told me that I could order cereal or other kinds of breakfast foods if I wanted. All I had to do was fill out the card that accompanied each meal, to order something for the next meal. I thought that this was decent of him to tell me about that and I apologized for causing them any hassles. They thanked me for being honest. Ken scowled.

In the end, I was glad that I'd stolen the food. While everyone else was playing cards and ping-pong in the community room during the free period after dinner, I talked with one of the doctors who was supervising us. I didn't know his name, but had seen him listening in on my "stealing the cereal" interviews. I introduced myself and asked him what it took to get released from the program. He told me to tell the truth, and added that an addict would have lied about stealing the cereal. The expression on my face was serious but inside I was smiling. I knew that telling the truth had gotten me some brownie points with the staff, and I was confident that they would soon be telling me that I could go back to school.

My confidence was short-lived. By the next day, Sunday, the only thing I felt was anger and frustration. I had already been in the hospital for four days and I was beginning to wonder how long it would take them to make up their minds. After all, I had a lot of homework to do and tests to make up. I was beginning to worry that this "little vacation" was going to cost me my good grades. It began to dawn on me that maybe, just maybe, I wasn't going to get out of the program as quickly as I had expected. I realized this when I went to the kitchen to get a juice and met up with Nicole. We talked for awhile and Nicole told me that she was in the program because her mom thought that she was addicted to speed and believed that she needed to stop "wasting her life." I told her what had happened to me at school and we agreed that neither of us were addicts. I asked Nicole how I could get out of the program. She told me that I probably wouldn't be allowed to leave because so far everyone she'd seen come through Phase One had been diagnosed an addict by the staff and sent on to Phase Two.

That morning, the staff made me move out of the Fishbowl to make room for some new patients. They put me with Scott and Dan. Much as I liked Scott and Dan, I didn't want to be moved like a piece of luggage. Rooming with two people instead of one meant less privacy.

My frustration began to build and little things began to get to me, like when Will's exception to the no-sugar rule backfired. He had saved me a piece of chocolate cake from a graduation party that was held for three Phase Two people who had finished up the program, saying I could have it on the condition that I didn't act-out at the next group meeting. The idea of eating a piece of cake was like heaven to me since I hadn't had anything sweet to eat in almost five days. I wrapped up the cake and put it in the refrigerator for later. I was so grateful to Will that I did as he said; I went to group and even made myself "share" my feelings.

After that group we were supposed to answer questions in our workbooks. Instead, I left my room to go see if Nicole might be in the community room. She was and so were the other members of Phase Two. It was their break time and most of them were just sitting around, talking and smoking. Nicole and I began to play ping-pong.

Will walked in the room and asked me what I was doing, then told me Phase One people are not supposed to be in contact with Phase Two. "Just let me finish the game," I said and kept playing. He came up to me and took the paddle out of my hand. I felt helpless, like a child. I wasn't used to being told what to do. I felt that Will, the one counselor who seemed decent, was really like all the other counselors after all. He gave me a shove on the shoulder and escorted me back to my room. I went in and shut the door. I laid down on my pillow and kept telling myself that I didn't belong in a drug rehab program and that I was too old for all this crap.

This was the first time I had broken down in years. I couldn't stop myself—I cried. This was the first time in years that I couldn't just freeze my emotions and become hard and cold. My frustration, anger and sadness kept pouring out of me, I sobbed into my pillow and hit it with my fists, yelling "Why me, why me?" I didn't know why I was the one that had the problem. As far as I was concerned my life was a continual flow of problems and hard times: allergies, dyslexia, cliques at school, my parent's problems, business problems with my dad, and now this.

I stayed in my room all alone for two hours, skipping "Feedback" and growth group meetings. I went to "task" group, and because I wouldn't answer any questions, Ken sent me back to my room. Dinner was delivered to my room by an orderly. I was forced to eat alone for not participating in task group. I was so angry at this point that I figured my only choices were to run away or commit suicide.

After dinner, I went into the kitchen to get my treasured piece of cake from the refrigerator only to discover that someone had taken it. Everyone from Phase One, except Tracy, was in the kitchen smoking their after-dinner cigarettes. They all denied eating the piece of cake. So I charged down to Tracy's room and demanded to know if she had eaten the cake I had saved in the fridge. She looked up at me calmly and said she had.

I threatened to rip her head off and told her that she was a little selfish fucking bitch. This started a huge fight. All our screaming and swearing brought everyone from the unit into Tracy's room. Will came running into the room as well. By this time, Tracy was crying hysterically. Seeing her so worked up almost made losing the cake worth it. When she tried to charge me, I held up my fist and let her crash right into it. Then Tracy started going berserk—punching, kicking and screaming. I wouldn't hit her back. Will had to physically separate her from me. John, Scott, and Dan each gave me thumbs up signals. Jan just smiled at me. Will put Tracy on room restriction, and, as we all went back to the kitchen, we could hear Tracy throwing the chairs against the walls in her room.

Things didn't get much better that night. Ken led us in playing the "Wish Game"; we each had to make two wishes, which he would write on the board. My wishes were for world peace and a cure for cancer, honestly. Some of the other wishes were for a Ferrari, an acre of pot in Mendocino and for a boyfriend to come back. Then we were given an imaginary $100,000 and told to bid on the wishes as if we were in an auction. Tracy said the game was fucking lame and refused to play. Much to my surprise, Scott, who was usually totally mellow, started a fight with her and said in a baby's voice, "Oh, poor Tracy, are you gonna have another fit?" Tracy started hitting Scott and was sent back to her room screaming. The game broke up soon after that. Ken left all of us in the kitchen to go have a private talk with Tracy.

That's when I decided that I had had it with being cooped up. I proposed that we all go outside to get some fresh air. It took some convincing, but soon everyone followed me out of the kitchen and down the hall to the exit door leading outside. We crossed the line of tape on the rug near the exit which marked the limits for people in Phase One. As we neared the door, counselors appeared telling us to get back to our rooms. Trying to speak steadily, I told everyone to keep walking. Ken ran out of his office saying, "What in Christ's name is going on here?" I told him that we had a right to get fresh air and we were tired of being inside. Just then, John began to have second thoughts, saying he was afraid that he'd be sent to Juvenile Hall. I pushed the door open to show Ken that we were serious and the buzzer went off. I didn't step outside. Then I told the group that we should do this only if everyone was one hundred percent behind the idea. We talked for a few minutes with the counselors hovering around behind us. We ended up having a three hour sit-in by the door before deciding to go back to our rooms for John's sake.

After lights out that night, I snuck into Nicole's room. I didn't expect to find three guys from Phase Two hiding in the closet and shower; they had been there visiting Nicole's roommates. In order to talk quietly with Nicole I had to sit on the floor between the bed and the wall. That way if a counselor came by for a room check, I could quickly duck my head under the bed. I told Nicole about how depressed I was and how much I wanted to go home. Nicole listened to me very carefully and said that I should try to make the best of it. While we were talking, I heard one of the night orderlies running down the hall muttering, "Where is he?" Since I didn't want to get Nicole in trouble, I said goodnight to her and slipped out. Back in my room, I could hear all the other guys in Nicole's room getting busted.

The next morning, Monday, we had another one of those serious meetings at which everyone from both Phase One and Phase Two was present. Ken, who looked really pissed, was staring directly at me. I assumed that he was going to get on my case for being in Nicole's' room. Instead he said, "Your friend was found running around the hospital last night and will now be leaving the program to pursue his life in Juvenile Hall." I knew that he meant John. Ken continued to stare me down when he told everyone that Monica tried to leave the unit as well and that she was on twenty-four hour room restriction. I had the impression that he was blaming me for what the others had done.

After breakfast we had to go to our rooms and work on our workbooks. Within a half hour we heard John and his mom in the hall. We all stood at our doors and John said good-bye to everyone. I knew that he had a major crush on Jan and was upset about having to leave her. John vowed to come back and get Jan out. He shook my hand and promised to send me a joint. Seeing him leave made me really sad. For a few moments, I felt as though he was a member of the family and that the family was breaking apart.

Except for John being thrown out and Tracy's "graduating" into Phase Two, not much new happened that day. We had group, we watched a movie about heroin and wrote in our workbooks. And I was getting more depressed and angry as the day went on.

In fact, during group, Pat asked me what I was going to do about my attitude if I were diagnosed as chemically dependent. I put my finger to my head, pulled an imaginary trigger, jerked my head, and rolled my eyes.

I was very unhappy. I didn't have much to look forward to. I was missing so much school that getting bad grades seemed inevitable. And my social position at school was clearly messed up. The only person I wanted to talk to was Nicole. I found myself thinking about her constantly. That day, I went to her room three times to see if she was around and three times the counselors brought me back to my room. On my fourth try, they revoked my privileges for the entire day. That meant I had to sit alone in my room. But it didn't really bother me because I was tired. I fell asleep and had a dream about driving off a bridge and drowning. In the dream, I was stuck inside my family's Toyota pick-up truck. I saw the water wash over the windshield and then everything faded to black. When I woke up, I felt more depressed than ever—someone I knew from public school had died that way recently. I wrote Nicole a note about how I would kill myself if they didn't let me out of this place soon. I crumpled the note into a ball and threw it across the hall into her room. She wrote me back that night saying that I'd better not kill myself because she wanted to get to know me better after we got out. This gave me new hope.

On Tuesday, I saw my name in a notice on the bulletin board. It said I was scheduled for a referral meeting at 10:30 A.M. the following morning. At such meetings, the staff tells the patient and his parents the results of the Phase One evaluation. Even though Nicole and Tracy had told me that everyone that comes into the program had been sent on to Phase Two, I was confident that I would finally be allowed to go home after the referral meeting. The idea that I could be a drug addict seemed impossible. So was the idea that I might have to stay at the program for another four weeks.

For the first time since I'd been in the program, I talked a lot about myself in group that day. I told the group about my allergies, dyslexia and unhappy home life. I did this to show the counselors that I had a reason for experimenting with drugs.

That night, before I went to bed, a shrink came to my room to give me a psychiatric evaluation because of the gesture I had made to Pat about shooting myself. At least that's what I assumed. Originally, I had wanted to come across as self-assured and stable, but when he started showing me ink blots, I decided to play with him and fry his mind a bit with some off-the-wall stuff. For example, when he held up a picture that looked like a butterfly and asked me what it looked like, I said in a grave tone, "It looks like a bad trip." His eyebrows shot up. "What do you mean by a bad trip?" he asked. "You know, like when you are on vacation and aren't having any fun." After the ink blots, he gave me a memory test and short word association test. When it was all over, I told everyone what a joke he was and how easy it was to fool him.

The next morning I refused to participate in group because I was certain that I would be going home that afternoon. I was very excited about leaving. When it was time for the meeting to start, Pat escorted me to her office and told me to wait by myself for a few minutes. Then she brought my parents in.

It was weird seeing my mom and dad under these circumstances. For the first time I didn't feel very close to them. We all hugged awkward hugs, then sat down. They asked me how I was doing and I told them that I was okay and that the food in the program made the food at Monticello look great. I told them how much I hated the place and how glad I was to see them. They seemed to be listening to me very carefully.

I told my dad that one of the counselors had pushed me and that I thought the program was in business to make money, not help people. My dad looked hurt and told me that wasn't true. Then Pat walked in carrying my patient folder under her arm. Ken followed her. The first thing she said was, "Now, how are we all doing?" Her bullshit smile told me everything: she was going to try and nail me and was very happy about it. Her insincere tone of voice and fake looks made me sick.

Pat sat down on a chair and opened the folder on her lap. Ken stood behind her. She said, "Well, Craig has been a very interesting patient. He has really tested his limits with the staff and other patients." My parents both looked at me surprised. I just smirked because I knew the real story and didn't really care what their perception of my experience was. I planned on telling my parents everything on the car ride back to school. Pat continued, "As you know, Craig said that the last time he had used cocaine was two months ago. But his blood test came up positive for it. When asked about this discrepancy, Craig said that he forgot. Forgetting or lying are common signs of denial." I thought, "Oh, fuck!"

Pat went on and on about how I was an addict. It seemed that every word from every interview I'd given the staff was on paper. All my explanations were being twisted. I was furious and called Pat and Ken every name in the book. I told my parents that Pat was lying and pleaded with them to take me home. I threatened to run away or kill myself if they didn't listen to me.

Then Ken said aggressively, "Why don't you just calm down, mister," and I screamed back, "Why don't you get the hell away from me before I kick your ass."

No one seemed to care that I was upset. In fact, Pat kept right on talking. She said, "It is also highly irregular for one student to report another student's drug use. And the fact that Craig said that they were out to get back at him implies a certain degree of paranoia, which is also a classic symptom." Her conclusion was that I needed to proceed onto Phase Two. My parents agreed with her. I looked at them coldly and said, "I hope you can live with this decision, because if you make it, I am no longer your child—I will never call, write or visit you again. I promise!" Then I walked out of the room.

Phase Two

That afternoon the harsh reality that I wasn't going back to school finally hit me. I was certain that my chances for getting into a good college were ruined and that I'd probably be kept back a year for missing so much work. Also, I was worried about what the people I'd left behind were saying about me. I was nervous about being unable to defend my reputation at school. And the idea that I had to spend the next month in such a fucked-up place seemed totally unfair; if I was an addict then everyone else I knew was too.

The day that I was admitted into Phase Two, two people graduated from the program, leaving ten people including myself. Within a day and a half, just as Tracy had predicted, the rest of the Phase One group were diagnosed as addicts. Like me, they were placed in Phase Two.

Even though I hated the program, Phase Two was better than Phase One. The counselors returned my clothes—but only after they searched through my bags for drugs, drug paraphernalia, and weapons. Just being able to wear my own shirts and pants made me feel like I had some of my identity back. Second, the counselors let us play "approved" tapes on the community room stereo during designated free time. All of the patients brought music with them but most of the best albums were censored by the staff. For example, heavy metal and all hard core music was forbidden, as were certain songs from the sixties. Even Yaz, a New Wave group, was "too sexual" for their tastes. Basically, any record that mentioned depression, drugs, sex, or anything "satanic" was off-limits. The staff felt that certain lyrics were "not good for developing minds" and might influence us in a negative way.

The biggest improvement during Phase Two was that we were allowed to go outside. Every other day, during a forty-five minute time slot, we'd take a walk to a nearby park or go for a one mile jog together. Just having the chance to get out of the unit and breathe fresh air improved my frame of mind 100 percent. When I was outside, I always made sure I picked a flower or found some sour grass to give to Nicole, the blond who'd helped me hide in the community room.

The schedule in Phase Two was a little more intense than in Phase One. There were things to do, group meetings to attend, and assignments to work on from early in the morning till late at night. On a typical day, for example, all of us in Phase Two would get up at 6:30, shower, and then go to the community room for a meeting where we would bring up issues and problems. Then we'd each set our daily goals. My daily goals were typically things like "To listen better in group" or "To stop gleeking on people." (Gleeking, something I've been doing since third grade to annoy my friends, involves using the salivary glands to voluntarily shoot a spray of saliva out of my mouth as if I had just bit a lemon. A "gleek" looks like the spray from an orange when it's squeezed.)

Before breakfast we'd do Tai Chi, the Chinese exercise designed to strengthen inner balance. After breakfast, we'd have "school," a period where everyone did assignments from their schools. "School" was sort of a joke because the people in treatment weren't exactly academically motivated. In fact, over half the group had dropped out of school. Most of the time, the staff sat everyone down at tables in the community room and made them do easy math problems or write "creative essays" on topics like "What Truth Means to Me."

Since I had a lot of homework to catch up on, I requested to be put on independent study. After contacting my school, the staff agreed to let me go to my room and work by myself. Nicole was also on independent study, and the staff gave her permission to help me with my algebra. Neither of us really wanted to work, so most of the time we would go to the kitchen and just talk. Whenever a staff member came by we'd pretend to be engrossed in an algebraic equation.

Before lunch, Phase Two had an exercise period at the local community boys and girls club where there were indoor sports facilities. There we'd play basketball or soccer. After the exercise period, we'd all sit around on the ground in a circle and rate ourselves on honesty, participation, and cooperation.

Next on the schedule was a hospital-style lunch of something offensive, like vegetable lasagna or pressed turkey with instant mashed potatoes—what I assumed prison food must be like. After lunch, we'd either have "contracts" or "process" group. In contracts group, we'd bring our completed assignments—like "Name the ten most negative consequences of your drug use"—into the meeting with us. Then we'd each discuss what we'd written. In process group, on the other hand, the counselor would ask questions and try to get us to talk about ourselves. For example, the counselor leading the group might say, "You probably feel bad for treating your parents like shit," or "You feel guilty for stealing and lying, don't you?" The patients who'd been in the program for awhile would do most of the talking; the newer patients had little to say. But when it came time for the "feedback" part of the session, I'd get right in there and offer my reactions to what different people said. I really liked helping people with their problems, and they seemed to like my advice. Also, helping others also put me in a position of power. I felt like an authority. But although I loved giving feedback, I hated receiving it because the "receiver" wasn't allowed to talk back to the group and stand up for himself. I hated not being able to fight back.

Each afternoon, a counselor named Marlene led a "Step" study in which we talked about the Twelve Steps to Recovery.

THE 12 STEPS OF RECOVERY

1. We admitted that we were powerless over our addiction, that our lives had become unmanageable.
2. We came to believe that a power greater than ourselves could restore us to sanity.
3. We made a decision to turn our will and our lives over to the care of God as we understood Him.
4. We made a searching and fearless moral inventory of ourselves.
5. We admitted to God, to ourselves, and to another human being the exact nature of our wrongs.
6. We were entirely ready to have God remove all these defects of character.
7. We humbly asked Him to remove our shortcomings.
8. We made a list of all persons we had harmed, and became willing to make amends to them all.
9. We made direct amends to such people wherever possible, except when to do so would injure them or others.
10. We continued to take personal inventory, and when we were wrong promptly admitted it.
11. We sought through prayer and meditation to improve our conscious contact with God as we understood God, praying only for knowledge of God's will for us, and the power to carry that out.
12. Having had a spiritual awakening as a result of these steps, we tried to carry this message to addicts and to practice these principles in all our affairs.

We never got beyond Step Three. In fact, most of the group was stuck on Step One. Before dinner we'd usually have a break, and everyone, except me, would light up cigarettes immediately. Instead, I'd just hang around and talk with the others or play hackey sack.

After dinner we'd either see a movie about drugs such as *Midnight Run*, or have a chair meeting, where a member of

Narcotics Anonymous (N.A.) or Alcoholics Anonymous (A.A.) would come talk to us about their experiences. On Saturday nights, we'd leave the unit to go attend an actual N.A. meeting. N.A. meetings were organized on the basis of the Twelve Steps. At these meetings, addicts and alcoholics from both inside and outside the hospital got together to talk about their problems. Recent graduates of the program were required to attend ninety meetings in ninety days after release, (in order to fulfill their Aftercare contracts) so some of the faces were familiar. At N.A. meetings, people introduced themselves by saying, "Hi, my name is Amy. I'm an addict." Then, in unison, everyone would say, "Hi Amy," and they'd clap their hands to show support. When my turn came, I'd leave off the addict part and say, "Hi. My name is Craig." I wasn't about to admit to a problem that I knew I didn't have.

Although I wouldn't admit I was an addict, I liked the N.A. meetings. For one thing, people told some cool stories about drugs and danger. Hearing and talking about drugs was still one of my favorite pastimes. Second, coffee was served at the meetings and we got to drink it with a lot of sugar. I hadn't had any sugar since I'd left Monticello because there was a no-sugar rule. The counselors said sugar was a stimulant. After these N.A. meetings, I'd always manage to snag a handful of sugar packets on my way out.

One of the only people I knew who got anything out of the early N.A. meetings was Tracy. She would talk dramatically about the severity of her addiction and how she would die if she ever used again. Like Tracy, most of the old Phase Two members, people who'd been in the program for at least three weeks, were big on participating in the meetings. They, too, considered themselves addicts and they were close to being discharged from the program. I didn't feel that I had anything in common with them, especially because most of them were dropouts or rockers. The people that I felt closest to were the ones that had just come out of Phase One with me. None of us thought we were addicts and we all stuck together.

At night after an N.A. meeting or movie, we'd do our assigned chores like vacuuming the hallway and cleaning up the kitchen. Then we'd all meet in the community room to have another process group. Our final meeting of the day was called feedback/review, where we'd discuss how the day had gone and whether we'd met our individual goals. At around 9:30, we'd all lie down on the floor of the community room for meditation period and listen to tapes of waves crashing on the sand. I suspected that there were subliminal messages in these "calming" tapes. I'd seen them sold in stores at home—tapes that promised to help the listener "overcome obstacles" and "build self-esteem." Lights out was at ten, but I'd usually stay up late sneaking around the unit talking to the other patients or visiting Nicole. Sometimes, when the night staff was in the community room watching TV, I'd sneak into the staff offices and see what I could find or steal. But the most exciting things I came across were a bunch of vitamin pills, banned music tapes and the progress files.

I would probably have run away at this point if it hadn't been for Nicole, who was almost done with Phase Two. I desperately needed someone to connect with, someone I could plug into like an emotional outlet. My last good relationship with a girl had been with Katherine, and I'd screwed that up by partying instead of dealing with the fact that our relationship had to end.

I think I needed Nicole because I needed to be understood. Ever since I can remember, I've felt I had something of a split personality. There has always been the me the teachers knew, the me my friends knew, and the me I was always trying to figure out and express. At the hospital, my confusion only got worse.

The friends I'd made in Phase One seemed to get a charge out of the me that acted confident and pretended to know everything. This was the me I was the most comfortable being. They liked it when I cut down the counselors or stood up for our rights. But at the same time I felt really alone—as if no one understood me. I really needed love from someone. I knew that I had to go out with

Nicole to make the whole situation bearable. I craved female companionship. I could be more candid and intimate with a girl such as Nicole. She was smart and very articulate but usually quiet in group. However, when she was just around me or the others, she was usually laughing or joking around. I liked her a lot—she seemed to have everything under control and was making the "best out of it," as she had suggested I do. She was my reason for not leaving.

During that first part of Phase Two, being with Nicole was my reason for living. Even though Nicole wasn't as interested in me as I was in her, I concentrated all my energy on her. I did everything I could to be with her. The love that I thought I was feeling was like a drug.

But as my interest in Nicole became more and more obvious, the staff became very critical because the rules in the program prohibited physical contact between the sexes. The counselors always said that, "During the first year of sobriety, recovering addicts should stay out of relationships and focus solely on their recovery." Since I knew I wasn't an addict, this meant little to me. I considered their policies a challenge, and took every opportunity I could to be with Nicole.

Certain rules were changed because of us. Lights stayed on during meditation after a counselor saw Nicole and me kissing in the dark. And we were told that there had to be at least two people sitting between us during movies. Sometimes the new rules went too far, like the time the counselors forbade thumb wrestling. Nicole and I were thumb wrestling in the community room during lunch. The counselor who saw us said that thumb wrestling "would lead to fucking in the bathrooms."

As a result of such absurdities, my relationship with the staff went even further downhill. Basically, I resented being told what to do and when to do it because I'd been taught how to make my own decisions both at home and at Monticello. But since the staff treated everyone like five-year olds, I decided to make my own rules: Treat me like a child, and I'll be a big pain in the ass.

The shit really hit the fan during the first week of Phase Two, when John, the patient who had been thrown out of the program a few days earlier, came back to get Jan out. He stood outside in the rain one night, knocking on all our windows and telling us to get Jan. About fifteen minutes later, when we were in group, the sliding glass, which was usually locked, slid open. Into the community room walked two dripping wet guys I'd never seen before. One had brown hair down to his shoulders and looked a lot older than the rest of us. With him was a short, bald guy who was about sixty and was dressed like a skid row bum. Both of them smelled of liquor; they were heavily slurring their words. The younger guy said that he was Jan's boyfriend and that he'd come to take her home.

This sent the group into an uproar. When Jan ran up to the younger guy and kissed him, the counselor yelled to one of the older Phase Two-ers, "Get Ken, now!" A fight nearly broke out as Ken tried to escort the two intruders out of the unit. For a few minutes, the two men stood behind the wire mesh door calling out to Jan and telling her that it was time to go. When security was called to take them away, Jan's boyfriend yelled out, "We'll be waiting for you out in the parking lot."

For almost an hour Jan stood in the doorway of her room, holding her clothes and other belongings, trying to decide what to do. Several staff members stood there and pleaded with her to stay and talked to her about the importance of "completing the program." She really wanted to go, but they were blocking her way so I yelled from my door and told her the counselors were full of shit. I encouraged her to go, telling her that I'd meet her on the outside soon. Then Scott and a few others joined in.

After hesitating for a few more minutes, Jan left. The staff was pissed about losing a patient and furious with me and the others for interfering. Ken was so angry that for a moment I thought he was going to try and punch me. I tried to egg him on and called him a "sorry son of a bitch," and that he was "unable to provide effective counseling to patients in crisis." I really wanted him to take a punch at me because I knew if he did I could leave the program too.

Following the Jan incident, the biggest and most thoughtless counselor on the unit, Jack, was assigned to "keep me in line." Jack, who had a long ponytail and a receding hair line, was a total asshole. Everyone hated him because he was so hard on us. He made Ken look like a really friendly guy.

As it turned out, Jack ran many of our groups in Phase Two. During the first part of Phase Two, my story in group remained the same. I would use the phrase "recreational use" and explain to everyone that I just did drugs to have fun and relax. Jack would yell at me and tell me that I was full of shit. He'd try to pit the others against me. My old friends from Phase One never questioned what I said, but sometimes the Phase Two-ers who'd been there the longest, patients who thought they were addicts, would try to confront me and say things like, "I don't think Craig is being honest." These discussions always erupted into big arguments, during which I vehemently defended my action and tried to turn the focus back on the ones who were criticizing me. I wasn't one to forget an attack easily, and for the rest of the day I'd continue to cut down the other patients who'd made the mistake of getting on my case.

Then, one day for contracts group assignment, Jack asked me to write down, "Who is Craig without the argument?" I've saved my answer:

Without the argument, I'm Craig E. Fraser without the "E."

Without an argument, I'm always wrong and feel like I don't know anything. I get defensive if my space is trespassed or my authenticity is questioned. When I'm told that I know nothing, I get even more defensive and you'd better believe that I'll argue my point to the fullest!

Jack looked at what I wrote down, read it to himself and frowned at me.

Another counselor, Marlene, continually questioned me, only she did it in a nice way. Marlene had a teenage son and was pretty hip to what was going on. Unlike Jack, she never yelled or told me I was full of shit. Instead, she would raise her eyebrows and give me an "I know what you're up to" look. Then she'd expect some sort of answer from me.

Even though I liked Marlene, I considered the Step studies she led a joke. For example, everyone in Phase Two was required to read a handout and write a paper on Step One: "Our lives had become unmanageable and we are powerless over drugs and alcohol." Working on Step One was easy for me since I didn't believe a word of it. I wrote a very poignant but totally bullshit essay about how "we must admit that we are different than other users...that we must not minimize or rationalize....Sobriety is a high in itself." I got most of my ideas from reading material that was passed around at an N.A. meeting and then reworded it for my presentation. Marlene just frowned and rolled her eyes.

After I'd been in Phase Two for about a week and a half, Nicole graduated from the program. At her graduation ceremony, I told her that I loved her and she said the same to me—although I wasn't sure if she meant it as much as I did. While she was packing up and getting ready to leave, I sat in the kitchen listening to the counselors talk to her. Suddenly, I felt a flashback coming on. Then I saw the floor turn into a pond of water a couple of inches deep. Water began dripping off the chairs onto the floor, creating rings. For several minutes, I sat there staring at the rings, getting more upset with each moment. The only good thing about my life was going away.

That night after Nicole left, I became very depressed and called Brad, my "little brother" at school. I told him how fucking harsh treatment was and how much I missed everybody at school. Brad told me that there had been a big coke bust in one of the dorms. We talked about this for awhile. Jack, the counselor who was supposed to "keep me under control," overheard this conversation and consequently my phone privileges were semi-suspended. The next day he produced a list of the people I was permitted to call: my mom, dad, sister, and grandparents. Jack knew how upset I was over Nicole, and pointed out that patients like myself weren't permitted to talk to graduates of the program. He said that if I started a relationship during my first year of sobriety, I was setting myself up for failure. He added that from now on, he would dial all my calls for me.

Once Nicole was gone, I thought seriously about leaving the program. But I knew that if I ran away, I'd never see Nicole in Aftercare, nor would I be accepted back at Monticello. A few days later, I decided I was done with being depressed and wanted to do an "about-face" and really "work my program" (treatment lingo for getting healthy), so that I could get out soon and be with Nicole. When my mother came to a meeting of the parents' group, I told her that I wanted to work my program and then go on to Aftercare; I didn't tell her exactly why. She seemed very happy, but then we got into a huge fight when I told her that I wanted to get a motorcycle to use as transportation to Aftercare. I was infuriated when she said I couldn't buy one. This was the first time I can ever remember her saying no to me. I figured that it didn't really matter though since I would buy it with my own money.

The counselors weren't quick to accept my reversal. At an N.A. meeting, I said that I wanted to live a "sober life." Then I went on to explain that I didn't have a problem and that I had planned on giving up drugs anyway for a month during MWA, Monticello Wilderness Adventure. During the day on the unit, I tried to have a positive attitude and be helpful toward the staff and other patients. I thought that I was giving everyone what they wanted, but Jack still told me that I was full of shit. He'd say, "Craig, I know you're not being sincere in your program," and "You seem to be just putting in your time."

Even though Jack was right and I was just "putting in my time," I couldn't help but notice how different I began to feel. After all, the last time I'd been sober for more than a week was during the Est training—over a year and a half before. When I'd first gotten to the program I'd sweated a lot and had very pungent body odor—just as I had in eighth grade, but worse. The counselors said that my body was releasing all the toxins trapped in my body from drugs. By the first week in Phase Two, the smell had disappeared and I had stopped sweating so much. Another big change was in the morning—I'd wake up with a clear head. Before when I was doing drugs, I'd wake up and my thoughts would be scattered and my body would feel heavy. And I wasn't coughing up black chunks anymore. Also, my memory seemed to be returning. But regaining my memory was both good and bad. I liked having better recall, but a lot of painful events were resurfacing for me. I felt horrible about the way I'd treated Katherine over the summer and about ditching Zack at Monticello. I also felt really guilty for all the times I had told Zack that I would go see his band perform, but flaked and got high with someone instead. I also began to feel guilt for all the problems I was causing my parents.

Around this time, Jack had me list the ten most harmful consequences of my drug abuse as an assignment for contracts group. I wrote down things like, "I'd steal from stores for thrills and not take care of myself physically or mentally." Jack and I talked about my list privately. Because I wasn't "bringing up my problems," he told me to increase my harmful consequences list to twenty. The next day I presented my list in group. My harmful consequences included:

1. Almost getting raped in San Francisco because a dealer was a coked up freak.
2. Losing my girlfriend over the summer because I took too much fry.
3. Fishtailing my parents' car all over the road and almost hitting another car when I was on LSD.
4. Getting drunk and jumping off a seventy-foot bridge.

5. Not being close to my parents because I "used" instead of spending time with them.
6. Driving under the influence of a lot of 'shrooms and trusting my karma to take me safely where I needed to go.
7. Doing blow until I almost had heart attacks.
8. Getting stoned at school and work where I could have been busted for it.

Writing this list really got me thinking about the way I'd been living my life, and I began to feel guiltier than ever.

That night, we all attended an N.A. meeting, during which a black poet from Los Angeles and a white guy who looked like a Hell's Angel told their stories. I really related to what the poet said. He talked about doing coke all night long at homes of people he didn't even know. He described crashing hard and then going back for more, getting shot at and not eating for days on end. During the meeting, I told him that I could identify with his story—particularly the parts about crashing so hard.

Afterward, I went up and talked to him for a few minutes. Then he took me aside and handed me his three year chip, which represented three years of "no coke." He said that a recovering addict had given it to him when he first got sober and dared him to "earn" it. Then he looked me in the eyes and said, "Craig, I dare you to earn this chip, so you can say it's really yours." These chips are the only material signs that recovering addicts have of their success. When I realized that he truly seemed to believe in me, I felt a rush of excitement inside. No one had ever trusted and challenged me like this and I felt unconditionally loved. For the first time, I wanted to stop doing cocaine for three years too—no bullshitting. I thought that if this poet could do it, then so could I. But I kept telling myself I wasn't an addict—I just had a problem with cocaine.

As I began to consider the idea of not doing coke, I became better friends with Tracy. Since she was Nicole's roommate for a few days, I'd gotten to see a different side of her and learned that she was really smart. Her bitchiness was just a defense. In group, rather than harp on each other, Tracy and I began to "match energy" and would struggle for the support of the others. It was a constant game to see who would win the most followers. But the main reason why I became better friends with Tracy was that things weren't going too well with Nicole. I'd tried calling Nicole, but she never seemed to be at home. At the one Saturday N.A. meeting where I finally saw her, she seemed to be more excited about sitting with another guy who'd graduated from the program than about seeing me. I wanted to kill this guy even though Nicole assured me that there was "nothing going on." What it came down to was that I really missed Nicole and needed a close friend with whom I could confide—and Tracy fit the bill.

By this point, the second week, there were also a number of new people who'd recently come up from Phase One. One kid, Kurt, who was only twelve, became everybody's favorite scapegoat because he lied all the time and did things like breaking ping-pong paddles for no reason. I took it upon myself to be sort of a big brother to him and teach him how to be more cool. I'd also defend him if he were being blamed for something. In some ways he reminded me of me when I was younger with my problems of dyslexia and allergies. Ever since that time in my life, I have always fought for the underdogs. My friends in Phase Two relied on me for their defense. I'd defend Kurt or act as group spokesman. For example, I'd steal cigarettes from the nurse's station and bring them to people who wanted to sneak a smoke in the bathroom before free time. At other times, I'd read their progress reports and then tell them what they had to work on.

But it wasn't always me doing everything for others. My Phase Two friends would quickly come to my defense if I needed them, as happened once in group when I talked about stealing and how I used to shoplift all the time. Jack got on my case and started asking the rest of the group, "So how does it feel to have a thief among you?" Then he went around the group and asked each person individually if they trusted me. "Do you trust Craig?" One by one each person said yes. I was really glad that they trusted me— and I loved pissing Jack off, and so did they.

During the second week of Phase Two, my relationship with the staff hit an all time low. First, I stole my psychiatric chart from under the nose of one of the staff members after he told me that there was no way that I could get it out of the cabinets. Once I had my chart, I took it back to my room and began reading it. Scott, Dan and a couple of the others sat there just staring at me. They couldn't believe that I'd actually taken something that was so strongly forbidden. Even though I had done it for each of them in the past, but in each of their cases I had only removed the "progress" notes. That way I was able to tell them exactly what they had to improve on.

My chart didn't say much that surprised me. Different counselors marked down that I was "superficial in my program" and that my "acting out" was a source of concern. They said that I "acted grandiose," "had all the right answers," and "constantly tested the limits of the staff and program." Once the staff member realized that the file was gone, he came storming into my room and took it away.

It wasn't until the next day, Sunday, that I realized what deep shit I was in. On Sundays, parents came to the unit for group therapy and parent/staff consultations. At my meeting, Jack made me sign a contract saying that if I took my file again that I'd be dishonorably discharged. Then Ken told me that I had violated several federal laws by taking my file and he pointed out that dishonorable discharge would mean that I couldn't go back to Monticello; instead I'd be sent to a lock-down program in Oakland. What made the whole thing worse was that they took away two days of my free time and made me wear scrubs for twenty-four hours.

From that point on, I was angry at everyone. One day, when everyone in Phase Two was really tired and no one would say anything in group, Jack got really pissed-off and said, "Okay, fine, we'll just sit here for an hour." I saw an opportunity to burn him bad so I began leading the group and getting people like Scott, who never said anything, to open up. We all talked and totally ignored Jack. For the first time, I even told everyone about my learning disabilities and how I had grown up thinking I was a loser. Since I was in charge of the group and trying to prove a point to Jack, talking about myself became easier. Jack just closed his eyes and folded his arms. When the forty-five minute period was over, and we all got up, Jack followed me back to my room.

Just as I was expecting, he said he was "pissed as hell and sick of my little stunts." But then, in a nice voice, he asked what my "real" problems were. This confused me because I thought that dyslexia and allergies were my "real problems," or at least a major part of them. And I'd been expecting him to yell at me, not have a discussion. Then, much to my astonishment, Jack said, "Craig, I like you and I hope you can come to like me too. I want you to take more risks in this group." I was stunned. I thought Jack hated me.

Being defensive, I told him that I was trying to but that it really pissed me off when he didn't believe me. Jack then said that he did believe me but that he sensed that there were some other things bothering me inside. Then he said, "Let's work on them together."

I was thrown off balance and a little intimidated by Jack's friendliness because he was usually so mean to me. But I really wanted his acceptance. Deep down, I wanted him to like and even respect me. Before I left the room, he gave me a book called *Young, Sober, and Free*, and suggested that I make a presentation to the group after I'd read it. I took the book from him and we hugged awkwardly. I felt that maybe, just maybe, we could be friends.

Cured?

Young, Sober, and Free taught me many new things about addiction. As I sat there in my hospital room with time to absorb the information in the book, it dawned on me that maybe I didn't know as much about drugs as I thought I did.

I had always pictured drug addicts as weak skid-row types, usually much older than me; people who couldn't control themselves.. But the book said that there was no age limit for addiction and that anyone could be an addict—even a five-year old child. This blew me away. For all the reading I'd done on drugs before, I never heard that even little kids could become addicts. The book also pointed out that the amount of drugs different people used was directly related to their addictions and that addicts have naturally high levels of tolerance. And addicts, it said, will use until their drugs are gone; they often sell their possessions to get more. There was no way I could reason around this: the book's definition of "addict" sounded a lot like me.

I began to think back to all the times I had used drugs, especially coke, when I hadn't really wanted to but felt I *had* to. I remembered all those nights when I'd whiteout and when my heart felt like it was going to burst inside my chest. I remembered always coming down, crashing hard and then needing a joint or two just to block out the pain. I thought about the Friday night when I'd taken all of my monthly allowance out of the bank because I'd done some coke at school and then *had* to do more. For the next three weeks, I had to borrow money from Brad. I thought about how easy it was to rationalize scamming Sharon's eightball. I remembered how I couldn't stop doing coke over Christmas vacation.

Far away from drugs and school, I began to wonder—for the first time ever—why I did this to myself over and over again. I craved the high of cocaine, but the downside was pretty harsh. I began to think that I *might* be addicted to cocaine. While I was working on *Young, Sober, and Free*, Jack asked me to rework Step One and then make a presentation to the group. But Step One was still very difficult for me. I could not bring myself to admit that I was powerless over drugs. Instead, I told the group that at times my life was a "little crazy"; that during the last few months at school, I felt like I was living on the "brink of insanity." I also told them that I could never trust anyone, and that when I thought about the people back home and at school, I really wasn't sure anymore who my real friends were. I compared my life to a string with a candle burning under it.

Then something happened that really changed my mind about Step One and how I felt about the program. Will took me aside and asked me very seriously if I knew the definition of "surrender." I gave him a look as if to say, "Of course I do," and then said, "Sure, to surrender is to give up."

Will's eyes lit up; his expression was rapt. He said, "The true definition of surrender is to 'join the winners,' and that's a choice you have with addiction."

For the first time I felt that I wasn't necessarily a weak person if I were addicted to drugs, and that I wasn't at fault or a bad person. Even though I still wouldn't admit defeat, I began to accept what Will was getting at. I really liked this concept of surrender and considered it seriously because I respected Will a lot.

What also made the idea that I might be addicted to drugs seem less threatening was the fact that each day I was getting three or more cards and letters from my entire family, including my uncles, aunts, mom and my dad—everyone. My sister mailed me a couple of bracelets from Italy, where she was spending a semester abroad, and my four-year old cousin sent me a picture she drew in nursery school. Getting all this mail made me feel less guilty about having a problem. I didn't feel so dirty and weak. The support of my family showed me that I was still a lovable person and that people still cared about me; I had been half expecting to be abandoned. My family, especially my dad, showed me that it was okay to have a problem as long as I was doing something about it. This was important because more than anything I didn't want to be looked down upon.

By contrast, I didn't receive one letter from any friends at Monticello or from the Napa Valley during this whole time. I began to see that my friends were the people—both guys and girls—I was currently surrounded by. This was important to me, especially now that Nicole was no longer around. Having new friends made me feel less obsessed about my relationship with her. In treatment, my new friends and I could laugh and cry together. I could hug them and tell them that I loved them. It seemed like all we ever talked about at school were drugs, music, and girls—never family problems or what was going on inside ourselves.

Most important, for the first time in my life, I felt that I was with a group of people my age whom I could trust; this was new for me. I had never really felt I could trust anyone, even about simple things. For example, if a friend said he was going to be somewhere at a certain time, I never really believed it until he actually arrived. But now I felt I could trust this new group of friends, and this feeling blew me away. My opinion about the treatment program changed drastically.

At the end of the second week I realized that what we had in the program—all that candor and the opportunity to talk—was rare. In fact it was what I had been trying all along to create with my using friends when we did cocaine. The difference was after we crashed from the drugs we never really remembered what we had talked about and, if we did, it seemed less important somehow. In treatment this wasn't the case. I told everyone that I wanted to take advantage of this chance to "quit the bullshit" and "get the most from each other." Tracy backed me up 100 percent and, pointed out that we were "stuck here anyway." From this point on, things really changed. I began to make the best of the program and in a way, surrendered to my situation. That's not to say I was an angel. Even though I felt better about being in the program, I still liked to wrestle with Scott and steal food and mess with the night staff. One morning I started an uproar on the unit by throwing Scott in the shower with all his clothes on—a typical boarding school prank.

Once I decided to make the best of it, my attitude toward the counselors began to sincerely change. For instance, Marlene the counselor who ran most of our Step studies, gave me a lot of grief when I screwed around in her group, even kicking me out occasionally. But when things got out of control, most of the time the blame would fall on someone else because I was very good at maintaining an innocent expression on my face. One day, Marlene was very upset with me and asked why I was so disruptive. I suggested that if she treated me like a person instead of a child, she might be surprised. "Ask nicely and I'll stop it," I told her.

Marlene found this hard to believe, snapping her gum while she looked me over doubtfully. But she said that she'd give it a try. From then on I kept myself under control—most of the time, anyway. Since she respected me, I respected her back. When she would tell me to "stop it," I did. Marlene was really surprised that I kept my word and that my screwing around was really an act and not the way I really was.

Putting on an act for every situation was how I got by. Ever since I was little, I had always worried that I wasn't "good enough." That's part of the reason why I worked so hard on my homework as a kid and then later on took the Est training. By the third week of treatment, after many intense conversations with Will, I began to see my drug use as a handicap—something that was holding me back from being "good enough." I began to think that doing drugs might be my biggest act.

Many of the people I knew at school talked a lot about what they really were "going to do," like travel around the world or take a year off from school. At the same time, they'd always say, "If I hadn't been so high I would have or I could have..." Their lives revolved around making great plans, then great excuses. I began to see myself as one of those people.

One day, Will said something very important to me. He said that there are people out there doing drugs who are hurting and miserable. He said those people try to pull you down by getting you high, too, so you can feel their pain. "So, Craig," he said, "when someone asks you to get high, it's like he is saying 'come see how much I hurt, share my pain, take a hit.'" Will's words blew me away. He was so right. I suddenly realized that a real friend wouldn't want to hurt me and that if I really cared about myself I wouldn't want to hurt myself, either. It dawned on me that a friend would say, "Hey, I think you are using too much." At this point, I began to wonder how I would live my life without drugs as a main focus and what kind of person I had become.

At the next N.A. meeting, I introduced myself by saying, "Hi, my name is Craig. I'm an addict." Tracy's jaw dropped when she heard this. Then she got a big smile on her face and said, "Fuckin' A!" It wasn't that hard for me anymore to admit that I was a cocaine addict. After all, I was practically staring at the proof. As for the other drugs, my attitude at this point was, addiction is an elevator and I can get off at any floor. In other words, I just hadn't bottomed out on the other drugs as far as I had with cocaine. That night, I wrote a letter to Nicole to tell her about how much my ideas had changed about treatment, drugs and my life.

Once I became more committed to sobriety, I focused on becoming the peer coordinator. At the Pegasus Program, peer coordinator status is given only to the most trusted patient, someone who is really "working his program." A peer coordinator runs groups and organizes activities. He gets to live with just one roommate and has the luxury of a private bathroom.

Patients who wanted to be the peer coordinator had to write a short essay stating why. Both Tracy and I really wanted this honor, but we knew that only one of us would be selected. So every few days, I'd write an essay and say that I really wanted to be peer coordinator because I felt the added responsibility would be good for me and keep me working my program. Once I got serious about this goal, I shifted gears again and decided that not only would I give the counselors what they were looking for but I'd do everything I could to be a success in their eyes. So that third week I began to do everything they told me to—in the manner that they wanted it done. In fact, after I honestly tried to change my attitude, the only time I got kicked out of group was when something truly wonderful happened: Scott and I couldn't stop laughing. It was the first sober laugh I'd had in as long as I could remember. We were in group with Marlene when our long laugh started. To this day, I don't know what set us off but every time we'd even look at each other we'd laugh. When we both got kicked out of group, we staggered into the hall and fell on the flooring clutching our sides, rolling around. Marlene tried to look annoyed but instead she cracked a smile and said, "Go to your rooms until you can control yourselves." I went to my room to calm down. Then I heard Scott who was in the bathroom, let out a belly-wrenching howl. That made me start in all over again. Soon the bursts of laughter were coming from the rest of group we left behind; they could hear everything that was going on.

"I don't appreciate you doing that in my group," Marlene said later, trying to be stern. I told her that I was sorry but that I had never thought that I would be able to laugh like that unless I was on drugs. Just thinking about it started to make me snicker and I begin laughing again. She just smiled and walked away. I felt great, like I was okay just being me.

The next afternoon, something very strange happened, something that I will remember until I die. All of us from Phase Two went for a walk up into the mountains behind the hospital. Walking outside was an activity I treasured because I loved the fresh air. Tracy and I were about twenty paces ahead of the others, when along the bank of a stream, we both spotted a plastic bag filled with a white substance. My first thought was that it was melted crank. Jack caught up with us wanting to know what we had found. Then we heard some grumbling and mumbling noises coming from a bush by the stream. Behind the bush was a kid, no more than fifteen, breathing in and out of a white coated plastic bag. Next to him were five empty bottles of liquid erase. He didn't look at us as we walked by, and Jack told us to steer clear of him. Curious I walked over to the kid and said, "What's up?" I noticed he had dirt and the white liquid all over his shirt. He looked in my direction and took the bag from his face. There was liquid correction fluid all over his nose and lips. He muttered some sort of gibberish. I had no idea what he was trying to say. He then went down on all fours and began searching the ground for something that was obviously not there.

It made me sick and sad to see someone in that condition. I felt like throwing up. As we all continued our walk along the river bank, Jack talked about how fifty percent of all people who try inhalants die the first time. I wondered if that kid would be one of the fifty percent that died. Suddenly I felt a surge of gratitude for being given a chance not to just be a statistic for deaths due to overdose. I had come close so many times with coke, but like the kid back on the bank I, too, had kept going.

By the third week, people in Phase Two really began to open up in group. The older members, myself included, were no longer in massive denial. My position at this time was different from the others. I would state that I was one of those people who could quit using on my own; that I didn't need the support of Narcotics Anonymous. *The Big Book,* a guide for addicts that we had to read in treatment, talked about people who do it on their own. When I told Will how I felt, he said, "I don't think you are one of those people," but I felt compelled to prove him wrong.

I was getting along better than ever with the staff, even though they told me periodically that my good behavior was only an act. I felt that life itself is an act; at this time, I believed that I could change myself the way some people change a suit of clothes. But, although I made a conscious effort to change my behavior, not all my changes were planned. Some kept surprising me—for example, that it became easier to smile. When we'd go for walks, I smiled at the people we passed. This felt good. I found myself beginning to appreciate the smaller things in life, like breathing fresh air and eating pizza. When I picked a wildflower to mail to Nicole, I found myself enjoying them more than I ever had before. Even colors looked brighter, more vivid and so picture-perfect. My mind was becoming very clear, my body felt strong and healthy. For the first time in years I was really able to enjoy just being me.

At the end of my third week in Phase Two, Will took me into the community room after group and said that the staff had decided to make me peer coordinator on a twenty-four hour trial basis. The reason for the trial period was that many of the staff members didn't feel that I could handle the responsibility. Will said that my behavior would be reviewed each day to see if I still deserved the honor and the privileges that went with the position of peer coordinator.

I was stoked that I'd finally been given the authority and responsibility that I wanted. I knew that getting this position would force me to work harder on myself and for once I sincerely wanted to. Still, many of the staff members were pessimistic and very hesitant about congratulating me. The same went for some of the patients. Tracy, for example, was pissed that she hadn't been picked. After my first day as peer coordinator, one of the new patients started complaining that I wasn't doing a good job, so I called a special meeting and offered to step down. We took a vote and I stayed on.

One of the key parts to being peer coordinator was representing the views of Phase Two patients to the staff. I had always spoken up for the group, but as peer coordinator I had more power. One of the first things I requested was that we be allowed to go outside more often. I arranged with the counselors to let us do our chores before, instead of after, dinner so that way we could go for a nightly walk before bed.

One of my jobs as peer coordinator was orienting the newer members of Phase Two. When they joined the program, I gave them a tour of the unit and explained the rules. I was expected to set an example for the new people. I knew that if I were to be perceived as a role model I'd better get fully with the program, so I began to talk more in group about how I had been denying the truth all along and then admitted that "Yes, I'm an addict."

I was also responsible for running group. If people got disruptive, I'd ask them to calm down. If that didn't work, I'd ask them to leave. If they had a hard time sharing their experiences, I'd take them aside after group and talk to them privately. Tracy, who quickly got over her jealousy, decided to work with me, instead of against me. We were a good team, and the other patients began to call us Momma-Trace and Papa-Craig. The fact that she had been through the program once already gave her a lot of clout with the others. We worked hard to be role models and to set a good example.

Another one of my responsibilities was to assign and organize chores. Since Tracy was such a big help to me, I gave her the easiest jobs. I also gave my roommate easy jobs because he, too, worked hard at contributing during groups. I considered him my little brother. I gave Scott the worst jobs because he was always screwing off and causing trouble. And now that it was my job to see that no one got out of control, I didn't think Scott was all that funny.

After the first few days of being peer coordinator, I felt like I was on a real high, a mood people in the program called the "pink cloud." Will took me aside and asked me if I knew what HALT meant. I listened intently because I really respected him. Will told me that HALT stands for don't get too Hungry, Angry, Lonely or Tired. "In other words," he explained, "Easy does it. You must take life one step and one day at a time. That's the only way your sobriety will last." I was so moved by his words that I went back to my room and wrote them down so I wouldn't forget.

At this point, I saw myself as basically cured. I knew I was an addict. I was proud to admit my problem. I believed that addiction was a progressive illness and that I'd become addicted to cocaine and even speed because once I started snorting speed I'd always want more and more and more. As for other drugs, I knew that I would have become addicted to them in time. I just hadn't gotten as far with them as I had with coke. My only problem at this point was with Step One; I still didn't like admitting I was powerless over something. Step One annoyed me, so I sort of skipped it and concentrated on Step Two, which says, "We came to believe that a Power greater than ourselves can restore us to sanity."

At first I wasn't able to accept the second step either. I thought a Higher Power had to be God or Jesus, which no one was going to "make" me believe in. Then Will told me that a Higher Power is anything that has more power than I had. He gave me the example of a truck. He said, "You know you can't stop a truck coming at you full speed if you stand in it's way, right?" I nodded in agreement, "Then the truck could be your Higher Power, or the sun or God or anything you choose, but it's important to choose one. It is what you will rely upon when times get tough—and you will, so choose wisely." I still didn't really understand, but I had an idea of what he meant and I knew that it was important. I went back to my room and closed my eyes and asked in my mind, *What is my Higher Power?* I saw a little light while my eyes were closed. It floated around and then disappeared. I didn't know what it was, but I knew it was my Higher Power. I had often seen that light as a child, but had lost "it" while doing drugs. Now it was back. I chose *it*, what ever it was as my Higher Power.

The days went by quickly during my last week of treatment, and my whole focus was to "fix" everyone's problems before I left. Because Nicole had just written me a letter saying how depressed she was, quoting some depressing lyrics from a Grateful Dead song, I worried that she was going to begin using drugs again and I wanted to help her. I wanted everyone else to be as cured as I saw myself being. I thought that Tracy and I almost had Scott cured too, because he was making a lot of progress. In fact, one of the group's most emotional moments that last week was getting Scott to read a paragraph. Instead of letting him get away with saying he didn't want to read, I began the group by asking him how we could support him with his reading. I knew how he was feeling because of my experiences with dyslexia and told him so. I said, "Just ask if you don't know a word. We don't care how fast or slow you go." The others began encouraging him to participate, saying things like:

"Come on, Scott."

"Just give it a try. No one is going to make fun of you, and if they do I'll kick their ass."

"You can do it Scott."

"We are here for you."

I remember him staring at the picnic table and scraping it with his fingernails, the paint scraping off under his nails, exposing wood. Then he yelled out, "No!" I gave him my most solemn promise that no one would laugh, and then someone else said, "Come on, Scott. Do it, you know you can."

He squirmed and grinned. Then he read a sentence slowly, sounding out every word. Everyone stared in amazement, then broke into applause. From that point on, he read whenever it was his turn. Then he began sharing some of his feelings in group and once even cried in front of everybody.

Unfortunately, just as Scott was beginning to really work his program, his family ran out of money and couldn't afford to pay the hospital bill. Scott had to leave. The moment he heard this, the light went right out of his eyes. I could just feel him crawl back into his shell.

I was outraged that Scott had to leave, and leave that very day. I completely blew out—didn't follow the program guidelines. I yelled at Ken for being a capitalist, money-hungry fucker, with no commitment to helping anyone but himself. I was so upset that I hid inside my closet. When the nurses saw that I wasn't in my room, they assumed that I'd run away. Within ten minutes, everyone else had freaked out and started blowing out too. From inside the closet, I could hear all the commotion on the unit. Knowing that I was creating an uproar didn't bother me, I was too upset about Scott leaving. He had been just about ready to change, I knew it. I stayed there for a little longer, while the counselors looked all through my room but not in the pile of clothes I was hiding under in my closet. Things started to get really out of hand: Tracy was screaming and saying that she was going to "run" too.

After thinking about how bad things were already, I decided I didn't want them to get any worse so I came out of my room. Counselors and patients in the hall stopped and stared in awe. "Where did you come from Craig?" asked Will.

"I was pissed off so I took a time out in my closet." The rest of the group poked their heads out of their rooms, and I said, "Special meeting in the community room right now." This was one of the privileges I had for being the peer coordinator. I arranged so that there would be no staff in our group meeting. We all talked about what had happened with Scott and how angry it made us. The only thing that calmed us was the fact that Scott was going to be allowed to attend Aftercare with us.

One Thursday—weeks after I entered Phase Two—I was given a notice saying that I would be leaving in three days. Tracy received a notice too; she would be leaving in four days. But at this point, I didn't want to leave. Treatment had started out as my worst nightmare. But by the end of the program I felt I was in heaven. In the past, I never was able to say, "I love you" to my friends. Now I couldn't stop telling them.

During those last three days, a lot happened. Jack had me sign an Aftercare contract stating that:

A. I would not associate with "slippery" people. (Then I had to make a list of all my old drug-using friends. So I wrote down the friends from home, but not from school. I know it sounds crazy, but the friends from home seemed more "slippery." Plus, I knew that I'd be running into them right away.)

B. I would not go to places were drugs were used (another list required).

C. I would attend the Pegasus Aftercare program and ninety meetings in ninety days of either N.A. or A.A. meetings in my community. (This didn't bother me because I wanted to go to Aftercare to see Nicole and, at this point, I also wanted to go to N.A. meetings. I wanted to be sober.)

D. I would stay in contact with my sponsor.

So after signing my Aftercare contract, Jack handed me a slip of paper with a phone number on it and said, "Here's the number of someone who might want to be your sponsor." (In programs like N.A. and A.A., each addict has a sponsor who is also a recovering addict or alcoholic. I learned during treatment that a sponsor is someone you confide in and "work the steps" with. A sponsor is the one person you are supposed to be able to tell anything to, at any time of the day or night. They are the ones you are supposed to call when you want to use drugs.)

I thought Jack was doing me a big favor by giving me some-one's phone number. I was also a little nervous about having a sponsor I had never met. So I called up Joe and he asked me a cou-ple of questions about myself. Then he said he'd be my sponsor and that he'd meet with me once I got out of the program. I didn't know much about Joe except that he was a recovering addict and that he worked in a carpet store.

With just a few days left, Tracy and I—"Momma and Papa"—decided to give the program our best efforts. With so little time left, everything took on a new sense of meaning and importance. I felt safe. I felt that I could trust others. More than anything, I did-n't want to lose those feelings. To make the most of the few precious days we had left, Tracy and I got special permission for more nightly walks and a picnic. We also organized a marathon group, which lasted three hours. When we weren't in group, we met and talked intensely among ourselves in the kitchen. For the first time in my life I felt good for just who I was. I finally felt like I had the friends I'd always wanted—ones who accepted me just for who I was, ones who I didn't feel I had to put on a show for or have to give drugs to, sell or use drugs with so I would be accepted.

Friends are what really changed my mind about wanting to become and stay sober. Many of my friends from both Monticello and back home knew where I was. Only my old friend, Ben, from home called. He had called to see how I was doing and if he could visit. He didn't ask me anything about drugs. I knew I wanted more friends like that, and that I'd rather have one good friend than a bunch of party friends who didn't really care about me. I just didn't know where to find them and I was scared to be alone. I was hoping Nicole would be this one friend since Ben was on my Aftercare contract of people I could no longer see.

I graduated from the program on a Saturday afternoon. My mom was there and I didn't know if my father would be because he was on a business trip in Japan. He came home early to be there too. During the ceremony, a coin was passed around a circle to each patient and counselor. Whoever held the coin would say something to the graduating patient. As each person spoke, most of them were crying. I felt warm all over. Most of us were crying with joy.

Jack, who I once hated, talked about how far I had come and about how far I still had to go. He talked about how proud he was of me. Jason, my roommate, talked about how much he loved me, and how much our friendship meant to him. Marlene, the Step study counselor, talked about all the changes I'd gone through. Dan told me how much I'd helped him and how he knew that I'd be a "success." Will reminded me to use HALT in my daily life and to "take it one day at a time."

When it was my turn to talk, I gave from my heart in words similar to the ones they all had given me. I talked about finally feeling loved by people that I loved too. I was crying most of the time. When I started to talk about my parents, I couldn't get any words out and started to bawl harder than ever. My dad and mom were crying too. The three of us clasped each other tightly and hugged on the couch. On that day, I realized that the program gave me a chance at a new life.

At the end of the ceremony, while people were still milling around, I walked outside to bring some of my stuff to the car. As I looked at the beautiful sunset and wisps of red and pink clouds, the first thing that hit me was, "Wow, that's gorgeous. I want to get high." I slapped myself mentally because I couldn't believe that such a thought would cross my mind. Then I remembered what Will had said: that my mind will still be telling me to do drugs all the time for the first year and that I had to learn to ignore those crazy thoughts, and when I got them to call my sponsor or get my ass to a meeting.

I walked back into the hospital to get the rest of my stuff. Back in my room, Jason was waiting for me. I took out a folder and gave him the best of the drawings I'd done during the program. He knew I prized these drawings, and that the one I gave him was my favorite. I handed it to him and signed it "To Jason my brother, your best friend, Craig E. Fraser." By the time I'd gathered all my things together, Jason was fighting back the tears. My tears, though, had been exhausted from the coin ceremony. We looked at each other again. I said, "Till I see you again, Jason—I love you, stay sober." As I left the room, I could hear him crying into his pillow. But I couldn't go back to the room. It was my time to leave.

On the way home, my parents let me drive. Then they took me out for a steak and lobster dinner. After eating so much disgusting hospital food, I really appreciated such a delicious meal. Every bite was like heaven; I was overwhelmed with being "free." We made a lot of small talk as usual. I asked my dad about his business. I talked to my mom about tennis and asked her how my birds and snakes were doing. It was strange being away from all my new friends. I already missed them and wished that I was back on the unit. I wondered how I would be able to stay sober alone.

The first thing I did when I got back to the house was call Nicole, but her mom said that she wasn't home. I had thought she would have called me since she knew when I was getting out. I was really upset and my mind said, "Just get high." I took Will's advice and decided I needed to do just the opposite. I went up stairs to my closet and took out a shoe box filled with all my old drug paraphernalia. There were pipes of all shapes and sizes, bongs, vials, and small mirrors for cocaine. I looked at them as if they were completely foreign objects. Then I went down to the basement and, from a secret hiding spot, pulled out the rest of my stuff, including several large bongs, some big awkward home-made pipes, and my coke kit with gold razor blades and straws. Also in this stash was a bag of buds and some coke.

My father was in the den reading, so I showed all the paraphernalia to my mother. She was surprised at the number of things I had stashed in the house. She asked about some of the things, saying "What's this for?" or "How does that work?" I answered her questions because I still enjoyed talking about drugs. After all, they had been my life for the past few years.

Then I took everything out to my dad's car and drove over to Dirk's house to give it all to him. I thought, *Since I'm not going to use this stuff, Dirk might as well have it.* When he wasn't home, I drove by all our old hangouts down and around town. All of a sudden, I realized what I should do. I think it was my Higher Power telling me: *Why are you giving your burden to someone else? It's crazy, don't do it.*

I suddenly realized that by giving Dirk all my leftover drugs and paraphernalia, I would only be helping him hurt himself. So I drove out to the reservoir, stopping at the bridge that I had jumped off the summer before. I parked the car along the side of the road, but I left the music on, blasting Marvin Gaye's, "I Heard It Through the Grapevine" from my tape of the movie, *The Big Chill.* The sky was pitch black but the stars were out as I carried all my pipes and bongs and everything else a few yards up to the bridge. I looked at all the things that used to be so important to me. Then I threw what represented the greatest temptation—the coke—over the bridge and let it drop through the darkness into the water. Then I threw the pipes and bongs. After they hit the water with a crash, I chucked my favorite wooden box—the one my parents discovered when we stayed at the beach—right over the side as hard as I could.

I felt free and exhilarated. I remember yelling after I threw the last pipe into the water, "You fucked up my life and all the people in it. For this I will never forgive you or see you again. Good bye."

Anyone who might have seen me would have thought I was a crazy person. I probably was crazy, but I also felt that I was finally free.

Relapse

left Phase Two thinking I was cured of my problems. I was wrong.

The first thing I had to deal with was deciding whether or not I'd go back to Monticello. My parents said I could live at home and go to public school if I wanted, but I knew that there would be even more drugs in my hometown than at boarding school. Also, all the people I'd "contracted" to stay away from were old public school friends—I knew that it would be impossible for me to stay sober at the old school. Lastly, my parents had already paid my tuition bill and I didn't want the money to go to waste. I decided to finish the semester at Monticello, but I wanted to be really strong in my program before I went back.

I was eager to start Aftercare. I knew that Aftercare was supposed to help support me in the new life I had begun. And I was aware that I needed all the help I could get. I was already missing treatment and all my friends there. It quickly felt like it had been a different world all together. The one thing I had to look forward to was seeing Nicole. After being without her for so long I really wanted to see her again. I knew since she was sober that my parents would let us hangout. Otherwise there wasn't one person in my home town that was a friend and didn't use drugs. I was scared to be alone. I hated being alone. So I planned on Nicole being my sober friend and girlfriend.

Aftercare was fairly involved. It consisted of meeting with the other Phase Two graduates for five hours a day, five days a week, at the community center near the hospital. I was also required to go to an N.A. or A.A. meeting seven days a week on my own. The counselors encouraged Phase Two graduates, like newly sober alcoholics, to go to "ninety meetings in ninety days."

I expected to find in Aftercare a safe and loving environment like the one I had just left in Phase Two. Instead, I felt like I had been slapped in the face. People in Aftercare weren't very welcoming; they had their own sets of friends, little cliques, just like my public high school. I hated it! After all, many of them had been going to Aftercare for months. Even Tracy, who'd been let out the day after me, had hooked up with all her old friends; people she knew from her first time through the program. My other close friends from the unit were either still in Phase Two, or had been kicked out altogether. I felt as alienated and as lonely as a kid in a new school. The only people that seemed even remotely cool were two guys who'd come from another treatment program and joined the Pegasus Aftercare because it was the closest to their homes.

For the first week, I really hated Aftercare. All everyone seemed to do was talk about their parents putting pressure on them to get a job or to go back to school. Also, I didn't much like the idea of sitting around and listening to a bunch of people who smoked incessantly congratulate each other for "not doing drugs." My attitude was, "Okay, I've been through the program. Now I want to get on with my life." But the worst part about Aftercare was that Nicole was distant. She would say hi and then go sit with her friends. This really confused and hurt me. Even though she hadn't answered my last two letters, I thought Nicole loved me. But during the first week of Aftercare, she acted as though I didn't exist. I also got the impression that she was still seeing the other patient, Brett. Although this made me so angry that I wanted to kill him, I decided against starting a fight because I knew I'd get kicked out. If I were to get kicked out, then I'd never see Nicole.

I decided that the only way I'd be able to get through Aftercare was if Nicole were my girlfriend. Then I knew I'd be able to handle the fact that the others weren't very nice. So I kept pressing Nicole to make her see my point. I was aware that I was ignoring Will's advice about getting into a relationship, but I believed that I was different from everyone else. I thought that I was an addict who could quit on his own accord, who didn't really need group support. Since I believed I was different, I decided it was perfectly okay to follow rules and suggestions differently too.

For the first week of Aftercare, I basically kept to myself and didn't say much. Whenever I got bored with the bullshit, I'd just walk out of the room; everyone did this when they got mad. Then I'd go downtown with one of the patients who'd come from another program, drink coffee, and shoplift tapes. Shoplifting was the only illegal thing I allowed myself to do. And since I didn't have Nicole and I didn't do drugs, I needed some excitement. I felt the program had done away with my wild and rebellious side. Shoplifting gave me a little of my wildness back—not to mention an adrenaline rush when I got away with it.

The A.A. and N.A. meetings I was required to attend were generally held at night in the basement of a church in my town. From having grown up in the Valley, I already knew some of the people in the meeting. I liked going to these meetings because the people unconditionally accepted me. It helped that I was a local and they knew my family. Sometimes my sponsor came with me to these meetings, but this usually didn't work out because he lived so far away and we really didn't have anything in common.

By the second week of Aftercare, Nicole was convinced of my sincerity and decided to go out with me. I asked my parents if Nicole could stay at our house a couple days out of the week since she was the only sober person I knew and so we could drive together to Aftercare. My parents knew Nicole from parents' days at the program, and I told them how close I was to her and that we supported each other in our sobriety. My father thought it would be a good idea for me to be going out with her, and said it would be okay if she stayed over and used my sister's room.

During the third week of Aftercare, things got rougher. Three of the guys who had gotten out before me "slipped"—got stoned. They shared about it in our group and that night did it again with two others. Tracy blew-out about it because she was now dating one of the guys who got loaded. Not knowing how to handle it, she tried to hang herself, but failed. I don't think she really wanted to do it. But now we were so distant towards each other I couldn't even ask her about it. Over all, the group was of no "support" or "care" to my recovery program. On top of that, the counselor in charge of our group was also working through her own pain from a recent miscarriage.

After the third week, I told my parents that I wanted to quit Aftercare. I told them the whole thing was really depressing me and that everyone was getting suicidal. I said that I hated the fact that all everyone did was complain all day; no one seemed to want to get on with their lives. After a long discussion, my parents said that if I thought Aftercare was so horrible, then I didn't have to go. They also said it was okay for Nicole to continue staying at the house over the weekends. I told them that we would go to N.A. meetings together.

I had two weeks left before I had to go back to school, so I asked my parents if I could call up my old friends—even though I said in my Aftercare contract that I wouldn't hang out with these people that I used to party with. I explained to my parents that I wanted to take these friends—Dave, Dirk and Ben—to an N.A. meeting to show them what I had learned. My parents said, "Are you sure you should be doing this?" I explained that I felt I owed it to these friends, especially Ben, since he had called me while I was in treatment. Part of me felt guilty for having introduced them to drugs, but I also wanted to see them because I was lonely. Breaking my Aftercare contract didn't seem wrong at all because I hadn't been given what the contract had promised me. Aftercare, their so-called "safe environment of sharing and support," was a crock of shit. The contract no longer seemed valid.

Dave and Dirk really seemed to like the N.A. meetings. In fact, after two meetings, Dave introduced himself as "an addict" and talked about his "problems." I think he was just copying me and that the only reason Ben ever went was for the free cookies and coffee. Dirk sat in a couple of meetings, but never said anything. After about three weeks, both of them stopped going. As did I, once I went back to Monticello.

I arrived at my dorm one night as mysteriously as I had left. My father helped me carry my books and bags to my room. After a hug and deep sigh, he left. Brad, "my" freshman, had seen us drive up. He came into my room in Boys Dorm C and watched my parents and me with dancing eyes. I could tell he was on speed by the way he kept grinding his teeth and tapping his fingers. As the door shut behind my father, Brad yelled out, "Dude, where have you been?" I told him about treatment. He kept saying, "Harsh, harsh, that sucks," and it had—but not compared to being back at my school and sober.

I didn't know what to tell my friends or teachers. While I put my clothes away, I listened to Pink Floyd's *Dark Side of the Moon*. I didn't really want to see anyone. Brad went out to get stoned and told a few people I was back. Some stopped by—mostly girls— and told me they were happy I was back. But I was not. I wanted to be at home with Nicole and not have to deal with any of this shit. I was not sure what was going to happen, but I knew I wouldn't like it. I had no choice but to tough it out.

That night, to celebrate my return, Zack and Dexter wanted me to get high. I told them I was being piss-tested weekly and would be expelled if caught with a dirty test. This was not true, but it gave me a good excuse, because even though part of me wanted to get high, another part didn't. I had made a promise to my parents and myself that I wouldn't use drugs. Scared, I thought I might relapse my first night back.

So much had changed while I was away. Many of my friends had been busted for dealing or using, and several were thrown out of school. A few other friends had dropped out. I felt like a stranger. I wanted to hide. The people left were still using drugs every day. Staying sober, while everyone else was getting high, was like being in hell with a good view of heaven.

Brad was now heavily into drugs. He would get stoned all the time, do speed, coke, ecstasy, or 'shrooms. I longed to be part of it. There was always something for him to do and people to do it with. I had no idea where I fit without drugs. Just two months before, they were all I knew and cared for. Now I wanted them, but knew I shouldn't. I wanted to feel good, but how?

School sucked. Only one of my teachers talked to me about what happened; it all seemed to be a big secret. Many avoided me all together, and I felt like a leper. My old friends just wanted to get high together. They said they supported my decision, but at first they would still ask me to get high.

After a week of hearing 'no' every time, I was no longer asked to get high with them. In fact, I was no longer asked to do anything, because that was all my friends did. When I'd go to someone's room, they would usually be sparking a bowl or just finishing bong hits. At first, I would just leave the room if they were going to get stoned. I had no idea where or how to find new friends. All I knew was drugs. I saw nowhere to turn.

Since I was sober and no longer in the "in" crowd, I didn't have a chance to be in student government or the yearbook. As for sports, I had gained about twenty pounds while I was in treatment, which prevented me from playing on the volleyball team. It had been the one place where I thought I could find fun and friends without drugs. I remember the first day I went back to the gym. The coach just looked at me and said, "You gained some weight, Fraser." I had not realized it, but she was right. I was no longer lean. She told me that I could go to the games, but would be unable to play or even practice due to all the time I had missed. I felt like shit. Didn't she understand that my life sucked and I barely wanted to be alive anymore?

There was only one teacher who offered me a hand. He was my history teacher, Art Bacon. Art and I had spent many hours talking during study hours and sparring in judo class before I went into treatment. Art was a real adventurer and I admired him greatly. He had traveled through South America on a mountain bike for six months. I thought of him as a modern-day Indiana Jones. Instead of failing me or giving me an incomplete, he gave me a project. Art told me to write a paper on my experiences in treatment. That night, I spent several hours typing a thirty-page paper titled, "Evaluation My Ass." He gave me an A for it and a B for the overall class. At the time, I had no idea where this assignment was going to lead, but it eventually became the foundation for *BURNT*.

By this time, the school year was practically over. My sobriety was weak. My sponsor never called, I couldn't find any good meetings, and I was having urges and using dreams all the time. The first stage of my relapse began with the loss of my support system. In those days, Narcotics Anonymous didn't mention alcohol as a drug, so Nicole and I began drinking hard alcohol on the weekends. We would finish a large bottle of rum with a six-pack of Coke each weekend. My relapse with drugs soon followed.

I missed drugs and thought about them every day. I began to deal small quantities of a designer drug called ecstasy at school. I had a connection for good stuff at low prices, so I bought a bunch and sold it to old friends. A guy down the hall let me use his coke scale to weigh it before I filled old aspirin capsules with the powder. Instantly I had people to hang around, and even though we could not connect once they were high, it felt good to be wanted.

For the first time in years I was no longer perpetually stoned, and many feelings inside were different. My dyslexia, which I had thought was gone, came back. I could no longer concentrate, spell, do math, or write papers. All my skills seemed to be back at my junior high level when I had begun using drugs. Most of the time I felt nervous and insecure. I was having to grow up a second time. The first time was so hard I had gotten wasted on drugs. Now I had to do it sober, and I wasn't sure I could or wanted to.

Each day after school, I spent hours doing make-up assignments to pass the classes I had missed while in treatment. I was told by the dean that if I didn't complete this work, I would be held back a year. There were piles of assignments in algebra, Spanish, history, art, and geology. All my free time was spent doing this work. I stopped attending school meetings and missed many meals. I would eat off campus or in my room because I was afraid to see anyone. I was sure they were all talking about me and saying how I was a loser, drug addict, fat, stupid—all the things I had feared I was. I hated my life. Fortunately, summer vacation was coming soon, and I knew that I could spend time with Nicole.

Lasting Recovery

When summer vacation rolled around, I had lost my foundation of sobriety. I bought some pot from my friend Dirk the same week I moved home. He tried to talk me out of it at first, but soon gave in. Nicole and I had discussed it and decided that pot was okay—that we could use it in moderation. My sponsor had not called me in two months. I didn't go to meetings and my parents never asked any questions. I was sick and tired of feeling like shit, I could not find any recovering people my age to talk to about how hard being sober was. I had no one to tell that I was alone, scared, and wanting to use again. I got stoned.

Dirk and I were in the dungeon, a properly named cement basement below his parents' house. There were a few gray rooms the size of jail cells that you had to duck while standing in. There were no windows, just an old wooden door with a large bolt-lock on the inside. Stained and torn blankets hung between the rooms. The air was stale, and an odor of rotten newspapers and wet dogs permeated the air.

Furnished with whatever his parents no longer used, the dungeon was a mess. There were a couple of torn sleeper couches, fold-up chairs, stained pillows, and an old bed with a stained mattress. Scattered over the rooms were various stolen bikes and motorcycle and car parts. In one corner there was an amp and a bass guitar. In the other sat a large wood cage where Ben kept a rattlesnake. I looked around slowly, remembering all the lunch breaks and weekends I had spent stoned, amped, or frying in this place. I felt at home.

Dirk had scored an eighth of bud for me but was questioning me whether or not I should use it. "Are you sure you want to?" he asked.

"Yes, I want it. I haven't been stoned in three months, that's longer than I have ever gone."

"Yeah, but you went through treatment, you sure you want to blow all that?"

"You know I don't have a problem, now let me see it," I said. I was laughing but inside I wondered if I was making the right decision. I was so full of energy that I was shaking inside and my knee kept twitching. He asked me again if I was sure I wanted to get stoned. I assured him that everything was under control and I knew what I was doing.

Slowly, he reached into his jeans jacket and pulled out a tightly rolled ziplock bag. I could see that it was a healthy eighth—a good deal. Unrolling the bag, he tossed it across the table for me to inspect. I was so excited that I felt as if my heart would explode. I opened the bag and breathed in deeply, a sweet aroma of earth and skunk filled my head. Exhaling, I slumped back against the couch smiling in appreciation of good quality. I tossed the bag over to him; I had no pipe.

He packed a bud into a wooden pipe the size of my thumb. We had used it many times at school because it was easy to hide. Taking a deep hit, he passed the pipe to me. "To old times," he said, holding his breath. The smell gave me great peace. I took a deep hit and coughed, my eyes turned red and filled with tears, my throat felt as if it were on fire. I drew in again, much slower. A calm feeling flooded my body. Smiling, I passed the pipe back to Dirk, who drew on it casually. For him, this was like every other night. For me, I was reentering a world where I knew I shouldn't be. I had signed a contract saying I wouldn't see Dirk or anyone else with whom I had ever used drugs.

I thought about my parents. They had stood by me and now I was doing drugs again. I kept on smoking to make myself forget. Before long, I felt stoned. It hit my body like a warm breeze on a cold day; my mind began to drift, my mouth went dry, and my eyes were heavy. I began to giggle a bit, then forced myself to stop. Dirk told me what all my old friends were doing, but I could barely concentrate on what he was saying. I was feeling paranoid again, as I had in Berkeley. I thought I was going to have a full flashback. I tried not to show any signs of this, but I was starting to feel crazy. I began to wonder, "Does Dirk really like me or is it only because I bought pot from him; and did the people he talked about really miss me or was he lying?" I tried to dismiss all these thoughts, but they kept coming. I began to feel uncomfortable. Instead of leaving, I just sat there as I had in Berkeley, paranoid.

Before I left the dungeon I put some of Dirk's eye drops in. It ran all over my face—a rookie move. I was really stoned and wondering how I would hide it from my parents. I had told them I was going to a meeting. It was past ten and the meetings were always out by nine. I walked outside and was distracted by everything. I was unable to concentrate, and I began to worry about riding my scooter home. I started it up and almost dumped it trying to turn around. Dirk waved and went back down to the dungeon. My parents weren't up when I got home, I munched out and fell asleep in front of the TV, just like old times.

As the summer went by, I began to think I was not an addict any more. I didn't use my pot up right away or drink every day like most people I knew did, parents included. Nicole and I got stoned once or twice each weekend when we were together. I didn't use it by myself, even though I wanted to.

I was still afraid of my parents finding out. I only drank or got stoned when I was not going to be near them. For the first time, I felt guilty about using, which was completely new to me. I had never felt guilty for anything before. I often thought to myself, "Am I supposed to be 'cured,' even though my family is still all screwed up?" There was no communication at home, my mother was drinking daily, and my father would travel most of the time on business. I had no way of telling them that I hated my life. The only thing keeping me around was Nicole. She lived at my parent's house for the summer doing odd jobs. I worked on a bottling line for a winery: labeling, packing, filling, corking, foiling, and cleaning the bottles.

I loved Nicole but, really, we were just a distraction for each others' pain. Nicole had been using drugs since she was released from treatment, without telling me. Instead of drugs, I used her for my emotional escape. I often told her she was the source of my problems. She would cry, scream, and sometimes hit me. Those were the worst times. Usually, we enjoyed each other as best we could, but our addictive personalities had turned us into insecure and jealous people.

Instead of looking at my own problems, I tried to solve Nicole's. It was easier to fix her than myself. I would spend long hours counseling her on how to have a better life and what she should do about her mother's negativity or her using friends at school. Helping her made me feel as if I were alive for a reason.

No matter what her problems were, I was always right there to fix them. This way, she didn't have to deal with them, and I didn't have to deal with my own. I was lonely and started to get depressed thinking about returning to Monticello. My father, sensing that I was having a hard time, took me along on one of his business trips. We went to Italy and Switzerland. This was the first time we had taken a long trip together since my childhood. I didn't really want to go; I knew I would miss Nicole and thought that she would be unfaithful. The trip was fun, but all I thought about was Nicole.

I returned from Europe with my father the week before school started, when Nicole and I received some bad news: two of the people we were in treatment with had died. My friend Scott had hung himself after relapsing. His girlfriend Jan—the one who ran from the Pegasus Program—crashed her car into a tree while loaded on ludes (depressants) soon after. When Nicole called my house and told me the news, I went numb. I didn't know what to feel. I thought back on all the good times Scott and I had in treatment. He was the one guy who could always make me laugh back then. Now he, too, was gone.

I was alive, but I often wanted to be dead. I just didn't understand the big deal with death—life sucked most of the time; the things and people I loved or cared about always seemed to be taken away. I couldn't find any purpose in life, until I went to Jan's funeral.

Nicole and I drove to a neighboring city for the funeral. Scott had already been buried while I was away. Jan's funeral was held in a church the size of a mobile home. Many people were there from treatment, even some of the counselors. I looked for Will. I knew he could help me with how I was feeling. I saw Jack and asked, "Where is Will?" Jack looked at me for a minute, he was different, his ponytail was gone and he had lost weight. Solemnly he replied, "Will went back."

"What do you mean, 'went back'?" I couldn't and didn't want to understand what he meant.

"Will relapsed. He's using again." I was blown away. Will had helped me so many times in treatment, I never thought he could go back. He had been my model of sobriety. I walked away feeling more lost than before. I had trusted Will. I wondered why he had chosen not to "surrender," as he had told me to do. Where could he be?

As we walked further into the church, many people were crying. Tracy saw me coming and ran up to give me a hug. I could tell Nicole was jealous, but I didn't care. Tracy told us in detail what happened; "Scott and Jan had been going out all summer. After Jan bailed from the Program, her boyfriend dumped her and she ended up in Juvy (Juvenile detention) for dealing speed. When she got out, she was sober and moved back to Napa with her mother. Scott had gone back to live with his father in Santa Barbara. His father was still a drunk and usually working. Scott started drinking too, then getting stoned. He tried to get away from it by moving to Napa and living with Jan. Her mother had agreed, as long as he stayed clean and worked. Scott found a job making pizzas and had stopped using. After a month, Scott started to do fry (use LSD). Jan's mother told him he had to get out; instead, he hung himself. Jan called me right after she found him. He had hung himself in her mother's bedroom."

Nicole and I looked at each other in shock, I began to feel sick to my stomach. "I can't fucking believe it," I said. Nodding in agreement, eyes tearing up, Tracy went on. "Jan was so fucked up over Scott, she relapsed."

Tracy looked at the floor and started to cry. I held her while she shook in my arms. I too wanted to cry, but didn't. My jacket was wet from her tears when Nicole asked, "What happened to Jan?" Tracy looked at us, eyes full of tears, "She was on her way to pick me up for a meeting. As usual, she was late." Tracy laughed and so did I. "I was about to call her, when the phone rang. It was her mother. She told me Jan had hit a tree. Jan died that night." We were all silent for a long while.

"She couldn't handle losing Scott." I looked past Tracy to the coffin. It was closed. Jan hadn't been wearing a seat-belt.

After the funeral, we said good-bye to everyone and promised to call each other, but never did. I thought back on the times we had all spent in treatment and wondered what had gone wrong in Aftercare. Those days seemed so long ago. I still had a picture from treatment on my wall, with Nicole, Jan, Scott, Tracy, and me. Nicole and I drove home in silence, grateful to still have each other. The deaths of our friends intensified our relationship. We didn't fight at all the last week of summer. I was glad to be alive and have someone I cared about in my life. Nicole was all that mattered to me.

There had been talk about keeping me back a year for all the classes I had missed. I did not want this to happen. I hated school and agreed to do whatever it took to get out on time. I had to do all the makeup work to pass my junior year. I worked on it every day until it was done. I felt like such a loner. I was friends only with Brad and a few foreign students. None of us would go to school meetings, instead we would hang out in the dorm doing homework or eating. The foreign students didn't use drugs or speak much English, but that didn't stop us from having fun sometimes.

My friend, Brad, was now next door to me in a single room like mine. He was still using drugs constantly. I spent my free time alone in my room studying. I stopped going to meals; I would eat only in my room. I feared everybody but the few foreign students and Brad. I hated my life. I was using pot more frequently on the weekends and sometimes at school. Stoned, I was able to spell, write, and do my math. I didn't know why, and I didn't really care, just as long as it was easier. I didn't realize it at the time, but this showed how dependent I was on drugs—I couldn't do anything without them.

The only person I got high with was Brad, late at night. He would tell me what my old friends were doing. He was my only link to the old crowd. Brad was young and in the drug scene, but not very educated about drugs. Late at night, he would have me test the drugs he bought to make sure they were good. This made me feel important.

It was good to talk to Brad. Everyone else seemed to have life all figured out. They appeared confident, smart, and happy—all the things I no longer was. I was sure they all hated me, even though they had no reason to. I was paranoid. Each time I walked through my dorm's door and onto campus, I felt as if I were in a living nightmare.

Walking around on campus, I would often look at someone and hear them thinking terrible things about me, no matter who it was, even teachers. I was sure I was losing my mind and would end up in the state hospital for crazy people. I didn't tell anybody about these feelings or experiences. I was afraid of what would happen if I did. Unfortunately, they kept getting worse. For awhile I was hallucinating.

One night as I sat at my desk studying Spanish, I suddenly looked at my hand and saw ants all over it and my table. Some people might not be bothered by this, but I hated ants and I was covered with them. At first I stared in awe, then I flung my chair to the ground and backed away from the table, trying to brush them off. Suddenly they were gone; I realized there were no real ants.

I stood inside my little room, slowly sat down on the floor, and started to cry. I was crazy. I thought to myself, "What in the hell am I going to do with my life now?" The worst thing was, I didn't have anyone I could talk to about it. I was afraid that if I told Nicole she would leave me, and that my parents might make me go back to the hospital. None of my dorm-mates would be able to understand. I pushed my fears deep inside.

For months my life stayed the same, until Christmas break. We were released two weeks early because a guy named Steve, who lived in the dorm next to mine, hung himself. Steve was from a high-pressure military family and was often upset about his father, who used to beat him. He was into sports, had good grades, and wasn't into the party scene very much. Everyone liked him and he was even friendly to me. He had always had a hangman's noose hung from one of the rafters in his room, and one night he used it. The stars were just coming out when I heard yelling across the courtyard, then sirens howling up the road towards us. Steve was not dead, but he quickly slipped into a coma and died a few days later.

His death brought up a lot of shit for me. Before he hung himself, I was feeling depressed and more alone than anyone. I often contemplated suicide. Then Steve, a guy with many friends and what looked like a perfect life, killed himself. His death brought up new feelings in me for the deaths of my friends from treatment. Once again, I didn't know how to feel. I, too, wanted to be dead, yet part of me needed to get through what was happening. I sat in my room and began to cry. Until this point, I really had not cried about my life; I had been numb for over a year. Suddenly a flood of emotions was being released. I felt a deep mourning come over me, and I sobbed for the deaths of Steve, Jan, and Scott—and I finally cried for myself.

For the three days Steve was in the hospital, most of the boarding students walked around like zombies with distant gazes and faces swollen from crying. Many people visited him. I stayed in my room thinking about my life. There were school meetings and, for the first time since returning from treatment, I decided to go. I wanted to see and hear how other students were handling this. The boarding students all stuck together in one area of the dining hall, looking sad, some crying, others comforting those who were hurting. The day students, not having the same feeling of community, were not so affected by his death. Some joked, saying that they hoped we would get out early for Christmas. We did. I hated them for not caring, for not understanding that Steve was never coming back. Never.

The dean announced Steve's death at 1 o'clock in the morning on the third day. Even though the boarding students knew he was going to die, sobs broke out, and the dean's voice cracked as he shared his memories of Steve. During the days we were waiting for the news, several other boarding students had become suicidal and, due to the rising alarm from teachers and the school psychologist, we were all sent home early. I didn't feel happy or sad about this. I returned to that numb state I had been in. There was nothing at home for me. Nicole would be in school for two more weeks while I was alone.

I packed a few things and went home that day. The school gave all boarding students a letter telling our parents of the situation and to be aware of any signs of depression. As with most papers from school, I threw it away. I had been depressed before it happened, so no one noticed anything new with me. I spent those days hiking in the hills above my parents' house.

One day, while hiking in the local hills, I found a partially fallen rock wall in the middle of a field. I stopped and began to rebuild the wall. The rocks were covered with dark moss. It took all my strength to lift them. My shirt was soon soaked with sweat. I wanted the wall to be whole again. As I worked in the open field, I often thought about Steve, Jan, and Scott. I wondered what had been going on in their minds. Was death what they expected? Had they been scared? Before the wall was completed, my hands were blistered and my back and arms were sore. I laid the final rock into place and leaned against the wall, watching the high reeds blowing in the winter breeze. The sun was setting; clouds turned slowly from silver to gold.

I began to wonder about my own life. Why did it have to be so hard? Everyone else seemed to have it easy. Why did I have to stop using drugs. Why was I using them again? Nothing had changed since I started using pot again; I was still depressed, often paranoid. Nicole and I still argued, and I felt guilty about using drugs and lying to my parents. As I sat there, I thought for the first time that I might want to stop getting high for good. Not because someone told me to, but because I wanted to.

The next week went by quickly. I spent most of my time watching rented movies, Christmas shopping, hiking, or cooking with my mom. Before Nicole came over for Christmas, I bought one killer bud. It was the size of my hand. I was so proud of it I couldn't wait to show her. It was our insurance for a good holiday. That was on December 17, the day before my eighteenth birthday. Later that evening, my older cousin arrived from L.A. Otis was a born-again Christian who had very strong beliefs. We had been friends since childhood, and I had always admired him. He was a blue belt in judo, a rock climber and surfer, and was always generous.

After dinner, we went upstairs to my room to hang out. We talked about school, and played my SEGA video game. After we were done playing, I asked him if he wanted to see something cool. He had a past in the party scene, but not nearly as bad as mine. I thought he might get high with me. I brought out my prize bud and showed it to him. I will never forget the expression on his face. His brow pushed forward and he stared at me, not the pot. Looking me in the eyes, Otis said, "That's bad." His reaction was so honest and direct, I didn't know what to do; I just looked down and put it away. His two words changed my life. I went out walking once everyone was asleep. I made a promise to the stars. They were my chosen Higher Power—the second step in a twelve step program. I said, "I am done with it, help me." That night was the last time I had any illegal drugs.

The rest of Christmas went along smoothly. There were many relatives around, and we played games at night and went on walks during the day. I was happy, and for once I was not worried what people were thinking about me. I spent the rest of my break studying for finals. My school work was hard again now that I was not getting stoned.

Back at school, I started to run each day. In the beginning, I only ran a mile or two, but slowly worked up to a few miles. My father had always been a runner and I began to realize why. I would feel completely energized and happy for no reason. I also began to drop some of the extra weight I had gained in treatment.

During this quarter, I was still working very hard at school and spending the weekends with Nicole. I branched out a bit and joined a small madrigal choir. Unfortunately, I was still addicted to Nicole and missed all the concerts so I could be with her. I began to go to recovery meetings once a week. I never talked because it was an A.A. meeting and not my recovery group, but it was still about sobriety. I didn't pay much attention to the fact that I drank occasionally. I was sure I didn't have a problem with alcohol.

As the quarter dragged on, I was still depressed but no longer all the time. I had made some new friends, we would talk in class and sometimes study together before tests. I had known them before I was in treatment. They were never part of the "in" crowd and now neither was I. School was hard. Nicole and I would often fight. I missed drugs. During this low point, something amazing happened.

My father had sent the paper I had written for Art's history class to New York, and a publisher was interested. I remember the day he told me. Over breakfast with Nicole and me one Saturday morning, he had asked me to come down to his office later in the day. Sitting behind his desk, my father looked at me very seriously, which was uncommon for him. He said, "As you know, I sent your paper 'Evaluation My Ass' to some friends in New York. After reading it, one of them asked if you would be able to write a book. This is a big commitment and if you agree you will have to see it through to the end."

I tried to swallow but my throat was dry as a bone. I couldn't believe my ears. Someone wanted to hear my story, wanted me, the dyslexic drug addict, to write a book. I was terrified about writing my story. I didn't want to remember those years. I was afraid more people would hate me if I told them what happened.

I thought about it until Wednesday, then called my father to tell him I would write my story. Those five days I had spent thinking about my friends who had died because of drugs and all the people who I thought had been my friends but were gone as soon as I got sober. I decided I wanted to tell my story so that many others wouldn't have to make the same mistakes I did.

That weekend I was told that I had to get an agent and a co-author to help me. Dad had already been given the name of an agent and she had some ideas about a co-author. My co-author's name was Kate, and both she and my agent lived in New York. Within two weeks, we were writing. Kate would send me letters or faxes telling me what to write about, and I would write it all down and send it back to her. For the first time in months, I was happy. Even though I had dyslexia, I had always loved to write, and dreamed of one day being an author. Now my dream seemed to be coming true. It was too good to believe.

When I was not studying, I was writing for Kate. Without her guidance, there was no way I could have done it. Before the quarter was up, we had finished the book proposal and our agent had sent it to ten publishers. Even though there were no immediate responses, we kept writing.

Toward the end of the school year, I applied to several colleges in California. On the weekends, my mother helped me type applications, because my spelling and handwriting were so poor. My grades were average and extracurricular activities were nonexistent. On top of that, I didn't even know if I wanted to go to college. Up to that point, school had really sucked. I had enough stress in my life trying to stay clean, write my story, and graduate from high school; I could hardly think about the future. My mind and body were still recuperating from my addiction—and not very well, much of the time. Plus I was still paranoid.

During class I often could not think straight. When I was asked a question, I would respond with nonsense. Knowing this, the teachers did not call on me unless they had to. One day before break, my communications class had to discuss a movie. When it was my turn, I could not put my thoughts together at all. I felt the others staring at me while I fumbled through. I had been paying attention and trying very hard, but my mind was unable to do it. The teacher suggested we take a break because we were all tired. I knew she was making an excuse for me.

During the break, I sat in my chair, sure that these two guys on the other side of the room had been talking about me. I got up and went over to their desks. I used to party with them, but I had not talked to either of them for several months. I flipped up a piece of scratch paper on one of their desks and it said, "Fraser's next stop is the loony bin." All of my paranoid feelings were finally justified, and the worst part was that he was right, I felt as if I was only a step away from insanity. All of the feelings I had kept hidden away for so many years were now pouring in and there was no way to stop them.

His note helped me, though. Thanks to him, I was able to focus my anger and other emotions on proving him wrong. At that moment, I committed myself to getting better no matter what the cost . I was not going to give him the satisfaction of predicting my future. I started to run further, write more, study harder, and stay away from drinking and people who were still using drugs.

I was feeling a little more confident and would even go to meals now and then. Soon it was time to graduate. I remember that day as if it were yesterday. A few family members attended with two friends from my home town. They will never know how much it meant to me that they were there. I walked alone in that line; I had lived at Monticello for two years, yet hardly knew anyone.

There were many students in the audience who had graduated the past year. These former friends of mine yelled and cheered for the people I once was friends with. When it was my turn, there was only the usual pathetic applause that comes from clapping for over an hour for people you don't know. Then, as the applause was dying, my friend Dave yelled out, "All right, Craig!" loud enough to turn every head in the audience. He sat there with a big grin on his face, and then the grin was suddenly on mine too. For an instant I forgot everyone else. For a moment I felt proud.

College and Life

It was summer, and I hadn't heard from colleges or publishers. I started working in a winery on the bottling line again to make some money while I waited. After a month, all the schools had rejected my applications. I didn't care. I kept on writing day after day. During these weeks I was very lonely. Home was no better than school; I hid from all my old friends in town. I didn't know what to say to them. I didn't think they would want to talk to me. I was afraid that if I tried to talk to them they might just ignore me. Instead of enduring that humiliation, I avoided them all together.

One night everything changed. There was a full moon and I could not sleep. I walked around town until two or three in the morning, as I used to do when I was loaded. On my way back home up a gravel road full of potholes, I stopped and looked to the stars. Out loud I said, "I need a sign. I am walking my talk. I'm not using drugs and it's hard. Please show me I'm doing the right thing. I think I am, but I don't know any more." Wiping the tears from my face, I walked home and went to bed.

Three days later, I came home to a congratulations banner, made by my parents, hung over the front door. I had received bids from the two largest publishers in the U.S. I didn't know what to do. I stood there with tears in my eyes. My prayer had been answered. Within a month, all the contracts were done; I was writing for Signet books. I was filled with new passion. I wrote day and night. Kate would ask for a few pages and I would send her twenty. My father gave me a car for my graduation, a Volkswagen Rabbit. I would drive to the beach on my days off and walk barefoot in the sand, wondering where these new things were going to lead me. I had no idea, but knew that I couldn't live at home.

I moved to Santa Rosa, a city an hour from my parents' house, with my old friend Ryan. He had been in Chicago for a year opening a Hard Rock Cafe, but was now back and needing a place to live. We got a small two-bedroom apartment. He was a waiter at a fancy restaurant nearby, and I spent my days writing and working out at a YMCA across the street. Each day during lunch I would jog around a nearby lake.

The city had a large recovering population. Any time of the day or night there was a meeting. I went to several a week. Some were really good, where people were talking about their feelings and what they would do if they got an urge to use drugs or had a using dream. Their sharing helped me learn new skills for leading a sober life.

Each day I would wake and be excited to write, even though the things I was writing were painful. I could not believe the person drugs had turned me into. My program of recovery required me to make amends to all the people I had harmed in any way. At first I hated the idea and didn't do it. I had never had to admit I was wrong before and didn't want to now, but I had to. Slowly, with the help of other recovering people, I was shown how to admit I was wrong, something I had never learned growing up.

I didn't know how to begin apologizing to some people. My sister was one of them. I basically had to be sorry for my whole life; I had always been horrible to her and I knew it. I sent her letters saying I was sorry, but I would never get a response. She was still too angry to talk with me. I didn't blame her. For the first time in my life, I understood guilt. Before I got sober I had never regretted any of my actions. I had been able to justify them all to myself.

Another person I had to make amends with was my old girl-friend, Katherine. I had left her without looking back and caused her much pain. I hid from my pain with drugs, she did not. After we broke up, a friend back home said she had tried to kill herself by sitting in a closed garage with the car running. I had no idea she was hurt by our break up. I had been troubled too, but drugs had taken the pain away.

I spent a week tracking her down. She was now going to college on the East Coast. My fingers shook as I pushed the buttons. I had to try twice before I got her number right. She was there. I was hoping that I could leave a message, but I said, "Hello Katherine, this is Craig Fraser." There was silence for a couple of seconds, then she spoke, "Hum, hi." I could tell she was suspicious of my call. My hands were sweating as I tried to gather my courage to apologize. I blurted out, "I was just calling to say I was sorry for being such a jerk to you when we broke up. I know you probably don't care, but I have felt bad about it for a long time and needed to tell you. So once again, sorry."

I had no idea what her response would be. I really didn't want to wait around for it, but it was worth it. She answered, "That's okay Craig. How are you doing now?" I couldn't believe it. I had made it into such a big deal. After our conversation was over, I felt a huge weight lifted from me. I was finally taking responsibility for my life, past and present. It was hard, but it felt good. The next big step was about to come.

After moving in with Ryan, we took a trip together to a Club Med in Mexico. I had received the first and only check I would get from my publisher. It was for four thousand dollars. I thought I deserved a vacation. I thought long and hard about the trip; I knew there would probably be a lot of drinking. The night before we left, I told Ryan that I was not drinking anymore. The N.A. literature still never said that alcohol was a drug, but something inside of me was finished with drinking. In fact, I was not even tempted during our trip and we both had a great time. I didn't have another drink for eight years.

Drinking was just like drugs. I used it to feel numb or to relax. Writing *BURNT* helped me to want my life back. It made me realize life was worth having, and that I no longer had to be controlled by drugs or alcohol; that I could be the one who controlled my life. My roommate was very supportive, he didn't care about drinking or drugs, there were so many other things to do. I had always thought of myself as a failure, because I had been one in school and sports. I was finally getting an opportunity to change who I was and what my life was all about.

Nicole and I were still dating, but more on and off. I had found pot in her purse, but she assured me it was not hers. "It's a friend's at the junior college," she told me. I felt she was lying but because I loved her, I believed her. Our relationship was sad. I wanted to save her from drugs and alcohol, but it was impossible. Eventually, I had to let go and begin working on myself instead of trying to fix her. Once we were separated, we both were able to get better, but we would never again go out together. My life was becoming very full of positive people and activities. I no longer had room or desires for my old life.

When I was not writing, I attended lectures and seminars on drug addiction. At one of these weekend workshops, I met a woman by the name of Kathy Young. Kathy was to become my close friend, mentor and boss. Her husband was a psychologist, and she had two young children and was the kindest person I had ever known. After speaking with her during a break, she offered me a job as a teen facilitator for her nonprofit organization. This organization, Choices for Change, taught children from addicted and dysfunctional homes skills such as effective communication, and the constructive use of anger, feelings, and defenses. It also educated them about the symptoms of chemical dependency, codependency, and many other valuable life lessons. I was so surprised she wanted me to work for her. No one had ever offered me a job before.

The next month, I attended a training seminar for her organization, where I learned about all of these topics and how to teach them to children and adolescents. I also learned how to use them in my own life, which at the time was still a mess. Before the training, I had no idea what to do with my anger or how to communicate with people without putting them down. I had just left a codependent relationship, and hadn't even realized it until I took her training. Choices for Change taught me the basic life skills I had not received while growing up. The training taught me how to be with people without pushing them away. All the people that worked for Choices were in recovery. They were much older and had families. I began to pattern my new life after these people. With time, they grew to be my extended family.

This new family showed me how to have fun and enjoy life without drugs. They taught me about intimacy, unconditional love, and friendship. No matter what I went through, they were there for me, especially Kathy. She was the first person outside of treatment who was completely honest with me about areas where I needed to change and grow.

One night during my first week of groups, I was teaching a section on effective communication. This was taught in many ways. First, we used some common arguments and did a role-play where each person would get the chance to be the parent, then the child, in the argument. Afterwards, they would repeat the same argument using new skills, such as using "I" statements or taking a time-out. I had no idea that I would be in a position to use these very skills that night.

At the beginning of class, I noticed a brother and sister who were acting out and obviously stoned. They were slow to respond, their eyes were glassy and red. I confronted them about being high, and they denied it. The others in the group agreed they were high and began to pressure them to leave. I took Kevin and Sarah outside, and they admitted they had gotten stoned earlier. I told them they had to leave for the night, but could come back to the next class if they were clean.

Instead of being cool about it, they got their mother and had a meeting with Kathy and me after group. They were very angry, and so was I. Kevin and Sarah told their mother that they were not high, but we all knew they were lying. Choices had rules that no one could come to group high; they had, and therefore they had to suffer the consequence. They continued to deny being high and said that I was the one who was lying. I thought I was keeping my cool, but afterwards Kathy said, "Craig you really have to work on your anger, you were explosive in there."

"What do you mean? I didn't yell," I quickly replied.

"That's not what I mean. You were so mad that I could feel your rage, and they could too."

"I thought it's okay to be angry," I said defensively.

"It is," she replied, "but when you work for Choices, I need you to show your anger in healthy ways. It's not good to hold it all inside and smile when you really want to explode." Shocked, I looked at her in disbelief. How could she tell I had been so angry. I had never known anyone who could tell how I was feeling by looking at me, or tell me in a way that didn't make me more angry. A few days later, I called her and asked what she thought I should do about my anger.

I trusted Kathy more than anyone in my life, so when she suggested that I see a therapist, I agreed. I didn't think I needed one, but I thought maybe Kathy knew something I didn't. And she did. I told my parents. They were a bit skeptical, but agreed to help me pay. No one had ever had psychiatric help in our family. I was worried at first. I didn't know what to expect. I thought the people who went to therapy had to be crazy or really messed up. I was wrong.

My therapist was a short, middle-aged woman with a kind face. I felt as if she really cared about me. It took a long time to learn how therapy works. At first I would spend most of my time analyzing what was going on and how she worked, so I could be who she wanted me to be. Most of my actions back then were used to manipulate the people. Until therapy I did not realize this. In my life I was never just me; I didn't know who I was any more. I had spent my life either pleasing people or getting stoned.

In therapy I began to learn who and what I was all about. At first I would just sit there feeling uncomfortable as she asked me why I thought I was there. I would say, "I don't know why I'm here. Kathy said I should come, so I came." I often wondered why I had to pay someone to listen to my problems, especially when I thought I didn't have any. It took awhile for me to start really using therapy for me, instead of doing it to please Kathy.

I was frozen emotionally. I had no idea that my life was not perfect even though, on several occasions during my life, I had considered suicide. After months of introspection, I learned how to express my feelings. The first one was anger. My anger revolved around my parents, especially my father.

The issues I had with my father took a long time to unwind. I didn't realize then that I was so similar to him. He had been my only male role model, and from him I had learned practically everything—good and bad. I learned that a man is always right and doesn't cry or show his feelings. A man who has a family is the sole provider and is in control. I learned good things too. However, I spent my time in therapy on the problems that were continuing to mess up my life.

For several months, until I finished the book, I went to therapy weekly; taught at Choices for Change; spent time writing, running, and going to meetings. In late July, I received a call from Kate saying that the book was done. I couldn't believe after all that work, it was actually done. When we hung up, I began to feel depressed. I thought to myself, "What are you going to do now?" I had no idea. The next day, Greg, my friend from home called. He had cleaned up his act and was attending college. It was a state university only fifteen minutes from where I lived. I told him what was going on and he suggested that I apply to his college. I said, "Okay, what do I need to do?" He gave me the information and within three weeks I was registered and attending Sonoma State University.

I was scared about being around a group of people my age. I wondered what it would be like. Would everyone be on drugs like high school? I couldn't believe I was going to college. High school had been so difficult, I had no idea how I'd get through. Greg assured me that it was not so hard, that I just had to know how to manage my time. I already knew about that, after the deadlines from writing *BURNT*.

BURNT wasn't due to be published until December, so I didn't think about it. Kate, my co-author, had taught me a lot about working with people and what my rights were as a dyslexic. Once I began at the university, I was tested and registered at the school as learning disabled, which entitled me to readers, note takers, and untimed tests. I used these services the first semester, but soon realized I didn't need them, so I began doing it all on my own. It felt really good.

My roommate, Ryan, needed to live closer to his new job, so we agreed to move out of our apartment. I moved into the dorms at school. It was a lot like being at Monticello. The school was full of hippies and the dorms were built in the seventies. There were large sprawling lawns all over the place, with ponds and trees. It was beautiful. I was finally in control of my own life and where it was headed.

I soon found out that the dorms had constant parties. I began looking around for other activities. My friend, Greg, who had persuaded me to go to college in the first place, told me about fraternities. I had no clue what they were, other than my father had been the president of one. Greg told me that there was only one fraternity on campus for me, and that was Sigma Alpha Epsilon. The rest were just party fraternities.

SAE's campus and community focus was on philanthropic activities for children. The group was composed mainly of the front line of the school's football team. These guys were huge—practically twice my size—the kind of guys you look at in awe but would never talk to. When I met with them, they shared their experience of fraternal life in SAE. I was impressed that never once was drinking mentioned. They talked about brotherhood, the importance of community involvement, and grades. I could tell all thirty brothers cared about each other. I knew I wanted to be one of them.

This group was unique; the average age was twenty-three, practically everyone worked, played sports, and maintained a B average. Many of the brothers had long-term goals for their lives. Some were working towards medical or law school. I had heard "stories" about fraternities, and had seen the movie *Animal House*. Fortunately, my fraternity did not believe in hazing (tormenting pledges). During my pledge-ship, no one was forced to do anything they didn't want to. Not once was I ever pressured to drink. They all respected my sobriety and supported it. By the time I graduated, there were several brothers that did not drink, some were sober, others just didn't drink.

After a fraternity meeting one night, my pledge brothers Mike and Greg came to my room to study. When I opened the door, my father was sitting in my room. Shocked, I wondered, "What would have brought him over late in the evening during the week?" My stomach felt as if it had dropped to the floor. I felt sick. He looked at me sadly and handed me a clipping from our local paper. It said, "Youth Kills Himself With Handgun." As I read the article, I sank to the floor in disbelief. My closest childhood friend, Ben, had shot himself in the head playing Russian roulette by himself in the dungeon, while others watched the movie *Colors*. I didn't know what to do or how to feel, I was in shock. Once again I felt numb inside. Ben had been my best friend for so many years.

I couldn't even cry when I heard the news. I was numb inside. My father came over and held me. I sobbed as my friends stared uncomfortably at the floor. My father explained to them who Ben was. As children, we spent our summers and weekends together. When I was in treatment, he was the only friend who called me to see how I was doing and if he could help.

In elementary school he kept me from failing many subjects. Each day I would copy his work or correct my own against his before handing it in. When we would have oral spelling-bees, he always stood next to me and whispered the answers in my ear, saving me from the embarrassment of not being able to spell even simple words.

In those days, I would always bring an extra sandwich in my lunch to give to Ben, because his parents never made him lunch. In high school, Ben lived in foster homes; his parents had given up on him. He was always getting kicked out of these places for not going to school, or for smoking and drinking. When this would happen, he would show up at my house crying, saying that he was going to live in the hills. I would convince him that it would all work out and then go convince his foster home to take him back. I did this many times for him, until I went away to boarding school. Soon after I left, he ran away again and lived in the dungeon until Dirk's parents kicked him out. He was living on the streets or up in the hills by the time I was in college. I often thought about him and the good times we had growing up.

I will never forget one time when we were in the sixth grade. We were spending the night over at his grandparents' house. Once they had gone to bed, we snuck downstairs to see his father's gun collection. It was all locked up, but Ben knew where the key was hidden. He opened one of the large doors, exposing several racks of rifles and handguns. I stood there in awe, staring, my mouth wide open. I had never seen so many guns in my life. While I was looking at a 9mm pistol, he put his father's Colt 45 to his head, acting as if he was going to shoot. I knocked the gun from his hand, threw him to the ground and, sitting on his chest, yelled at him to never, never do that again or I would kick the shit out of him. Ben got mad at me for overreacting, but he had really scared me. He was the first best friend I had ever had.

There was no funeral for Ben. He was cremated and Dirk kept the ashes. Ben had left instructions behind that his ashes should be smoked over some really good pot. I don't know if that ever happened, I no longer talked to Dirk.

As I sat in my room surrounded by people who cared about me, all I could think was how alone Ben must have been feeling down in the dungeon, surrounded by his "friends." I spent that night drinking coffee with my fraternity brothers at Lyon's restaurant. They stayed with me until early in the morning when I finally fell asleep in my room. It was a good thing I was going to therapy at this point, because I needed it. Most importantly, I was not alone and my friends let me know it by constantly calling me or dropping by my room. I thanked my Higher Power everyday for my new life. I could have been Ben.

My old friends were on the same track as Ben. Some tried college and dropped out; a few were homeless; others became heroin addicts or prostitutes in San Francisco. These people had been no different from me, but once they left school, their drug addictions quickly consumed their lives.

During that first week after Ben's death, I often thought how easy it would be to get stoned and leave the pain behind. Instead, I went to N.A. meetings and spoke about it. I found solid support in those rooms—all I had to do was raise my hand and ask for help. This was new for me. Before, I would never have asked for help. Growing up I had learned that if you asked for help, you were a failure. Now I had to surrender to the fact that I needed help—and a lot of it.

To clear my thoughts, I often went hiking in the mountains by myself. I kept asking myself, why were my friends dying? Why was I alive? My friends from treatment, along with Ben and Steve, were just the start. Nine others would die in drug and alcohol-related incidents before I turned twenty-five. Some were killed while drinking and driving, others overdosed or committed suicide. Two girls died slowly from AIDS after having unsafe sex at parties.

During high school, I had believed nothing bad could ever happen to me. My friends thought the same. Now they were dying and I was left behind, stuck in the pain and confusion of their deaths, knowing that there was absolutely nothing I could do. I had to completely let go and focus on my new life of sobriety.

I had begun to surround myself with people I wanted to be like—people who had goals in their lives and knew how to work hard for the things they wanted. I found these people in many places: some in school, others at work and at N.A. meetings. These new friends liked me for me. In the past, my friends had used me for drugs and I had used them for company, or to boss around. At first it was hard to understand why people liked me, why I deserved them. I kept wondering if there was some hidden reason we were friends. There never was.

During my freshman year I would see my father once or twice a month at a church he had introduced me to. Afterwards, we would have lunch together and talk. With time our relationship changed dramatically. Instead of talking about school and work, we began talking about our feelings. I was finally learning how to express myself. It was difficult for him too. For the first time in my life, I could trust him to listen to me without interrupting. We spoke mainly about ourselves. But even though we talked, I had no idea how bad things were at home.

One evening, a month after Ben's death, I received a strange message from my sister who lived in Oregon. She never called me. The message said that I should come over to the house. She and my mother's two sisters had just done an intervention on mom, and tomorrow she would be on her way to a treatment center. I stood there in shock. I played the message again and sat down on my bed.

With hands cupped over my face, I cried—not for my mom but for my own blindness. My denial about her addiction was as bad as my parents' denial of my problems. I was teaching people about addiction every night, and yet I couldn't recognize it in my own family. I had forgotten her hidden bottles and broken promises. I was so wrapped up in my own life that I hadn't seen my own mother's cry for help. I drove home immediately.

My father was out of town at the time, and didn't know what was going on. I pulled up into the driveway, still in shock, and walked through the front door. There they all were, sitting around the kitchen table. I walked towards my mother who looked down and began to cry. Her face was already swollen from tears, as were the others faces. Feeling that I was an expert on all of this due to my training at Choices, I tried to take control by asking questions, then giving advice. All I should have done was sit there and thank everyone for the courage it took to confront my mother. Mom chose a facility in the Bay Area, only two hours away from home.

Most of that time is a blur to me, I really blocked it out. I remember going to the treatment center and she was not doing very well. She looked too thin and didn't talk much. My sister and I spent the time yelling at each other. I was so grateful to have the support of my meetings, friends, and work to help me understand that time in my life. My father was as stunned as I had been. He, like me, did not know how to react, but was relieved that something had been done.

I visited mom two times while she was in treatment. After she graduated from the program, she continued living in the Bay Area. Once school started for me, I was constantly busy. I soon forgot my family problems and focused on my own life. I was active in my fraternity, Choices for Change, and the Student Ambassador program. The first semester was quickly drawing to a close when *BURNT* was published in December of '89.

I was terrified about doing the publicity. Public speaking had always made me nervous. People assured me that I should not worry, that I probably wouldn't have to do much publicity. These were the same people that told me I would never get published. As before, I told them to keep their opinions to themselves if what they had to say was not positive.

During the last two years, I had taken time every morning to be with my Higher Power. Some call it prayer, others meditation. For me it was just a time each morning where I would sit quietly with my eyes closed and feel peaceful. One of these mornings, shortly after *BURNT* was published, I was sitting and suddenly heard myself thinking, "What do you want?" Without hesitation I responded, "A national talk show." I was told by many people that I would never get one. They were wrong.

That morning I returned from my first class to find my answering machine blinking. I listened to the message. It was my editor from New York telling me I had just been booked on the *Sally Jesse Raphael* and *Live with Regis and Kathy Lee* shows. I couldn't believe my ears. I listened to the message again, jumping up and down and screaming. Heart racing, I sat on the side of my bed, took a deep breath, closed my eyes and thanked my Higher Power for once again answering my prayer.

Later that day my shock wore off, and I realized that I was going to have to speak in front of a live audience, with cameras. I was terrified! What had I gotten myself into? I thought, "Oh shit, what am I going to do?" I called my editor and was told that I would be flown to New York that week.

I could hardly believe it: I had gone from a dyslexic addict to a sober author in two years. I was about to be on two of the nation's largest talk shows. What would I say? How would people react?

There were so many questions I couldn't answer. What would happen if they asked me about my family? I knew they would. What was I supposed to say? "Oh, my mom has just been released from treatment, my sister lives in a different state and I see my dad once a month for an hour or so." I knew they wanted a different answer, but I didn't have one; I was in recovery, I wasn't cured. I had ways to keep myself from using drugs, but my family was completely fucked up, and I was not going to lie.

This all happened on a Monday. By Wednesday, I was flying to New York. My father was with me. We were greeted at the airport by a limousine that took us to a lavish hotel on Park Avenue. My co-author, Kate, called and we talked for awhile about the show. I had never seen it before because I didn't have a TV. I had no idea what was going to happen. My father was supportive; it was good to have him there.

That night I laid in our room terrified. It was late and I should have been asleep, but I kept thinking that the next day I would be talking to millions of people. I prayed to my Higher Power to guide me, but it still took another hour to fall asleep. I awoke with a jerk. My father was up shaving. I looked around the room, remembering we were in New York and we were about to be on television. After breakfast a limousine picked us up and took us to the studio.

We walked in and were taken directly to makeup by one of the show coordinators. They spent fifteen minutes putting makeup all over my face so I didn't look pale. I felt pale, that's for sure; I was sweating and my hands felt like blocks of ice. I started wondering how I could get out of there. After makeup, I went to the "Green Room," where there were others waiting to go on. Kate came by to give me support. We talked and she gave me advice about the show, but I forgot it as soon as she was gone. We were both excited.

There was supposedly a lot of pressure riding on me. This show was known for helping authors sell a ton of books. I didn't really care about book sales. I just wanted to get the hell out of there—yet, at the same time, I was excited to reach so many people. I was completely unprepared. I knew the host was a psychologist and so I assumed she would be kind and interested since her profession was helping people. I was wrong. From the start the audience and host tried to place all of us guests on the defensive by blaming us for being morally weak.

The show didn't go well at all. Fortunately, each time I was verbally attacked by the audience, the panel members came to my defense. Because I became so defensive, people chose to attack me. I kept getting in arguments with audience members who told me that I looked too good to have ever been an addict, and that my bottom was not low enough. I fought them and in the end regretted it. I felt the show had been a real mess. A month later, I would find out that was not entirely true.

One evening during Christmas break, I was sitting at my parents' house eating dinner with my father when the phone rang. The person asked, "Does a Mr. Craig Fraser live there?"

"I'm Craig, but I don't go by Mr." I answered.

There was a long pause and then I heard, "Craig, you don't know me, my name is John, I saw you on that TV show a month ago." There was another long pause. I was suspicious—how could he have found me, was he one of the angry audience? "Anyway," he continued, "when the show came on I was in my living room with a gun to my head [I thought about Ben] ready to kill myself." Tears began to roll down my cheeks as I listened to this man; "I understood what you said and it helped. I am also a drug addict, now I'm sober. Your story was like mine, only I am a lot older than you. I was ready to end my life. I didn't see any way out. You helped me. Thank you."

I was speechless. I tried to wipe away my tears so I could say something, "Thanks, you will never know how much that means to me, John." John had called city-by-city through Northern California to thank me, when it was me that needed to thank him.

After the call I went out for a walk. I thought that I had really messed up the show. My publisher and co-author told me I had, and after I watched it I agreed with them. Suddenly my fears and feelings of being a failure were gone. What I said had helped. It never translated into book sales, but it helped save a life. As far as I was concerned, that was better than a million in sales. I walked for a long time that night, thanking my Higher Power for the opportunity to show others there was another way, and for helping me to live it.

Over the next few months I appeared on many shows. I began receiving more and more calls and piles of letters from addicts and their parents, spouses, and girlfriends. Many were in jails and institutions. For a few months my life was filled with travel and speaking. My professors were threatening to fail me because I was missing so many classes. In the end, I managed to work it out and pass all my classes with high marks. Then one day it was over.

It ended as quickly as it had begun. By summertime, my publicity tour was over, school was out, and I was glad to relax. I moved back to my parents' house for that summer. My mother was still living in the Bay Area near her treatment facility, where she could more easily keep on top of her sobriety. My father was working and traveling as usual. I spent my time visiting relatives and was back in school before I knew it.

Now that my work with the book was over, I had a lot more free time. I started dating a girl named Chris, one of my friend's roommates. I thought she was perfect. She didn't drink or do drugs and had some experience with recovery. She was the first woman that could truly understand me. Chris came from a family similar to mine and had been through many hard years. I quickly fell in love with her.

I went from working with *BURNT* and all its publicity hype to Chris. Once again, I had unknowingly switched my addiction from one thing to another; Chris became my new drug. I had changed a lot since Nicole, but still had a long way to go. I was now able to listen better and be emotionally available in relationships, thanks to Choices for Change and therapy. Unfortunately, I was still a constant manipulator and would do whatever it took to get my way. Because we came from similar backgrounds, she was a lot like me and was also used to getting her way. Chris had been living on her own and paying all her bills since she was seventeen. She worked forty hours a week and went to school full time.

My relationship with Chris brought out a side of me I had never known. Suddenly, I became jealous. I would spend our time apart wondering if she was cheating on me. I don't know where these thoughts came from, but they began to ruin our relationship. I began to accuse her of seeing other people and getting drunk, things she would never have done.

Before we broke up, I would have fits of rage when she would tell me she couldn't see me. I couldn't control myself: I would stomp around and yell like a child having a tantrum. The day she broke it off for good, I had put my fist through my bedroom wall during an argument. I didn't even realize I had done it, until I was pulling my hand out of the broken plaster. She had looked at me terrified, and said, "It's over." I just sat there staring at my fist and the hole in the wall as she walked out of my room. I knew I needed help.

I was codependent and did not realize it. My codependency was so subtle, I had not even noticed it. I taught about codependency at Choices for Change, so how could I be the one who was codependent? Chris split with me for what she said was an "undetermined amount of time." It drove me crazy: I would drive by her place late at night to see if anyone was with her; I would call to see if she was home and hang up ; I would ask her friends questions about what she was doing. It was worse than my addiction to drugs. Drugs I could always buy, but Chris was gone and there was no getting her back.

That night, I called Kathy from Choices for Change. As usual, she gave me the perfect advice and told me where to get help. She suggested that I go to Codependents Anonymous meetings. The next one was in two days. In that time, I called Chris several times, pleading with her not to break up with me. I tried apologizing, I sent her flowers, and I told her it would never happen again. Nothing worked. During those two days I didn't go to class or eat and I hardly slept. I wanted Chris back.

She was my first sober love, and I trusted her completely. Yet when I had been with her, I was frightened about losing her, even during the times I knew she truly loved me. We had been together for almost a year. Unfortunately for us, I was still emotionally immature due to all the years of drugs. Once again, drugs had made me lose what I cared for most.

Two days later I went to the meeting. I thought it was my one hope to get Chris back. Would it work? What would these people be like? What would I say? What would they think about me? I had many questions and no way to answer them until I went.

I left early so I would not be late, and ended up driving around completely lost for half an hour. I had turned into some winding back streets, a maze full of dead ends. At one of them I stopped my car to calm down. I said the serenity prayer. I felt like I was just about to explode. I finally decided that I should just go home and try again another night. Driving home, I stopped at a red light. I was feeling much more relaxed since I had decided to give up. I looked across the street and there was the church.

I parked and walked back to the Sunday School rooms. There was a brick courtyard with trees and a sign with an arrow pointing to a room in the corner. It said "Coda meeting 7:00 on Tues. and Fri." Even though I had been to recovery meetings before, my hands were sweaty and my heart was pounding. It felt as if I had just done a line of speed.

I stood there in the open door for a second before someone waved for me to come in. A woman pointed at chairs stacked against the wall. I took one, and the others made room for me to enter the circle. As they read the steps of Codependents Anonymous, I looked around the room. They were mostly women in their forties, a few younger women, and two other men; one of the men was my age. I listened to the Steps.

1. We admitted that we were powerless over others, that our lives had become unmanageable.
2. We came to believe that a Power greater than ourselves could restore us to sanity.
3. We made a decision to turn our will and our lives over to the care of God as we understood him.
4. We made a searching and fearless moral inventory of ourselves.
5. We admitted to God, to ourselves, and to another human being the exact nature of our wrongs.
6. We were entirely ready to have God remove all these defects of character.
7. We humbly asked God to remove our shortcomings.
8. We made a list of all persons we had harmed and became willing to make amends to them all.
9. We made direct amends to such people wherever possible, except when to do so would injure them or others.
10. We continued to take personal inventory, and when we were wrong promptly admitted it.
11. We sought through prayer and meditation to improve our conscious contact with God as we understood God, praying only for knowledge of God's will for us and the power to carry that out.
12. Having had a spiritual awakening as a result of these steps, we tried to carry this message to other codependents, and to practice these principles in all our affairs.

The steps were basically the same as I had in N.A. The only difference was, instead of drugs, they spoke of people. Unlike N.A., there were some ground rules in the meetings. One rule was not to give advice or comfort people in their pain, which most

codependents love to do. Another, was to only talk about ourselves and our experience of a situation, with an emphasis on our
own feelings. These rules were to help people experience their
own feelings instead of focusing on others.

I had spent the last year with Chris trying to fix her life, just as
I had done with Nicole. I was always giving advice and manipulating her so she would do what I wanted. I didn't know about
just letting people be. I thought that I was fixed and so now it was
my job to fix others. I had a lot to learn. Many people in the room
shared similar feelings and experiences. Most of them were
addicted to their partners, wives, or husbands. Some of their significant others were alcoholics, drug addicts, or obsessive
gamblers. My situation was not so extreme—I had never been
divorced or had children, but I was hurting and obsessing over
my break-up. I didn't know how to stop.

After listening for awhile, I shared what was going on with
me. I couldn't hold back the tears. I sobbed through most of my
story. It was good to be in a place where I could share my feelings.
After I was done, several others shared experiences that were similar. It helped to know I was not alone.

I called Chris the next morning and told her that I was going
to codependency meetings. I thought she would want to get back
together with me right away once she knew this. I was wrong. I
continued to go to the meetings twice a week for months. During
this time many things changed. I was finally able to see how I had
been repeating my father's relationship with my mother. He too
was a codependent—controlling, manipulating and intimidating
her, as his father had done to his wife.

As the months went by, I continued working at Choices for
Change, going to school, attending meetings, and speaking about
drug addiction. I still missed Chris, but not as much as I had in the
beginning. We were still apart, and she was dating, which really
upset me. I would see her at school and wonder whom she was talking to and why. Were they a couple? I wondered why it couldn't be

me. I had no idea what a healthy relationship was. I was angry with my parents. I blamed them for my failure with Chris because they had not showed me how to have a healthy relationship.

Of course, it was not their fault. They had done the best they knew how, but at the time it was easier to blame them than to change myself. They had learned the same way I had—from watching their parents. Instead of growing and learning, they had simply repeated what they had experienced growing up without ever questioning it. That style was not good enough for me or the people I wanted to date. With time, I stopped blaming them and spent more time working on my recovery.

Chris decided to spend her last year of college abroad. I went nuts. In the end there was nothing I could do except tell her that I still loved her and would miss her. Once again, the one thing I cared most about in my life was gone, and there was nothing I could do to stop it. I had many using dreams once she left, and often thought about how easy it would be to get high. I felt as if I was going to slip (use drugs). I started going to N.A. meetings a few times each week and found the support I needed. There were lots of people willing to help me. If it wasn't for those meetings, I would have probably gotten loaded.

My focus continued to be on Chris until she left for her new school. To ease the hurt, I went backpacking with my fraternity brother, John. The first night we were sitting around the fire reading out loud from a book our fraternity would use on retreats called *The Book of Questions*. John flipped to a page, and using the fire light, he asked, "Have you led a full life, would you mind dying?" I answered "No, I wouldn't mind dying." I had wanted to die many times after getting sober, but this was different. Now my life was full of true friends, interesting classes, and rewarding work; I didn't think it could get much better and did not mind dying.

The next day, I awakened with horrible dysentery. I was throwing up and had diarrhea. I could not even take a sip of water without getting sick. I thought it may just be a one-day bug. It was not. For the next eight months I was seriously ill and the doctors were unable to figure out what was wrong. The only symptom was that if I ate anything solid, I would get sick. Within two months, I had lost twenty-five pounds. I was sure I was dying, and I knew that I didn't want to. Chris was no longer an issue for me.

For the next six months, I spent hours upon hours in doctors' offices, having hundreds of tests. I was no longer worried about codependency, addiction, or Chris. I was worried about my life. They gave me pill after pill to try to kill whatever it was, but none worked. Eventually, the doctors ran out of ideas, and I had to find help somewhere else. I went to an old friend who was an acupuncturist and herbalist. He spent hours listening about my illness and about my losing Chris. When I was finished, John looked at me in perfect confidence and said, "I can help. We can get you better." I was relieved and placed my total faith in him.

With regular herbs and acupuncture, I began feeling stronger immediately. My symptoms were still there, but I was getting better. My healing was slow, and it took a lot of work. John suggested I spend an hour a day sitting quietly asking my Higher Power to heal me, so I did. I figured I had nothing to lose. Three weeks later, I was able to eat solid foods again. Within three months I was cured.

I look back on that time as a miracle. There were many times I thought I would never get better. One friend thought I had AIDS because I was so thin and weak due to lack of food. Once I was healed, I realized that I had been sick in many places, not just my body. My heart was sick from losing Chris, my mind was depressed, and my body was trying to tell me this.

Getting better gave me a new lease on life. My shyness and feelings of insecurity were finally gone. Over those eight months, I had dealt with much larger issues than what people thought of me, what Chris was doing, or how my grades were. I had worried about whether or not I would live. No longer would I allow myself to be afraid of taking risks. I was finally back to the healthy, sober, happy person I most enjoyed being.

I had one more semester of college before graduation, and everything seemed to be going right. I was so used to dealing with big problems in my life, but finally I was able to just be me. I felt so good that I stopped going to recovery meetings, and spent my time looking for a job and having fun.

I found a good job as a child care worker at a nearby facility. I spent four days a week living with twelve teenagers who came from dysfunctional homes. The work was emotionally difficult because the children were always swearing at the staff, fighting, and lying. They reminded me of myself and the friends I had grown up with. Working with them was one of the ways I made peace with my past. Overall, my life seemed perfect—and it was for awhile. My big mistake was to stop going to meetings. Part of me felt that, after not using drugs or drinking at all in college when there had been so many problems, I was cured of my addiction. I was wrong.

I began setting myself up for a relapse months before it actually happened. I constantly justified why I should be able to drink. I would think, "I'm twenty-five, I have a good job, I'm healthy, almost out of college, and life is great. I can handle a beer or a glass of wine at dinner. What's wrong with that? Everyone else does." It took months of convincing myself that I didn't have a problem before I took that first drink.

During spring break, I went on vacation to Mexico for a week with a friend from work. We drove down in a day and checked in to a resort a few hours south of the border. I couldn't stop thinking about drinking. We got a room and went to the pool, where many people were drinking cocktails from hollowed-out pineapples or coconuts. I began to look at the pros and cons of drinking. "What could happen," I thought to myself. My friend, Tom, who was not a big drinker in the first place, ordered a beer. I didn't join him, but instead jumped in the pool and swam for , all the time thinking about having a drink. Of course, I didn't tell him this.

My mind was in constant conflict about drinking. What would I have to lose? I had no idea. As far as I could tell, there was nothing to lose and a bit of fun to be had. My problem was that I still didn't consider alcohol one of my drugs. I had used everything else and did have problems with them. I thought alcohol was different. I had stopped on my own because I didn't like it; now I wanted to have it. What was the big deal?

The mistake was that I was comparing myself to people who had never had a problem with drugs or alcohol. I was also no longer going to meetings. I didn't have anyone or anything left in my life to prevent me from relapsing. The people I worked with only knew the Craig at work, not the recovering addict. The following night after much deliberation, I ordered a drink with dinner. The last thing I had drunk was a rum and Coke with Nicole, so I ordered one of those. It tasted foul but quickly went to my head.

I felt really good at first. Suddenly, everything became soft, relaxing, and funny. Tom drank with me. For him it was no big deal, but for me, it was one of the largest decisions I would ever make. I was curious; was I still an addict? I had not used alcohol or drugs for eight years. I wondered if I still had a problem.

I no longer had a tolerance for alcohol. At age ten, I drank more in one sitting than I did that night. I began by having two drinks at dinner, then went dancing at a club next to the resort. John bought us rounds of vodka shots to celebrate our vacation and I returned the favor. Suddenly, I had four more drinks in me and I felt the effects. I was off balance. For the first time in many years, I was not in control. The fun was over, I was feeling sick.

I walked back to my room and laid down. As soon as I closed my eyes, the room felt as if it was spinning. I ran to the bathroom and threw up. I began feeling less drunk and realized what I had done. I thought to myself, "Oh, shit!" John came in hours later, while I was still trying to stop the room's movement by staring at the ceiling. He went right to sleep and was snoring in minutes. I sat there wondering why I had gotten drunk and if I would again. I decided it was okay to drink as long as I didn't drink too much. From then on, I limited myself to two drinks. I often craved more but didn't give in.

Once we were back at work, my life went along smoothly. I was single and researching graduate schools for clinical psychology. During my time off, I would mountain bike, backpack, or go out to the beach. I spent a lot of time thinking about drinking. This went on for six months. Then for no reason, I became depressed.

I had no idea of where it came from. Suddenly I was sad, and everything looked horrible to me. Instead of using more alcohol, I stopped. Somewhere inside, I knew that it was not helping. I stopped drinking that day and began going to meetings again. In the meetings, I remembered why I had stopped in the first place. In high school, I had been miserable all the time and used drugs to hide my feelings, but when I wasn't high, the problems were still there.

Fortunately, there were no big problems in my life; I had a good job and close friends. As soon as I stopped drinking, my depression went away. It was such an easy solution. It's been over two years since then, and I wish I hadn't tried alcohol, because now it is an issue for me. I do desire it from time to time, but I know if I have one, I will want more. So I just don't take that first drink, and when I want to, I remind myself of what happens when I do. Sometimes it's harder than that, so I still go to meetings weekly and remind myself why that one beer or glass of wine is not worth it. Today, I have peace of mind and control of my life. I make the decisions and live with the consequences.

Epilogue

When I was in high school, I thought there was no way to have fun without drugs and alcohol. Now I realize that I was just lacking imagination; there are endless things to do, it just takes a little more work to find them. My life is still filled with excitement and adventure, and I don't have to hurt my body or mind to get to it. I also don't have to spend all my money to buy the fun, or surround myself with people who just want to use me. In my life today, I still look for adrenaline highs and ways in which I can push my physical and mental limits—now I just do it sober.

Over the last several years I have found many things to do that are fun and exciting. I go backpacking in the mountains, rock climb, mountain bike, fish, and do volunteer work in my community. After working in the field of psychology for a couple of years, I saved enough money to travel around the world. It didn't take much, about twenty dollars a day. During my travels, I rode hundreds of miles on my mountain bike, climbed Mount Olympus, Mount Kenya and Mount Sinai. I backpacked through over thirty-six countries and worked on farms in Israel: fishing, gardening, picking bananas, avocados and mangos. I trekked after gorillas in the jungles of Africa, climbed the great pyramids of Egypt, and discussed Higher Powers with spiritual teachers in the Middle East, India and South America. Life is finally the adventure I always knew it could be. It took me many years to find it, and it's a lot better than sitting at home watching TV and getting stoned.

It took me a long time to have the courage to go after my dreams. I had always wanted to be an author and world traveler. I used to have many dreams when I was using drugs, but none of them came true while I was getting high. Since I have been sober, every dream has become a reality. It has rarely happened overnight—usually dreams come true after months of hard work, patience and faith.

I believe that whatever our dreams or passions are, we must go after them! We are all here for a reason and part of our challenge is finding that dream inside of us. Usually it is what we love to do, yet, due to our surroundings, most of us choose dreams that are not ours, but our parents or friends. I ask you now to take a moment and dig deep inside and look. What is your dream? How do you picture your life? What do you want it to be like. Your dreams are there and can still come true, just believe. Believe in yourself and that miracles can happen to make your life new. Drugs prevented me from making my dreams come true for many years. Often I remind myself of a quote when I feel like giving up: "The last ten steps are worth the first hundred miles."

I have found that at the point when I am just about to succeed, I come across the largest obstacles. The difference is that today I don't give up. I never let anyone tell me I can't do something. People again and again said I would not be able to stay sober, write a book, or travel around the world. Those people are no longer in my life.

When I was a child, I was told that I was stupid and would never amount to anything. If I had believed this, I would not have seen any of my dreams come true. When I finally took responsibility for my life and got sober, I realized that I could do whatever I wanted. Being sober was the most important step for me in making my dreams become realities. Living day-by-day, my life has become more than I ever imagined it could.

Today I am well and happy; my whole family is healthy. We joke about the way it used to be. My parents are now happily divorced and creating the lives they had always dreamed of. My mom has been sober for over eight years, my father is remarried and taking time to enjoy his life and the people in it. My sister has two young children, and we talk on a regular basis. I am surrounded by friends who care about me. I go to meetings weekly and still exercise and spend quiet time with my Higher Power every day. My life is good, and I only see it getting better as I continue working a program and life based on honesty with myself and others.

It was a long road home for me. I had completely lost myself due to drugs. At age sixteen, I never thought there would be a time when I would be happy without them. I just want to let you know that all the tears, pain, paranoia, urges to use drugs, and suicidal thoughts I lived through to get sober were worth it. Day by day, my life is my own and I am grateful.

Reference Material

GLOSSARY OF TERMS

AMPED 1. (adj.) "Psyched" to do something. 2. To feel the effects of speed or cocaine.

BINDLE (n) Square pieces of glossy 3 x 5" paper, which are folded into smaller triangular packages, and usually hold cocaine or speed.

BLACK BEAUTY (n) A pill made with speed.

BLAZE (v) To trip on LSD.

BLOTTER (n) LSD that comes on paper.

BLOW (n) Cocaine.

BLOW-IT (n) Someone who gets out of control while on drugs or alcohol. For example, "Everyone thinks Tim is a blow-it because he got really loud and obnoxious."

BONG (n) A pipe for smoking pot; the smoke is cooled through a chamber filled with water.

BUD (n) Flowering portion of the marijuana plant; it hold the highest concentration of THC.

BULLET SHOT (n) A hit taken from a mechanical vial of cocaine.

BUNK (adj.) Impure drugs or drugs that have no effect.

BUST 1. (n) Someone who is "uncool" and who will report a drug user to authorities. 2. (n) A situation where people are caught for using drugs or alcohol.

CHOCOLATE THAI (n) Marijuana from Thailand; smells like chocolate when it's burned.

COKE SMOKE (n) Cocaine inside a cigarette; otherwise known as a 'moke.

CRANK (n) A powdered form of speed, usually snorted or injected.

CROSS TOP (n) A speed pill that has an "x" stamped into it.

CRYSTAL METH (n) A very potent form of speed, also known as meth.

DOSE (v) To slip someone LSD without them knowing.

DRY (adj.) An expression meaning that there are no drugs for sale.

DUSTED (adj.) 1. Completely wasted. (In some parts of California, it refers to being wasted on PCP). 2. To have finished smoking a bowl of pot and all that's left is the dust or ash.

ECSTASY or MDMA (n) a type of hallucinogen, sometimes called the Love Drug or X.

EIGHTBALL (n) 3.5 grams; usually refers to cocaine or speed.

FLOPPY (adj.) Used to describe the way your body feel as an LSD trip begins.

FRY (v) To trip on LSD.

FRIED (adj.) Completely burnt out from doing too many drugs, refers to both body and mind.

GREEN HASH UNDER GLASS (n) A method of smoking hashish; the smoldering hashish is placed under a glass to trap the maximum amount of smoke.

HOST (v) To provide drugs for free.

HOT OFF THE PRESS (adj.) Used to describe LSD when it is fresh or recently manufactured.

KGB (n) "Killer Green Buds," excellent marijuana.

LUDE (n) Short for quaalude, a kind of downer that has a lemon printed on it.

MOKE (n) Cocaine in a cigarette; also called coke smoke.

NARC (n) 1. An undercover cop. 2. A person who tells on someone else.

NARC OFF (v) to tell on someone for using drugs or doing something illegal.

NUMBIE (n) A method of cocaine use: putting cocaine on your gums to cause them to become numb.

PEAKY (adj.) Stoned but not tired, being high but having energy.

PINNER (n) A very thin joint.

PURPLE KUSH (n) Marijuana that has purple hairs intertwined in it.

QUAD (n) A quarter gram of cocaine or speed

ROCK (n) Solid chunks of cocaine not cut with other substances; usually very potent.

SHAKE (n) Leaves and stems of the marijuana plant.

SHEET (n) One hundred hits of LSD.

SNEAK-A-TOKE (n) A pipe used for smoking marijuana; smoke is emitted from only one chamber.

SNO-SEAL (n) Glossy white and blue paper used for making bindles to package cocaine and speed.

SONOMA COMA (n) High-grade pot grown in Sonoma County, California.

STONER (n) A daily pot smoker.

STROKE OUT (v) To have a heart attack.

THAI STICK (n) Marijuana from Thailand; it is fastened onto a stick the size of a pipe cleaner.

TRACER (n) A type of LSD hallucination; repeating patterns of the same image of object.

TWEAKED (adj.) Totally messed up on drugs or alcohol.

WALL HIT (n) The act of making someone pass out on purpose.

WHIPPIT (n) Nitrous oxide.

WHITE OUT (n) A cocaine-induced state of temporary visual blindness accompanied by a feeling of total bliss. (v) To white out; to achieve this state.

CLASSIC SIGNS AND SYMPTOMS OF DRUG ABUSE

As you go down the list there are many of these signs I showed throughout the beginning, middle and final stages of my addiction. However, my friends and I were able to hide many of them from our parents. The one thing I have always told parents is that you must trust your gut feelings when it comes to children and drugs. Most of the time an addict will lie, manipulate, and do whatever they can to keep using. I did for a long time, and my parent's denial and desire to picture me in the best light prevented them from helping me early on.

During a lecture I gave one night, a parent told me that his child who was using drugs was just in a "phase." I responded by saying, "You may be right, and it may be the last phase of your child's life, it was for many of my friends." Drugs are not a normal developmental phase, they are deadly.

1. A CHANGE IN FRIENDS—When I began using drugs my friends changed dramatically, if someone didn't do drugs we weren't friends. My parents told me they didn't want me to hang out with these kids, so I did it without them knowing.

2. GRADES GOING DOWN—In my case my grades were not affected negatively. However, most all of my using friends in public school had their grades drop. It was slow at first, it took about six months before they were getting "bad" grades.

3. LARGE EMOTIONAL SWINGS—I would often fly into fits of rage with my mother or peers over nothing. I also would go through days of deep depression after using stimulants. I would not eat, talk, or do much of anything other than watch TV and sleep.

4. REBELS AGAINST RULES—I would often fight any boundaries and try to manipulate curfews, allowance and places I could go.

5. BECOMING WITHDRAWN—For days at a time I would not talk at all to my parents, not even during meals. I would also not make phone calls or have people over.

6. LACK OF MOTIVATION—In public school, at the beginning of my addiction, I stopped playing sports and all other extracurricular activities. This is when my peer group changed dramatically.

7. SNEAKY BEHAVIOR—I would often tell people to "call back later," when my parents were by the phone and I was being called about drugs. I would sneak in and out of the house late at night to go to parties.

8. SELLING BELONGINGS—I sold/traded many belongings to pay for drugs, clothes, tapes, stereo equipment.

9. LACK OF COMMUNICATION—I was good at communicating but often would not tell my parents exactly where I was going, who I would be with and what we were going to do. If they demanded to know, I would usually lie.

10. STEALING FROM FAMILY MEMBERS—On several occasions, I took money from my father's desk or mother's purse to buy drugs.

11. MANIPULATING PARENTS—I would convince my mother to let me go out with a friend my father didn't like and, then, just tell my father I was going and that mom said it was all right."

12. PHYSICAL DETERIORATION—I lost a lot of weight when I was on speed and cocaine and my skin became pale and waxy. When I was smoking a lot of pot my appetite was usually unstoppable, my mind was slow to react to questions and my eyes were droopy and bloodshot.

13. MENTAL DETERIORATION—My short term memory would often fail me on simple things like past conversations I had with my parents. I didn't remember conversations we had the day before.

14. PROBLEMS WITH POLICE OR SCHOOL—I avoided these for the most part but other friends were constantly getting detentions for acting out in class, skipping class, sleeping in class, not doing homework or being high in class. Some were caught for doing/dealing drugs and driving drunk.

15. GETTING HIGH/DRUNK AT PARTIES OR HOME—I was caught on several occasions by my parents coming home from parties high or drunk. I would usually lie my way out of it or convince them it wasn't a big deal. They never followed through on consequences, so I kept using drugs.

16. FINDING PARAPHERNALIA—Early on, my father found drugs when we were at the beach and when I was growing pot in my closet. I had many pipes and other drug stuff in my drawers and closet at home.

If your child is exhibiting these symptoms I strongly encourage you to further educate yourself with some of the resources listed. Good luck, and trust your gut feelings.

SELF-TESTING FOR TEENAGERS

Circle each number that is answered with a yes.

1. Do you use alcohol or other drugs to build self-confidence?
2. Do you ever drink or get high immediately after you have a problem at home or at school?
3. Have you ever missed school due to alcohol or other drugs?
4. Does it bother you if someone says that you use too much alcohol or other drugs?
5. Have you started hanging out with a heavy drinking or drug using crowd?
6. Are alcohol or other drugs affecting your reputation?
7. Do you feel guilty or bummed out after using alcohol or other drugs?
8. Do you feel more at ease on a date when drinking or using other drugs?
9. Have you gotten into trouble at home for using alcohol or other drugs?
10. Do you borrow money or "do without" other things to buy alcohol and other drugs?
11. Do you feel a sense of power when you use alcohol or other drugs?
12. Have you lost friends since you started using alcohol or other drugs?
13. Do your friends use less alcohol or other drugs than you do?
14. Do you drink or use other drugs until your supply is all gone?
15. Do you ever wake up and wonder what happened the night before?
16. Have you ever been busted or hospitalized due to alcohol or use of illicit drugs?

17. Do you "turn off" any studies or lectures about alcohol or illicit drug use?
18. Do you think you have a problem with alcohol or other drugs?
19. Has there ever been someone in your family with a drinking or other drug problem?
20. Could you have a problem with alcohol or other drugs?

Purchase or public possession of alcohol is illegal for anyone under the age of 21 everywhere in the United States. Aside from the fact that you may be breaking the law by using alcohol and/or illicit drugs, if you answer "yes" to any three of the above questions, you may be at risk for developing alcoholism and/or dependence on another drug. If you answer "yes" to five of these questions, you should seek professional help immediately.

STEPS TO MAKE YOUR RECOVERY LAST

1. Go to ninety recovery meetings in ninety days.
2. Get a sponsor.
3. Read the A.A. or N.A. *Big Book.*
4. Stay away from old using friends and places.
5. Talk every day with someone who is recovering.
6. Find new non-drug related activities that you enjoy.
7. Do things with both sober and non-using people.
8. Do not get into a relationship during the first year.
9. Speak at meetings.
10. Chair a speakers' meeting.
11. Let your feelings out— tell people how you feel.
12. Exercise regularly.
13. Begin to work the steps.
14. Set short term goals for yourself: job, school, family and friends.
15. Try something new: biking, skiing, running, painting, writing.
16. Remember to forgive yourself.
17. Read books or articles about people who have stayed sober.
18. If you think about using drugs, call your sponsor and tell him or her.
19. At the end of each day, list all the positive things that happened.
20. Spend time daily with your Higher Power or relaxing without TV.

WAYS TO SUPPORT YOUR CHILD'S EARLY RECOVERY

1. Educate yourself on addiction and recovery issues teens face.
2. Stick firmly to the aftercare plan or family contract.
3. Support them in doing recovery-related activities.
4. Allow them to earn back your trust through stages.
5. Help them set goals to regain this trust.
6. In the first year, always know where they are and who they are with.
7. Do not allow your child to manipulate or lie to you.
8. Set up a list of reflective consequences if they relapse or break their contract.

9. Trust your gut feeling—if you think they are using again, find out.
10. Create healthy, interactive activities for them and your family to do together.
11. Set up weekly family meetings to discuss problems and successes.
12. To best support your child's new life, do not drink in front of him or her.
13. Try not to make them feel guilty for past actions.
14. Stay in close contact with their school.
15. Give them lots of positive support daily. Early recovery is hard.

WHERE TO GET HELP AND INFORMATION

TOLL-FREE INFORMATION

1-800-Cocaine National Helplines. A 24-hour information and national referral service for drug education and treatment.

1-800-662-HELP National Institute on Drug Abuse (NIDA), U.S. Department of Health and Human Services. Counselors offer advice and treatment referrals.

1-800-554-KIDS The National Federation of Parents for Drug-Free Youth (NFP) This national information referral service helps parents who are concerned that their child is using alcohol or drugs. Call between 9:00 A.M. and 5:00 P.M. Eastern Standard Time.

At-Risk Resources
135 Dupont Street
P.O. Box 760
Plainview New York 11803-0760
1-800-999-6884

American Council for Drug Education
204 Monroe Street, Suite 110
Rockville, MD 20850
1-800-488-3784

Center for Substance Abuse Prevention
Workplace Help line
1-800-WORKPLACE

Children of Alcoholics Foundation, Inc.
Box 4185
Grand Central Station
New York, NY 10115
1-800-359-2623

National Council on Alcoholism and Drug Dependence (NCADD)
12 West 21st Street
New York, NY 10010
1-800-622-2255

GENERAL INFORMATION

Families in Action National Drug Information Center, 2296 Henderson Mill Road, Suite 300, Atlanta, Georgia 30345; 1-770-934-6364.
http://WWW.emory.edu/NFIA. This non-profit organization maintains more than 300,000 documents on alcohol and drug abuse. The Center's staff will answer mail and phone queries. Their library is open five days a week. They also publish Drug Abuse Update, a quarterly abstract of over 100 articles chosen from those being added to the Center's library.

Narcotics Education, Inc. 680 Laurel Street NW, Washington D.C. 20012-9979; 1-800-548-8700. (In Alaska call 1-202-722-6740.) This organization publishes and distributes an array of materials that deal with substance abuse issues, including the magazine, *The Winner,* for grades 4-6 and *Listen* for grades 7-12.
National Clearinghouse for Alcohol and Drug Information, P.O. Box 2345, Rockville, MD, 20847-2345. 1-800-487-4889. Internet; http://www.health.org
This non-profit group publishes and distributes an array of materials, much of which focuses on prevention. The Clearinghouse has a reference service for people doing research on drug-related issues. 1-310-469-4000- Hablas Espanol

PRIDE, the National Parents Resource Institute for Drug Education, Inc. 100 Edgewood Avenue, Suite 1002, Atlanta, GA, 30303; 1-770-458-9900.
A private, non-profit organization, PRIDE's goal is to stem the epidemic of drug use, especially among young adults. PRIDE offers an array of information and provides help to parents and organizations who want to start drug prevention groups. PRIDE sponsors a World Drug Conference and World Prevention Exchange each year, drawing more than 6,000 participants from over 45 nations.

HOME TESTING

Parents Alert, Inc.
At Home Drug Tests
Phone 1-800-TEST-170
FAX 770-955-5338
E-MAIL
parentsalert@mindspring.com
Web site: www.parentsalert.com

Psychemedics Corporation
Hair Analysis Drug Testing
For information call:
1-800-997-3890

SELF HELP GROUPS

Local chapters of the following organizations can be found in communities across the country. If you have a problem finding a chapter nearby, contact the organizations' national headquarters.

Alcoholics Anonymous (AA)
World Services, Inc.
475 Riverside Drive
New York, NY 100115
212-870-3400

Adult Children of Alcoholics
Central Service Board
P.O. Box 3216
Torrance, CA 90505
213-534-1815

Al-Anon/Alateen Family Group
Headquarters, Inc.
1600 Corporate Landing Parkway
Virginia Beach Virginia 23454
1-800-344-2666
http://solar.rtd.utk.edu/~al-anon/

Cocaine Anonymous (CA)
3740 Overland Avenue, Suite G
Los Angeles, CA 90034
1-800-347-8998
http://www.ca.org/

CoAnon Family Groups
P.O. Box 64742-66
Los Angeles. CA 90064
310-859-2206

Families Anonymous, Inc.
P.O. Box 3475
Culver City Ca. 90231
818-989-7841

Marijuana Anonymous
P. O. Box 2912
Van Nuys, CA 91404
1-800-766-6779
info@marijuana-anonymous.org

Nar-Anon Family Groups
P.O. Box 2562
Palos Verdes Peninsula, CA 90274
310-547-5800

Narcotics Anonymous (NA)
P.O. Box 9999
Van Nuys, CA 91409
818-780-3951

HOW TO CONTACT CRAIG

If you would like to contact Craig, you can write to:
Craig E. Fraser, P.O. Box 335, St. Helena, CA 94574 USA
Or you can e-mail him at—BuySchool@aol.com
I am especially interested in your own story of recovery, questions
about addiction, and ways in which you stay sober.
Information in letters or e-mails sent may appear in a new book.
If so, all names will be changed to maintain anonymity.

ORDER FORM
CUT OUT/PHOTOCOPY/FILL OUT & SEND

Signed Copies of HIGH SCHOOL $ 13.95

To Order Books
Send this form with payment to:

> Craig Fraser
> AYNI Press
> P.O. Box 335
> St. Helena, CA 94574

Include your name, address, and phone number.
Please include bank name & check number for verification.

Please send me the following:

Books   qty ____ @ 13.95 = $ _____

Total Amount for Books Ordered   _____
                              Tax   _____
                Shipping/Handling   _____
Total amount of check enclosed $ _____

Shipping and Handling:
Book Rate: $4.00 for the first book and 1.50 for each additional book
            (Surface shipping may take three to four weeks)
Priority Mail: $5.50 for each item listed, 3-day delivery

TAX: Please add 7.75% for materials shipped to California addresses.